Understanding the Medical Diagnosis of Child Maltreatment

Understanding the Medical Diagnosis of Child Maltreatment

A Guide for Nonmedical Professionals

THIRD EDITION

Edited by

Charmaine R. Brittain

OXFORD
UNIVERSITY PRESS

2006

OXFORD

UNIVERSITY PRESS

Oxford University Press, Inc., publishes works that further
Oxford University's objective of excellence
in research, scholarship, and education.

Oxford   New York
Auckland   Cape Town   Dar es Salaam   Hong Kong   Karachi
Kuala Lumpur   Madrid   Melbourne   Mexico City   Nairobi
New Delhi   Shanghai   Taipei   Toronto

With offices in
Argentina   Austria   Brazil   Chile   Czech Republic   France   Greece
Guatemala   Hungary   Italy   Japan   Poland   Portugal   Singapore
South Korea   Switzerland   Thailand   Turkey   Ukraine   Vietnam

First edition published in 1989 by the American Humane Association
Second edition published in 1997 by the American Humane Association
First Oxford University Press edition, 2006

Published by Oxford University Press, Inc.
198 Madison Avenue, New York, New York 10016

www.oup.com

Oxford is a registered trademark of Oxford University Press

Library of Congress Cataloging-in-Publication Data
Understanding the medical diagnosis of child maltreatment : a guide for nonmedical
professionals / edited by Charmaine R. Brittain.—3rd ed.
      p.   cm.
Summary: "Provides a step-by-step guide to frequently asked questions concerning
the medical aspects of child abuse and neglect. Designed for the nonmedical professional,
this guide covers burns, fractures, poisoning, sexual abuse, neglect, substance abuse, and working
with medical providers. Includes charts, illustrations, checklists, and resources"—Provided by
publisher.
ISBN-13 978-0-19-517217-1; 978-0-19-517216-4 (pbk.)
ISBN 0-19-517217-5; 0-19-517216-7 (pbk.)
1. Child abuse—Diagnosis. 2. Battered child syndrome—Diagnosis. I. Brittain, Charmaine.
RA1122.5.U53 2005
617.1'0083—dc22   2004031031

9 8 7 6 5 4 3 2 1

Printed in the United States of America
on acid-free paper

For all child protective services professionals

who work so hard on behalf of children and families

It is just not possible to worry about all the needs of all the children all the time. . . . For each of us there must be only one patient at a time. Thus one keeps one's sanity and does the very best job. At the same time, all of us who are devoting our professional life to the cause of children must engage our minds and our hearts on their behalf, each of us, and wherever we can: by the quality of our work, by being the child's advocate in our towns, in our states, and by influencing national policy to our best ability. Do so with passion.

—C. Henry Kempe, MD

April 26, 1978, Presidential Address

of the American Pediatric Society, New York City

Preface

As the pursuits of medical science march on, the discovery of more information, the discernment of causes, and the breaking through of barriers from misinformation and nescience in order to reach a higher understanding of the human body continues. In response to this continual advancement of knowledge, this latest edition of *Understanding the Medical Diagnosis of Child Maltreatment* offers the most up-to-date knowledge on injuries and conditions that may result from child maltreatment.

Child protective services (CPS) workers interact frequently with medical providers to diagnose maltreatment, care for injured or ill children, and provide ongoing monitoring of children and families. Since the language of the medical world is typically unfamiliar (sometimes even confounding) to most CPS workers, a guide that translates and makes medical conditions and injuries understandable—especially as they may relate to child abuse and neglect—is a necessary addition to workers' knowledge base. This book will provide workers with the knowledge they need to engage in more meaningful, productive, and positive interactions with medical providers.

This edition greatly expands on the previous 1997 edition with the inclusion of new chapters, many case examples, and an increased focus on understanding differential diagnoses. In an acknowledgment of the realities of CPS practice, this book includes not just the content of interactions with medical providers but also the process of working with medical providers. Chapter 2 addresses the tension that can occur between medical providers and CPS workers, because of their differing philosophical views on how to address issues surrounding child abuse and neglect, and it offers strategies for enhancing these relationships for the benefit of children and their families. Other new chapters in this edition cover substance abuse, a topic that is relevant to the medical community for multiple reasons, and violence in the home, focusing on spousal abuse and its impact on children.

Because child abuse is diagnosed by excluding other possibilities that may explain an injury or condition, differential diagnoses must be considered by the medical provider and the CPS worker. Therefore this book includes detailed differentials when applicable. Case examples are also provided throughout the book to illustrate specific conditions or concepts. Efforts were also made to ensure that this book is culturally responsive and considers explanations that reflect cultural variations.

The use of the term "medical providers" reflects another reality of practice. Physicians and nurses are not the only professionals who provide medical care; a host of other professionals, including physicians' assistants, homeopathic practitioners, therapists, chiropractors, culturally based healers and others, also contribute to the medical care of children and families. Therefore "medical providers" is used throughout the book as a broad inclusion of multiple titles, specialties, and licensures within the professional medical community.

■ About the American Humane Association

The American Humane Association has sponsored the development of this latest version of *Understanding the Medical Diagnosis of Child Maltreatment.*

American Humane has a long history of protecting children from abuse and neglect. In 1877, a group of humane societies from across the United States—including the New York Society for the Prevention of Cruelty to Children and the American Society for the Prevention of Cruelty to Animals (ASPCA)—joined forces to establish the national American Humane Association. In 1886, American Humane formally amended its constitution to encompass the protection of children as well as animals. Emphasizing the important role that family plays in children's welfare, American Humane encouraged its member organizations to protect families and to remove children from their parents only when absolutely necessary.

Today, American Humane supports the development and implementation of effective community, state, tribal, and national systems to protect children and strengthen families. It provides consultation to courts, public and private child welfare agencies, and community organizations; trains workers and supervisors on best practice; conducts research and publishes findings; analyzes child protection systems and offers recommendations to improve practice; advocates for new legislation; and disseminates information about innovative practice models and procedures to not only child welfare and other professionals but also a wide audience of concerned citi-

---

Mission and Vision

The American Humane Association envisions a nation in which no child or animal will ever be a victim of abuse or neglect.

The mission of American Humane, as a national network of individuals and organizations, is to prevent cruelty to and abuse, neglect, and exploitation of children and animals and to ensure that their respective interests and well-being are fully, effectively, and humanely guaranteed by an aware and caring society.

zens. American Humane works to ensure that services are in place throughout the country to protect children from abuse, neglect, and exploitation and to increase families' ability to nurture and protect their children. American Humane recognizes that, to succeed in this work and truly help children, it will need to involve professional partners, community advocates, and concerned citizens to develop a broad array of effective supportive services. In addition, it must recognize the strong, protective elements of culture and seek to ensure that child protective services are truly culturally responsive to the increasing diversity within families.

■ Using the Book

Understanding the Medical Diagnosis of Child Maltreatment offers readers multiple functions. Workers and supervisors should use it as a desk reference to help understand medically related aspects of casework. For example, a worker in a rural county is reviewing a report from a physician regarding the injuries from a 9–month-old child with shaken baby syndrome. Many terms are unfamiliar to the worker and she is trying to complete her investigation report and assessment. She is apprehensive, and, because her supervisor is in the next county attending training, there is no one to turn to for help. Seeing *Understanding the Medical Diagnosis of Child Maltreatment* on her desk, the new worker turns to the chapter on head injuries and is able to translate the medical terms into appropriate language for her report. She continues to thumb through the book and finds some content on domestic violence and substance abuse, both of which appear to be factors in this case, which gives her more information to integrate into her report and helps to stimulate her thinking on appropriate interventions so the other children in the family can remain in the home. As a result she feels more confident and is ready to finish her report and meet with the nonoffending mother.

In another situation, a supervisor could use this book as a tool to support on-the-job training. The supervisor could assign a new worker to read the chapter on working with medical providers and then ask her to comment on key points after attending a staffing with medical providers. In another situation, a college professor might use the book as a text for a course on child protective services. For a field assignment, the professor could ask students to use the appendix on child development to assess the developmental level of several children. Other readers, such as attorneys, court-appointed special advocates, or foster parents, may find it useful it as a guide to understanding the specific medical diagnoses of children who have been abused or neglected.

Lastly, readers can use the companion Web site to this book (available on the Oxford University Press Web site) to provide background material that will reinforce content and illustrate conditions. Look for this icon—💻—

at the ends of sentences; this indicates the availability of more information on the Web site. Pictures of injuries and conditions are provided on the site in a slide-show format, which can be easily downloaded and used in training sessions. Pictures illustrating differential diagnoses are especially useful to CPS workers in order to more accurately assess situations. Other materials, such as protocols, sample memoranda of understanding, articles, and charts, are also available on this Web site. A warning, however: some pictures on the site are quite graphic and even disturbing, so be prepared to process the experience after viewing the slides. To access the Web site, go to http: //www.oup.com/us/AHA.medicaldiagnosis.

Whatever its specific application, American Humane hopes that this book will help guide practitioners through the complexities of the medical diagnosis of child maltreatment, so that they are able to make better assessments and provide appropriate services that result in better outcomes for children and families.

Acknowledgments

Many people contributed to this edition of *Understanding the Medical Diagnosis of Child Maltreatment*. Their contributions are acknowledged in no particular order of effort toward or importance to the final product.

This latest revision of *Understanding the Medical Diagnosis of Child Maltreatment* continues American Humane's long tradition of promoting excellence in CPS practice. The first edition was published in 1989 by American Humane and revised again in 1997 with both editions funded by the North Carolina Department of Human Resources. Authors of the previous editions were:

Jean C. Smith, MD;

Rebecca L. Benton, MD, MPH;

Joyce K. Moore, RN, MPH; and

Desmond K. Runyan, MD, Dr.PH.

Thank you all for laying the groundwork and bringing attention to this important topic for CPS workers to understand. I am especially grateful to Jean Smith and Joyce Moore for their contributions to this latest edition. A special thanks to North Carolina Child Protective Services and the North Carolina Department of Human Resources for their ongoing support of the Child Medical Evaluation Program at the Department of Pediatrics at the University of North Carolina at Chapel Hill. It was through this support and the work of Rebecca Benton, MD, MPH, and Desmond K. Runyan, MD, Dr.PH, on the original version that this manual has been revised, edited, and expanded to its current form.

Thank you to staff at Denver County Department of Human Services for your insights and recommendations for improving this latest edition. The contributions from Nicholas Axes, Sara Epstein, Judy Martinez. Kasey Matze, and Barb Salfisberg helped us to frame the content and make it that much more useful to CPS workers.

A world of gratitude goes to Jesse Rainey for her competent and diligent efforts. Without her, this book would not have come to fruition and I so appreciate her warm enthusiasm and endless patience for all the details involved in writing a book.

Many thanks to Maura Roessner, whose accessibility and good nature made the publishing aspect of writing this book a pleasure.

Thanks also to all the staff at American Humane, who are so passionately committed to protecting children and animals.

A special thank you to the authors for their significant real-world experience, expert contributions, and passion for the field that has made this book such a robust resource for CPS workers. In alphabetical order, these knowledgeable and perceptive individuals are:

Joyce K. Moore,

Andrew P. Sirotnak,

Jean C. Smith, and

Kathryn M. Wells.

On a personal note, I thank my family, Jeff, Devyn, and Colton Frasier, for a contrasting experience to the content of this book. The sweetness of our lives makes the scorching frankness of this subject matter easier to manage.

Lastly, thank you to all the CPS professionals for the amazing job you do in an environment of decreasing resources and increasing issues, so that children are better protected.

—Charmaine R. Brittain, MSW, PhD
Englewood, CO
December 2004

Contents

Contributors

Book Editor

Charmaine R. Brittain, MSW, PhD
Institute for Families
University of Denver
Denver, Colorado

Dr. Brittain is an expert on best child welfare practice and policy as a worker, researcher, and policy analyst, and on communicating that information to a wide variety of audiences including workers, supervisors, and managers. She was with the American Humane Association for 11 years as manager of education and professional development. Currently, she is a program and research manager for the Institute for Families at the University of Denver. She was the senior editor for the companion book to this publication, *Helping in Child Protective Services*, at American Humane. Her responsibilities include managing training projects, writing curricula on a range of topics, and developing professional educational materials.

Chapter Authors

Joyce K. Moore, RN, FNE, MPH
Nurse Consultant, Child Medical Evaluation Program
University of North Carolina–Chapel Hill
Department of Pediatrics
Chapel Hill, North Carolina

Ms. Moore joined the staff of the newly formed statewide maltreatment diagnostic program, the Child Medical Evaluation Program, in the North Carolina Office of the Chief Medical Examiner in 1976. She continues to serve as nurse consultant/coordinator of the CMEP in the Department of Pediatrics at the University of North Carolina at Chapel Hill (UNC–CH). She completed the UNC School of Nursing Sexual Assault Nurse Examiner Program in 1997 and serves as faculty for that program. Ms. Moore is a member of the UNC Hospitals child protection team, the Orange County (NC) community child protection and child fatality teams, and the Board of the North Carolina Society on the Abuse of Children.

Andrew P. Sirotnak, MD, FAAP
Associate Professor of Pediatrics
University of Colorado School of Medicine
Director, Kempe Child Protection Team
The Children's Hospital
Denver, Colorado

Dr. Sirotnak is Associate Professor of Pediatrics at the University of Colorado School of Medicine. He is the director of the Kempe Child Protection Team and Department Head for Child Abuse and Neglect at The Children's Hospital in Denver. He is also the director of the University of Colorado Health Sciences Center's Child Abuse and Neglect Fellowship Program at the Kempe Children's Center and The Children's Hospital. His current clinical work, education and outreach efforts, and research and administrative duties all focus on child maltreatment.

Jean C. Smith, MD
Associate Medical Director
North Carolina Child Medical Evaluation Program
Chapel Hill, North Carolina

Dr. Smith is Clinical Associate Professor of Pediatrics and Associate Medical Director of the North Carolina Child Medical Evaluation Program in the Department of Pediatrics at the University of North Carolina at Chapel Hill. In this capacity, she provides consultation and training to local providers and the North Carolina Department of Social Services for children with suspected abuse or neglect. Dr. Smith trained in developmental and behavioral pediatrics through fellowships and provides clinical services in developmental and behavioral pediatrics at the Public Health Center, Wake County Human Services in Raleigh, North Carolina.

Kathryn M. Wells, MD, FAAP
Denver Family Crisis Center
Denver, Colorado

Dr. Wells is currently the medical director of the Denver Family Crisis Center where she serves as the child abuse and neglect consultant for the Denver Health and Hospital Authority, the Denver Department of Human Services, the Denver Police Department, and the Denver District Attorney's Office. She is also an attending physician with the Kempe Child Protection Team at The Children's Hospital in Denver and has an academic appointment as Assistant Professor of Pediatrics at the University of Colorado Health Sciences Center.

Glossary compiled by

Jesse Rainey
Research Assistant
Children's Services
American Humane

Understanding the Medical Diagnosis
of Child Maltreatment

1

Charmaine R. Brittain

Defining Child Abuse and Neglect

Ever since the case of Mary Ellen Wilson garnered headlines as the first child rescued from an abusive situation in 1876, the plights of children who are abused and neglected have captured our attention and mobilized our resources. We have learned much about diagnosing child abuse and neglect and even more about providing effective intervention and treatment. The first step in helping maltreated children is to identify those who have been abused or neglected and often this is done through a medical diagnosis.

The Real Story of Mary Ellen Wilson

Over the years, in the retelling of Mary Ellen Wilson's story, myth has sometimes been confused with fact. Some of the inaccuracies may stem from colorful but erroneous journalism, others from simple misunderstanding of the facts, and still others from the complex history of the child protection movement in the United States and Great Britain and its link to the animal welfare movement. While it is true that Henry Bergh, president of the American Society for the Prevention of Cruelty to Animals (ASPCA), was instrumental in ensuring Mary Ellen's removal from an abusive home, it is not true that her attorney—who also worked for the ASPCA—argued that she deserved help because she was "a member of the animal kingdom." The real story—which can be pieced together from court documents, newspaper articles, and personal accounts—is quite compelling, and it illustrates the impact that a caring and committed individual can have on the life of a child.

Mary Ellen Wilson was born in 1864 to Frances and Thomas Wilson of New York City. Soon thereafter, Thomas died, and his widow took a job. No longer able to stay at home and care for her infant daughter, Francis boarded Mary Ellen (a common practice at the time) with a woman named Mary Score. As Frances's economic situation deteriorated, she slipped further into poverty, falling behind in payments for and missing visits with her daughter. As a result, Mary Score turned 2-year-old Mary Ellen over to the city's Department of Charities. The department made a decision that would have grave consequences for little Mary Ellen; it placed her illegally, without proper documentation of the relationship and with inadequate oversight, in the home of Mary and Thomas

McCormack, who claimed to be the child's biological father. In an eerie repetition of events, Thomas died shortly thereafter. His widow married Francis Connolly, and the new family moved to a tenement on West 41st Street. Mary McCormack Connolly badly mistreated Mary Ellen, and neighbors in the apartment building were aware of the child's plight. The Connollys soon moved to another tenement, but in 1874, one of their original neighbors asked Etta Angell Wheeler, a caring Methodist mission worker who visited the impoverished residents of the tenements regularly, to check on the child. At the new address, Etta encountered a chronically ill and homebound tenant, Mary Smitt, who confirmed that she often heard the cries of a child across the hall. Under the pretext of asking for help for Mrs. Smitt, Etta Wheeler introduced herself to Mary Connolly. She saw Mary Ellen's condition for herself. The 10-year-old appeared dirty and thin, was dressed in threadbare clothing, and had bruises and scars along her bare arms and legs. Mrs. Wheeler began to explore how to seek legal redress and protection for Mary Ellen.

At that time, some jurisdictions in the United States had laws that prohibited excessive physical discipline of children. New York, in fact, had a law that permitted the state to remove children who were neglected by their caregivers. Based on their interpretation of the laws and Mary Ellen's circumstances, however, New York City authorities were reluctant to intervene. Etta Wheeler continued her efforts to rescue Mary Ellen and, after much deliberation, turned to Henry Bergh, a leader of the animal humane movement in the United States and founder of the ASPCA. It was Etta Wheeler's niece who convinced her to contact Mr. Bergh by stating, "You are so troubled over that abused child, why not go to Mr. Bergh? She is a little animal surely" (Watkins, 1990, p. 3).

Mrs. Wheeler located several neighbors who were willing to testify to the mistreatment of the child and brought written documentation to Mr. Bergh. At a subsequent court hearing, Mr. Bergh said that his action was "that of a humane citizen," clarifying that he was not acting in his official capacity as president of the NYSPCA. He emphasized that he was "determined within the framework of the law to prevent the frequent cruelties practiced on children" (Watkins, 1990, p. 8). After reviewing the documentation collected by Etta Wheeler, Mr. Bergh sent an NYSPCA investigator (who posed as a census worker to gain entrance to Mary Ellen's home) to verify the allegations. Elbridge T. Gerry, an ASPCA attorney, prepared a petition to remove Mary Ellen from her home so she could testify to her mistreatment before a judge.

Mr. Bergh took action as a private citizen who was concerned about the humane treatment of a child. It was his role as president of the NYSPCA and his ties to the legal system and the press, however, that brought about Mary Ellen's rescue and the movement for a formalized child protection system.

Recognizing the value of public opinion and awareness in furthering the cause of the humane movement, Henry Bergh contacted *New York Times* reporters who took an interest in the case and attended the hearings. Thus, there were detailed newspaper accounts that described Mary Ellen's appalling physical condition.

When she was taken before Judge Lawrence, she was dressed in ragged clothing, was bruised all over her body, and had a gash over her left eye and on her cheek where Mary Connelly had struck her with a pair of scissors. On April 10, 1874, Mary Ellen testified as follows:

> My father and mother are both dead. I don't know how old I am. I have no recollection of a time when I did not live with the Connollys. . . . Mamma has been in the habit of whipping and beating me almost every day. She used to whip me with a twisted whip—a raw hide. The whip always left a black and blue mark on my body. I have now the black and blue marks on my head which were made by Mamma, and also a cut on the left side of my forehead which was made by a pair of scissors. She struck me with the scissors and cut me; I have no recollection of ever having been kissed by any one—have never been kissed by Mamma. I have never been taken on my mamma's lap and caressed or petted. I never dared to speak to anybody, because if I did I would get whipped. . . . I do not know for what I was whipped—Mamma never said anything to me when she whipped me. I do not want to go back to live with Mamma, because she beats me so. I have no recollection ever being on the street in my life. (Watkins, 1990, p. 502)

In response, Judge Lawrence immediately issued a writ de homine replagiando, provided for by Section 65 of the Habeas Corpus Act, to bring Mary Ellen under court control. The newspapers also provided extensive coverage of the caregiver Mary Connolly's trial, raising public awareness and helping to inspire various agencies and organizations to advocate for the enforcement of laws that would rescue and protect abused children (Watkins, 1990). On April 21, 1874, Mary Connolly was found guilty of felonious assault and was sentenced to one year of hard labor in the penitentiary (Watkins, 1990).

Less well known but as compelling as the details of her rescue is the rest of Mary Ellen's story. Etta Wheeler continued to play an important role in the child's life. Family correspondence and other accounts reveal that the court placed Mary Ellen in an institutional shelter for adolescent girls. Believing this to be an inappropriate setting for the 10-year-old, Mrs. Wheeler intervened. Judge Lawrence gave her permission to place the child with Mrs. Wheeler's own mother, Sally Angell, in northern New York. When Sally Angell died, Etta Wheeler's youngest sister, Elizabeth, and her husband, Darius Spencer, raised Mary Ellen. By all accounts, her life with the Spencer family was stable and nurturing.

At the age of 24, Mary Ellen married a widower and had two daughters—Etta, named after Etta Wheeler, and Florence. Later she became a foster mother to a young girl named Eunice. Etta and Florence both became teachers; Eunice was a businesswoman. Mary Ellen's children and grandchildren described her as gentle and not much of a disciplinarian. Reportedly, she lived in relative anonymity and rarely spoke with her family about her early years of abuse. In 1913, however, she agreed to attend the American Humane Association's national conference in Rochester, New York, with Etta Wheeler, her longtime advocate, who was a guest speaker at the conference. Her keynote address, "The Story of Mary Ellen Which

Started the Child Saving Crusade throughout the World" was published by American Humane. Mary Ellen died in 1956 at the age of 92.

Source: Brittain & Hunt (2004). Reprinted with permission from Oxford University Press.

◼ Incidence

Information on incidence rates comes from the National Child Abuse and Neglect Data System (NCANDS) and is collected from all states and provides statistical information; data is summarized in the yearly *Child Maltreatment* report, which is used for a variety of purposes by federal and state governments.

◼ Prevalence

Child abuse and neglect continue to concern our communities. According to *Child Maltreatment 2003*, an estimated 2.9 million referrals of child abuse or neglect (representing approximately 5.5 million children) were received by public child protective services (CPS) agencies. From these referrals, 67.9% were screened in or investigated while 32.1% were screened out. Of those referrals investigated, 906,000 children were confirmed or substantiated to be victims of abuse or neglect. The incidence rate is 12.4 children out of every 1,000 were found to be abused or neglected (U.S. Department of Health and Human Services, 2005; also see Figure 1.1). ◖

Sources of Reports

Twenty-one percent of referrals were made by family members, friends, or neighbors known to the family. More than half of referrals made (56.8%) were from professionals who are considered "mandated reporters." Most common mandated reporters are educators; legal, law enforcement, and criminal justice personnel; and social services, medical, and mental health professionals.

Types of Maltreatment in 2003

During 2003, child victims experienced the following types of maltreatment:

Neglect: 60.9%

Physical abuse: 18.9%

Sexual abuse: 9.9%

Emotional and psychological abuse: 4.9%

Other: 6.9% (includes abandonment, threats of harm, and congenital drug addiction)

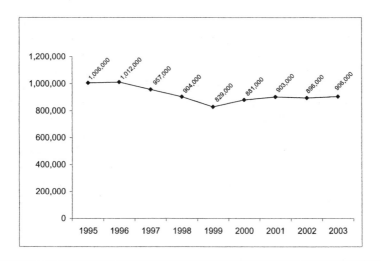

Figure 1.1. Number of Children Abused or Neglected.

For purposes of data collection and reporting, maltreatment was assigned one primary category, but in reality, child victims may experience multiple types of maltreatment. For example, a child may be physically abused and also emotionally abused.

In terms of gender, 48.3% of victims were male and 51.7% were female. Additionally, almost 74% of all victims of abuse and neglect were under the age of 12 and 22.6% were under the age of 3. Ethnicity rates of children who were abused and neglected, in comparison to the larger U.S. population, are shown in Table 1.1. (About 2.4% of the total U.S. population identified themselves as belonging to more than one race [U.S. Census Bureau, 2003].)

Table 1.1. Ethnicity Rates of Abused Children

	Ethnicity of Children Abused and Neglected	Ethnicity of U.S. Population
Caucasian	53.6%	69%
African American	25.5%	13%
Hispanic	11.5%	13.5%
Native Americans/Alaska Natives	1.7%	1%
Asian/Pacific Islanders	0.6%	4%

Sources: U.S. Census Bureau, 2003; U.S. Department of Health and Human Services, 2005.

Minority overrepresentation continues to concern the child welfare field. According to Earle and Cross (2001), relative to their numbers in the general population, children of African Americans, Native Americans, or native Alaskans are overrepresented in the child welfare system, and children of Whites, Asians, or Pacific Islanders are underrepresented. Research substantiates that minorities are overrepresented in foster care, spend a longer time in care, have a higher rate of reentry into care, have less stability in their out-of-home placements, and wait much longer to be adopted (Courtney et al., 1996; Derezotes & Poertner, 2002; Roberts, 2002). Speculated explanations (sometimes contradictory) for this overrepresentation include institutional racism, poverty, substance abuse, and poorly trained CPS staff (McDaniel & Lescher, 2004).

Child Fatalities

In 2003, 1,500 children died of abuse or neglect. Younger children are most vulnerable, with 43.6% of all child fatalities occurring in children younger than 1 year and 88.9% occurring in children younger than 8 years of age.

Between 1990 and 1993, child maltreatment incidence rates increased each year, decreased from 1993 through 1999, and have been steadily increasing again since 1999. The rate of victimization was 13.4 per 1,000 children in 1990. The rate peaked at 15.3 children per 1,000 in 1993, then decreased to 11.8 per 1,000 in 1999, while increasing slightly to 12.3 children per 1,000 in 2002.

■ Defining Child Abuse and Neglect

The federal government sets forth minimum guidelines for states to define child abuse and neglect in the Child Abuse Prevention and Treatment Act, or CAPTA (42 U.S.C.A. §5106g). From these minimum guidelines, states have developed their own statutory definitions. See the National Clearinghouse on Child Abuse and Neglect Web site at http://nccanch.acf.hhs.gov/general/legal/statutes/search/index.cfm to access each state's definitions. State definitions vary widely and guide each state's intervention and involvement to help ensure the safety and well-being of children.

CAPTA, as amended by the Keeping Children and Families Safe Act of 2003, defines child abuse and neglect as, at minimum, "any recent act or failure to act on the part of a parent or caretaker which results in death, serious physical or emotional harm, sexual abuse or exploitation; or an act or failure to act which presents an imminent risk of serious harm."

Most states recognize four major types of maltreatment: neglect, physical abuse, sexual abuse, and emotional abuse. Often, maltreatment types occur in combination and, in fact, a reasonable argument could be made that emotional maltreatment is inherent in all forms of maltreatment.

The examples provided below are for general information purposes only. Not all states' definitions will include all of the examples listed below, and individual states' definitions may cover additional situations not mentioned here or may define abuse more broadly, such as risk of harm.

Neglect is failure to provide for a child's basic needs. There are different types of neglect:

- Physical (e.g., failure to provide necessary food or shelter or lack of appropriate supervision)

- Medical (e.g., failure to provide necessary medical or mental health treatment)

- Educational (e.g., failure to educate a child or attend to special education needs)

- Emotional (e.g., inattention to a child's emotional needs, failure to provide psychological care, or permitting the child to use alcohol or other drugs)

All of these situations should not automatically be labeled neglect, as all neglectful situations should be evaluated within context. Workers should consider the cultural values, the standards of care in the community, and the circumstances surrounding the current situation. In and of itself, poverty is not neglect but may precipitate unsafe situations that could be mitigated through information and assistance. However, when a family ignores critical information that may protect a child or fails to access available resources, leaving the child's health or safety at risk, then CPS intervention may be required.

> *Physical abuse* is physical injury (ranging from minor bruises to severe fractures or death) as a result of punching, beating, kicking, biting, shaking, throwing, stabbing, choking, hitting (with a hand, stick, strap, or other object), burning, or otherwise harming a child. Such injury is considered abuse regardless of whether the caretaker intended to hurt the child.

> *Sexual abuse* includes activities by a parent or caretaker such as fondling a child's genitals, penetration, incest, rape, sodomy, indecent exposure, and exploitation through prostitution or the production of pornographic materials.

> *Emotional abuse* is a pattern of behavior that impairs a child's emotional development or sense of self-worth. This may include constant criticism, threats, or rejection, as well as withholding love, support, or guidance. Emotional abuse is often difficult to prove and, therefore, CPS may not be able to intervene without evidence of harm to the child. Emotional abuse is almost always present when other forms of abuse are identified.

The following chapters contain important information to guide CPS workers in understanding the medical diagnosis of child maltreatment. Better informed workers will make more effective decisions around case planning and intervention, which will lead to children and families who are safer, live in permanent homes, and have improved well-being.

References

Brittain, C., & Hunt, D. (2004). *Helping in child protective services: A competency-based casework handbook* (2nd ed.). New York: Oxford University Press.

Child Abuse Prevention and Treatment Act (CAPTA), 42 U.S.C.A. §5106g (1974).

Courtney, M., Barth, R., Berrick, J., Brooks, D., Needell, B., & Park, L. (1996). Race and child welfare services: Past research and future directions. *Child Welfare, 75*, 99–137.

Derezotes, D., & Poertner, J. (2002). *Factors contributing to the overrepresentation of African American children in the child welfare system: What we know and don't know.* Urbana-Champaign, IL: Children and Family Research Center, School of Social Work, University of Illinois at Urbana-Champaign.

Earle, K. A., & Cross, A. (2001). *Child abuse and neglect among American Indian/ Alaska Native children: An analysis of existing data.* Seattle, WA: Casey Family Programs.

McDaniel, N., & Lescher, N. (2004). The history of child protective services. In C. Brittain & D. Hunt (Eds.), *Helping in child protective services: A competency-based casework handbook* (2nd ed., pp. 31–49). New York: Oxford University Press.

Roberts, D. (2002). *Shattered bonds: The color of child welfare.* New York: Basic Books.

U.S. Census Bureau. (2003). *People: Race and ethnicity.* Retrieved from http://factfinder.census.gov/jsp/saff/SAFFInfo.jsp?_pageId=tp9_race_ethnicity

U.S. Department of Health and Human Services, Administration on Children, Youth, and Families. (2005). *Child maltreatment 2003.* Washington, DC: U.S. Government Printing Office.

Watkins, S. A. (1990). The Mary Ellen myth: Correcting child welfare history. *Social Work, 35*(6), 500–503.

2

Charmaine R. Brittain

Joyce K. Moore

Working With Medical Providers

■ Reasons for Working With Medical Providers

Medical providers play a key role alongside CPS workers when working with families experiencing child abuse or neglect. CPS workers' interactions with the medical community include receiving and making referrals, requesting consultations, and advocating and arranging for medical services. Medical providers include many diverse professionals such as physicians, nurses, nurse practitioners, physicians' assistants, clinicians, hospital social workers, psychiatrists, psychologists, and natural or traditional healers (e.g., curanderos, shamanic healers, acupuncturists).

Medical providers have an integral role on the team of professionals who work with children and families. Through expert consultation, medical providers provide information on the medical aspects of child abuse and neglect and will assess, diagnose, and treat injuries or conditions resulting from child abuse and neglect. Medical providers can also supply information about medical care prior to involvement with CPS and provide ongoing preventative care, as well as treat chronic medical conditions such as asthma or diabetes. They are a resource to parents, caregivers, and CPS workers on topics such as good nutrition and child development. For cases requiring court intervention, medical providers may act as expert witnesses to interpret complex medical information and present possible hypotheses for the causes of harm to children or conditions that may or may not be preexisting. Additionally, on an ongoing basis, medical providers offer another set of eyes to monitor at-risk children.

CPS workers interact with medical providers for many reasons, but this partnership especially helps with the diagnoses of nonaccidental injuries resulting from maltreatment. For example, a 16-day-old infant presents with a tear in his trachea and bruises on his bottom. While the parents deny harming the infant and no other caregivers watched the child, the medical provider supervising the case quickly disproves that the child could have hurt himself in the way the parents claim and informs the CPS worker and law enforcement that this case is clearly child abuse. After treatment for her injuries, the child is taken into protective custody and the parents are charged with criminal child abuse. Later, the medical provider will testify in court about the child's injuries.

Sometimes a worker senses that a child's injuries are inconsistent; perhaps something just does not seem right, leading the worker to contact a medical provider to discuss the situation. Some hospitals, especially children's hospitals, offer special consultation teams where workers can present information about a suspected case of child maltreatment for advice on how to proceed. Medical providers may help to discern inconsistencies or gaps in stories or give advice about adequate care or nutrition.

Case Example

A worker was perplexed about a case and decided to take it to the child protection team at the local children's hospital. A 2-year-old child had unexplained injuries at various ages of his life: none were too serious but were altogether suspicious. The CPS worker and the police detective assigned to the case presented the case information, including reports, interviews, and pictures, to the team. They assisted in making an assessment and decisions around custody and service planning for the family.

■ Typical Interactions With Medical Providers

Medical providers will call in cases to CPS that are clearly abuse or neglect. In fact, they are legally obligated to report all cases that raise reasonable concern of abuse or neglect. Therefore, they may call in reports on a variety of other situations such as the following:

- Unexplained injuries or injuries that do not match the caregivers' stories
- Accidental injuries to a child that occur when the child was clearly unsupervised
- Teenage girls delivering infants when there is concern about the babies' health or safety
- Drug-exposed infants
- Domestic violence situations when an adult is injured and a child is known to have been present

Calls to CPS agencies can be placed by a variety of medical providers depending on the medical provider's protocol or policies. Sometimes a referral call is made by the hospital social worker; sometimes by a nurse or physician. CPS agencies also receive referrals from midwives, psychiatrists, and traditional or natural healers like a curandero (a person in Mexican culture who helps heal various ailments by using traditional cultural methods).

At one time or another, workers will need to rely on medical providers for help with cases.

Case Example

One-year-old Jemma was missing her sixth chromosome, causing a failure-to-thrive condition. Her teenage mother was overwhelmed with two other children and so CPS was called by the medical provider to ensure the child's safety and support the family. Because of this devastating condition, the medical provider expected Jemma to pass away by the time she was 2. The family was prepared for her imminent death and even signed a "do not resuscitate order." The CPS worker's role started out more as a support to an overwhelmed family and as grief counselor to prepare the family for the loss. Jemma lived but seemed to be languishing at home so after thorough consultations with the medical staff, the CPS worker sought a medical foster care placement for the child. Once placed in this home and with teamwork from the medical staff, Jemma thrived and began to gain weight. During visitations, the foster parent coached the biological mother on the child's care and within a year, Jemma was reunified with her family and continued to thrive, despite the odds. Through teamwork with the medical staff and the CPS agency, the family's needs were addressed, resulting in a positive outcome for the family and a gratifying experience for the professionals.

Sometimes children or adolescents will be more candid with a medical provider than with a worker. For example, a 14-year-old taken to a local hospital for a medical exam may disclose sexual abuse to the physician's assistant but had previously never said anything about the molestation to the CPS worker assigned to the case. Adolescents may especially perceive a medical provider as a more trusting confidant, as they may fear that disclosure to a CPS worker could disrupt their current life by an unwanted placement or some other significant life change.

Medical providers also interact with CPS workers as part of ongoing casework with a child and family. CPS workers may contact pediatricians or clinics for medical information, medical records, or referrals. Every child should have a "medical home" where a central source manages medical care and records. This is especially important for children with chronic conditions who are placed in out-of-home care, which may necessitate a change in medical providers. For example, a child with cerebral palsy is placed in a medical foster home in a town 45 miles away from his home, necessitating a change in the child's physician on a temporary basis. The CPS worker contacts the original pediatrician to assure continuity of care, obtain medical records, and facilitate communication with the temporary medical provider. Such efforts ensure consistent care and accurate recording of the child's medical history.

■ Barriers to Working With Medical Providers

Like interactions with various community organizations, experiences of working with a medical provider can range from extraordinarily positive to frustratingly negative. Ongoing cases can become more contentious between medical providers and CPS workers when there is disagreement between them about a child's treatment or living arrangements. Sometimes a medical provider will have strong feelings about case decisions such as removing a child from a home and this might conflict with a worker's opinion.

Case Example

Two-year-old Cameron was diagnosed as morbidly obese, weighing 84 lbs. The local children's hospital staff treated the boy for a variety of health problems resulting from his weight and blamed the parents for his condition. None of the family's other children or his parents were overweight but the hospital was extremely concerned about the family's ability to attend to the child's nutrition. The CPS agency conducted an investigation and found that the parents were suitably concerned about the child's condition and determined that the child should remain in the home; however, the family lacked knowledge on appropriate nutrition and meal planning. After the investigation was complete, the staff members at the children's hospital were hostile to the worker because they perceived leaving the child in the home as dangerous. But the worker decided that the parents needed to be taught about nutrition instead of taking their child out of the home as hospital staff had openly advocated for. In order to ease tensions, the worker should have communicated more clearly that the CPS agency's job was to keep children in the home when at all possible and provide appropriate interventions to families in order to keep families together.

Sometimes medical providers wear "professional blinders," especially when dealing with economically advantaged families or those from rural communities, and they may be unable to speculate that abuse might have occurred in these families. Although it is stereotypical to think that abuse only occurs in lower income families or in urban settings, in reality these assumptions are not uncommon. Everyone needs to be conscious of and take measures to avoid perpetuating stereotypes.

Case Example

A young woman gave birth to a child who tested positive for cocaine. The child was the grandchild of a well-known and highly regarded physician in the community. Throughout the CPS investigation, the CPS agency was at odds with the medical providers and it became quite unpleasant as the medical providers were adamant that the family should not be involved with CPS. In court, a high-profile attorney intimidated the CPS agency but ultimately the CPS agency prevailed. A case was opened with intensive services—but not without a permanently damaged relationship between the medical provider and the CPS agency.

In situations like these, the CPS worker needs to avoid being intimidated and the medical provider needs to be open to the possibility of maltreatment.

Not every relationship or interaction can be improved; sometimes it is just as important to agree to disagree. Concern over liability may cause medical providers to appear to act defensively, when in fact they are only being vigilant. The medical provider's primary role is care of the patient and he or she will be protective of issues that he or she perceives will interfere with that primary goal. If a worker feels that a standard of care is not being followed, he or she should talk with a supervisor at the CPS agency and refrain from contacting a medical board or other oversight medical organization as that might only exacerbate the situation. Remember that medical providers think in terms of quality assurance as CPS workers do.

Medical providers receive varying levels of training regarding the detection of abuse and neglect. Most, especially physicians, will have had some formalized training on detecting abuse and will know their reporting responsibilities. All residency programs in pediatrics and emergency medicine will have some basic level of training. The level of training depends on the practice specialty. Most physicians belong to any number of national medical organizations that typically offer continuing medical resources on abuse and neglect. The American Academy of Pediatrics Web site (www.aap.org) provides specialized information on child abuse and neglect for medical providers. If a CPS worker is concerned about a medical provider's experience and training on abuse and neglect, he or she should ask about this and even inquire about previous experiences in dealing with traumatized children. See the section later in this chapter for ideas on working out differences and communicating more effectively with medical providers.

Confidentiality

Issues of confidentiality can be barriers for successful partnerships with medical providers, as one or both of the parties may use it as an excuse to inhibit communication, by saying, for example, "Sorry, I'm not allowed to talk about that subject because of the confidentiality rules." However, confidentiality should not impede successful collaboration because there are mechanisms to share information that balance the interests of children and families with those of agencies needing to exchange information (Soler & Peters, 1993).

Confidentiality is often expressed in statutes, policies, memorandums of understanding, or other agreements. To understand various confidentiality provisions expressed in statutes or policies, consider the following questions (Soler & Peters, 1993):

- What information is considered confidential?
- What information is not considered confidential?

- What exceptions are there to the confidentiality restriction? Who and for what purposes can information be shared?

- Can information be shared with the consent of the family? What information can be released with consent? What are the requirements for a consent release? Who is authorized to give consent for information related to the children?

The Health Insurance Portability and Accountability Act (commonly known as HIPAA) is a federal law intended to guard employees' medical and health information. It should not be used as a barrier to communicating with medical providers; as with all confidentiality requirements it can be attended to without jeopardizing communication or confidentiality. A clear exception to HIPAA rules is made when child abuse is alleged; during the investigation stage of a case these rules do not trump state law. When investigations are open, workers can communicate freely with medical providers to gather information and make an assessment of the current situation. Items such as photographs or imaging scans can be released to law enforcement or CPS agencies. However, HIPAA still only allows sharing of the minimum necessary medical information and the provider cannot and will not release information that they do not feel is important or related to the investigation (for example, a mother's medical records when the child is reported for a positive drug screen at birth). When the investigation is complete and a case is accepted for ongoing services, then HIPAA rules must be respected and appropriate confidentiality disclosure forms must be signed by a child's legal guardian in order to allow communication between medical providers and CPS agency staff regarding a child's medical condition. Disclosure forms regarding a child should include

- the name of the person authorizing the release;

- the name of the child's guardian;

- specific types of information to release (could be general medical information);

- the reason for the information being requested;

- the purpose of the release;

- the expiration date; and

- the explanation of the patient's rights about the release of information.

As part of the initial case investigation and case acceptance process, good practice dictates the routine gathering of medical release forms.

Because the HIPAA regulations are relatively new, not all medical providers may understand the child abuse exceptions during the investigation stage and may not be aware of the release forms that will facilitate communication once a case has been opened. These regulations do not necessarily change practice but it does change the procedures for interaction with medical providers beyond the investigation stage. If a worker is still uncertain on how to proceed, he or she should check with the agency's attorney or even with a privacy or information officer at the largest local hospital in the community. A local medical society might also be a useful resource (Soler & Peters, 1993).

Applying the confidentiality screening questions from above to the HIPAA regulations generates the following information, which should encourage communication between a medical provider and a CPS worker:

- What information is considered confidential?
  - All medical records related to a patient.
- What information is not considered confidential?
  - Any information relevant to an exception (e.g., child abuse).
- What exceptions are there to the confidentiality restriction? Who and for what purposes can information be shared?
  - An open child abuse investigation is considered an exception. Medical providers and CPS agency staff or law enforcement may freely exchange information during the investigatory stage of the case. However, only the minimum necessary personal health care information can be released. Once the case is opened for services, then appropriate confidentiality release forms must be signed prior to communication.
- Can information be shared with the consent of the family? What information can be released with consent? What are the requirements for a consent release? Who is authorized to give consent for information related to children?
  - Consent is not necessary during the investigation phase of a case. Once a case is opened, the child's legal guardian must give written consent on the standard HIPAA release of information form and/or any other form as designated by the medical provider or the CPS agency.

Strategies for Sharing Information

Agencies can successfully balance the privacy rights of families and their own needs to share information and find ways to share most of the necessary information. Some of these strategies include the following (Soler & Peters, 1993):

- Obtain a signed release of information from the person who is the subject of the information. Do this on a routine basis, typically when assessments are conducted or services commence.

- Provide notices to the family of the agency's need to release information both verbally and in writing. If the family does not speak English, be sure to have information translated.

- Develop formal interagency agreements and memoranda of understanding between CPS agencies and medical providers. 🖳

- Develop and use multiagency release forms that satisfy the confidentiality mandates of each agency and HIPAA regulations.

- Ask the medical provider up front what forms or other paperwork are needed to release information as it will vary from place to place.

■ Working Together

Successful partnerships can be achieved but it is important to clarify and reinforce what has to be in place in order to initiate, support, and maintain these partnerships on behalf of the children and families involved in the CPS system. Workers should discuss with supervisors and administrators how to collaboratively work with medical providers. Workers should also determine if written protocols, agreements, or memorandums of understanding exist between the CPS agency and the medical providers within a community. If these agreements are current and frequently reviewed and updated, they can help define roles, minimize conflicts, and assure the availability and quality of services (National Association of Public Child Welfare Administrators, 1999; Child Welfare League of America, 1989–1999).

Collaborating With Medical Providers

Principles for collaboratively working with a medical provider—or any community provider—are similar:

- Build and maintain trust.

- Communicate about core values. Explain that CPS works hard to keep children safe, achieve permanency, and improve their well-being. Remember that the medical provider's role is also to provide complete medical care for the patient, which includes participating in efforts to protect children. It is often helpful to explain the important role of the medical provider when working together in these difficult situations.

- Reach agreement and stay focused on common goals. Know what those goals are, as they may be different. For example, CPS agency staff's goals are to prevent child abuse and ensure safety and permanency; for medical providers, the goals are to treat the presenting condition and prevent it from occurring again. As a part of that they are also bound to confidentiality expectations and requirements.

- Develop a common language. Avoid jargon and acronyms. Achieve a common understanding of what terms mean: for example, "strengths-based" or "family involvement."

- Demonstrate respect for the knowledge and experience of each person.

- Assume positive intentions of all parties and that everyone is genuinely interested in working together.

- Recognize the strengths, needs, and limitations of all parties.

- Honor the knowledge and skills everyone brings to the process.

- Share decision making, risk taking, and accountability so that decisions are made and risks are taken as a team.

- Express appreciation to each other. A letter or a call to administration to let one another know their efforts made for a family are appreciated can be effective (Goldman, Salus, Wolcott, & Kennedy, 2003).

Methods for Enhancing the Relationship

Many strategies can be used to enhance the relationship between the worker and medical provider. The following ideas provide a partial list for improving the relationship and are similar to any strategies recommended for improving communication and cooperation.

Develop trust. Trust is best achieved when all members of the partnership can reach agreement about norms of behavior for working together. Also, by developing mutual respect, it is easier to take risks, be creative, and explore difficult issues. Trust will also allow all parties to correct misconceptions and be open to learning about each other's organizations. Most of all, trust will facilitate candor and ease in working together on behalf of children and families.

Mutually educate each other. Workers can help medical providers understand their role to protect children and families. They can help medical providers formulate questions of children and adult caregivers that might illuminate maltreatment and provide information on definitions and differentials. They can provide information on various cultures that might affect the medical relationship between the provider and patient. Additionally, workers offer a wealth of knowledge on community resources that a medical provider might not know. Likewise, medical providers can provide important information on diagnosing and treating medical conditions. They can also help workers understand why a caregiver's story is at odds with the child's current medical condition. Medical providers offer insight on the reality of future conditions and treatment on an ongoing basis.

Be professional. Workers should seek out medical providers and establish a working relationship for referral of children and payment for services, including indicated diagnostic studies (such as blood screens or imaging scans). Many agencies have a payment mechanism in place for these evaluations. Be sure to ask clear questions about the child's health and medical condition and make specific requests for diagnostic services that may help to clarify the presence or absence of maltreatment.

Maximize the medical provider's time. Medical providers will be most appreciative if all required authorizations and referral information and questions are completed and presented to the provider prior to the child's medical evaluation. CPS workers should make every effort to ensure that scheduled appointments are kept. If possible, workers should accompany children to the medical appointment. If a medical provider's court testimony is needed, CPS workers should also work with their agency's legal counsel to minimize time spent in legal proceedings by such measures as allowing the medical provider to be on "telephone standby" or by arranging a specific time for the medical testimony. CPS workers should also be familiar with sources of compensation for time spent in preparing and presenting testimony. All of these efforts minimize unnecessary use of the medical provider's time, which takes them away from caring for other patients in need of their services.

Refer less problematic cases. The working relationship between CPS workers and medical providers will be enhanced by referring children in need of more routine care such as a well-child checkup or a sports physical to primary care providers. Abuse and neglect specialists' expertise should be used for the abuse and neglect issues; children should be taken to the primary care provider for routine care and unrelated medical concerns.

Engage in case staffings. A powerful method for facilitating communication, staffings bring together all parties involved in a case including hospital staff, CPS agency staff, and community providers. They can be arranged on a formal, scheduled basis or an ad hoc basis to address more difficult cases. Staffings are sometimes the best way to talk about the facts, determine various perspectives, identify resources, make decisions, and plan for the future. These staffings can be integrated into family decision-making techniques, such as family group conferences, so that decisions are made with the family, not for the family.

Follow up often. Offer regular feedback and communicate with medical providers about the outcome of a referral. Let them know of future plans for working with the family and that their medical information and assistance was useful for the case outcome. One of the frustrations often voiced by medical providers is "I never hear if the work I did made any difference for the child" or "I never knew if the child was okay." Sometimes the follow-up boosts the medical providers' enthusiasm for working collaboratively, while other times it may be a lesson learned. Either way, this kind of follow-up helps to build relationships and trust that will facilitate future interactions.

Successfully Working Through Conflict

Conflict is healthy yet inevitable when people work together collaboratively, especially when working together on such an emotional issue as child maltreatment. Conflict is best handled in a trusting relationship. When all participants act as equal partners in designing and implementing collaborative efforts, then conflict can be minimized or at least resolved more quickly. When conflict does occur, strategies to resolve it include the following:

- Separate the people from the problem. Interpersonal issues need to be untangled from the real problem to be addressed. To do this, listen and try to hear the other's perspective.

- Avoid positional bargaining. Staking out a position means one party in the conflict digs in and refuses to give any ground in the negotiation, thus precluding a bargained resolution to the situation.

- Move from positions to interests. Try to find at least some areas of agreement and determine multiple interests.

- Refrain from rushing into premature solutions. It may be tempting to accept the first viable alternative to end the conflict but that may not serve the real purpose of helping children and families. Instead, generate multiple solutions to resolve the problem.

- Select and use objective criteria to evaluate the viability of the options generated (Strom-Gottfried, 1998).

If nothing seems to be working, it is time to call in a professional mediator to resolve barriers that interfere with working together on behalf of families.

An Example of an Interaction With a Medical Provider

Miguel, 7 years old, was brought to the emergency room with a black eye, a cut on the back of his head, and multiple other bruises. His father, Enrique, stated that Miguel had fallen from a neighborhood swing set. A resident physician, Dr. Kabal, examined the child and treated him for his injuries. Because the injuries were thought to be accidental, child protective services was not called.

Two days later, a report was called in to the CPS hotline by the school nurse, stating that Miguel had confided to a classmate that his dad had gotten mad and "beat him up" for spilling a gallon of milk on the floor. The CPS worker, Lionel, interviewed Miguel at school and observed his injuries. Miguel seemed confused and complained of a bad headache, so the CPS worker determined that a visit to the emergency room was in order in case there was a complication resulting from his injury. The school called his mother, who arrived to take him to the emergency room. Lionel followed in his car. At the emergency room, the same physician who conducted the initial exam two days prior was assigned to Miguel's case. After Miguel was examined and treated, Lionel asked to speak to the physician. A portion of the conversation went something like this:

> **Lionel:** How could you miss this as a case of child abuse? It's clear this couldn't have happened on a playground. What were you thinking?!?
>
> **Dr. Kabal:** The story seemed credible to me and in any case, even if it was, you just would have taken him from his family and they seemed to be like good, caring people who probably just made a mistake.
>
> **Lionel:** A mistake! A mistake that could've cost this kid his eyesight or worse, his life! All you docs are the same: you don't know anything about how to protect kids!
>
> **Dr. Kabal:** That's right; that is your job, not mine. My job is to care for my patients' injuries and illnesses. Don't come in here again, and next time, you can talk to our legal department.

It is safe to say that the worker blew this opportunity to engage the physician in a productive exchange of information. In fact, Lionel has now colored Dr. Kabal's perception of all CPS workers and confirmed his opinion on the motives of a CPS agency.

Instead, a more productive conversation could have gone like this:

> **Lionel:** What was the parent's story when he was brought in two days ago?
>
> **Dr. Kabal:** His dad said he fell from the top of the monkey bars on the playground and landed so that his head banged against a pole and his cheek landed on a rock. He said most of the bruises were just play bruises that he got from falling off his bike and roughhousing with his uncle. Frankly, I was concerned but it seemed like a plausible story. Miguel wouldn't say much when asked; he seemed really upset about having to get stitches.
>
> **Lionel:** Geez, that must have been disconcerting and puzzling as well. I'm wondering if you've received any training on child abuse because if not, I know of a great resource at the local children's hospital.
>
> **Dr. Kabal:** Oh, yeah, I heard about that and it sounds like a good idea because I sure don't want to miss something like this again. I did receive training in my residency program and we've certainly

attended the continuing education at the hospital, but more information would be helpful. But what if I had called it in, wouldn't you all have just yanked him out of the house? He was already so traumatized by his injuries.

Lionel: I understand how you might feel that way. Some people actually think our motto is, "you hatch 'em, we'll snatch 'em." But really, nothing could be further from the truth—we are trained to systematically assess a situation to determine if a child can safely remain with his parents. If that is not possible, we put the child in a permanent living situation as soon as possible. We work hard to find relatives for children to stay with if it becomes apparent they cannot stay at home and be safe. Like you, we want the best possible treatment outcome that addresses a child's physical and emotional health. I can help make arrangements to have that speaker come in from the children's hospital. But back to Miguel, could you please explain that medical term you used a little while ago and tell me what kind of special care he'll need over the next week or so?

In this exchange, the CPS worker made his motives clear, communicated respect and empathy to the physician, and made available educational information that might inform future decision making around situations that may present as abuse or neglect in the future.

In conclusion, when working together, medical providers and CPS workers can protect children and strengthen families. Both parties must commit to a respectful and mutually beneficial relationship through ongoing positive interactions. Like all relationships, it takes self- awareness, focused effort, and communication.

References

Child Welfare League of America. (1989–1999). *Standards for child welfare services.* (Rev. ed.). Washington, DC: Author.

Goldman, J., Salus, M., Wolcott, D., & Kennedy, K. (2003). *A coordinated response to child abuse and neglect: The foundation for practice.* Retrieved from http://nccanch.acf.hhs.gov/pubs/usermanuals/foundation/index.cfm

National Association of Public Child Welfare Administrators. (1999). *Guidelines for a model system of protective services for abused and neglected children and their families.* Washington, DC: American Public Human Services Association.

Soler, M. I., & Peters, C. M. (1993). *Who should know what? Confidentiality and information sharing in service integration.* New York: National Center for Service Integration.

Strom-Gottfried, G. (1998). Applying a conflict resolution framework to disputes in managed care. *Social Work, 43*(5), 393–401.

3

Joyce K. Moore

Jean C. Smith

Cutaneous Manifestations of Abuse

Cutaneous manifestations of abuse are injuries such as bruises and abrasions located on the skin. Recognizing and interpreting their significance is one of the most frequently utilized skills of the CPS worker. Remember, however, that the worker is not alone in determining the nature of these injuries. The medical provider will play a crucial role in helping distinguish abuse from differential skin conditions, diseases, or accidental trauma. Child abuse is considered a diagnosis of exclusion, which means that while the safety of the child is protected, all other possible causes of the injury must be excluded. Another explanation of an accidental cause is the differential diagnosis.

All children sustain some bruises and scratches in their normal, everyday play. In the attempt to distinguish these play injuries from abusive ones, it is crucial that the worker obtain a detailed and concise history. In relating this history to the doctor, be sure to include details such as how long ago the incident occurred and the exact details of the accident. For example, how tall the table was from which he fell, or what game he was playing when he bruised his legs or buttocks. In determining the etiology of cutaneous injuries, the medical provider must consider several aspects, such as the age and developmental status of the child and the specific location, shape, and size of the injuries.

■ The Pathophysiology of Bruises

Bruising occurs when some force disrupts the small vessels under the skin, allowing blood to escape. Bleeding usually starts immediately following the injury and may continue briefly or for hours, depending on the force of the injury, the size of the damaged vessels, the type of tissue injured, and the adequacy of the victim's coagulation mechanism (the body's ability to stop bleeding by itself). For a child who has no coagulation deficiencies or blood disorders, use the following general guidelines in assessing the bruise.

1. How old is the child? Bruises and abrasions in a child who is not yet walking should always be cause for question. An infant who can roll or crawl may sustain a fall from a bed or couch, producing minor soft tissue injury, frequently to the head. However, if there is extensive bruising or swelling or if the injuries are noted over several body surfaces, a simple fall is not an acceptable history. As children begin to pull up, cruise, and walk independently, the frequency of activity-related bruises naturally increases (Sugar, Taylor, & Feldman, 1999).

2. Where is the bruise? Loose skin with vessels unsupported by underlying bony or muscular structures will bruise more easily than supported skin. This makes the eyelids and genitalia predisposed to bruising following even minor trauma. Sometimes the injured vessels are located so deeply under the skin that it takes days for the blood to migrate to the surface and become visible. These deep-seated bruises may remain dark for days or weeks.

3. Can the age of the bruise be determined? Early child abuse literature suggested that the estimated age of a bruise could be reliably determined from its color. However, more recent literature does not support this belief. The color of a bruise is dependent on many variables, including the type of tissue, the depth of the injury, the individual's skin tone, and re-injury to the site. The only published controlled research on color changes in bruises suggests that red, blue, or purple coloration may be present at any time during the "life" of the bruise and that yellow coloration usually means that the bruise is older than 18 hours (Langois & Gresham, 1991; Schwartz & Ricci, 1996).

4. What size is the bruise? The color of the bruise begins to fade from the edges inward, causing the bruise to get smaller and smaller as it begins to heal. If the size of the bruise is no longer compatible with the size of the force that caused it, then the bruise is most likely old enough to have started healing.

5. Document the injury with photographs. It is essential that either the worker or the medical provider carefully document the bruises with color photographs or slides. The pictures should be taken early within the first few days of the incident. Photographs should clearly show the location, size, and color of the injury. A measurement scale, the child's name, and the date the photo was taken should be included in every photograph. ⬛ The worker should keep in mind that the bruises may not appear on the skin until a few days after the trauma; thus the photos taken on the same day of the incident may not show the true extent of the injury. If the child is accessible, try to take another set of photos a few days after the first set. The changes in color at this stage may greatly enhance the credibility of the evidence. The worker should not assume that the medical provider's documentation will always be adequate. Taking the time to re-photograph the child may provide crucial evidence for the case. If the worker and the medical provider lack experience or expertise with photography, it may be useful to contact the local police department for an experienced photographer. Any photographs of a child's genitals or a girl's developing breasts should be performed in the private context of the medical examination. Digital photography is now in widespread use and accepted for medical and legal purposes. All photographs should be accompanied by written descriptions of the injuries.

Common Sites of Bruises—Accident Versus Abuse

The actual location of the bruise is helpful in differentiating an abusive contusion from one that is accidental or a "play bruise." Bruises occurring over the bony prominences, such as the knees, shins, forehead, or elbows, are more likely to be accidental than those occurring over areas of soft tissue, such as the cheeks, buttocks, or stomach. Most falls produce one bruise on a single surface, while abusive bruises frequently cover many areas of the body.

Face and Head

Accidental bruises usually occur over the bony prominences, such as the forehead or chin. It is not uncommon for babies in the first few months of life to scratch their cheeks, ears, nose, and eyes with their fingernails, which are often long and hard to trim. Bruises of the forehead are not uncommon for the child who is just learning to walk and climb. Injuries to the soft tissue of the cheeks may be due to slapping or pinching.

Upper Lip and Frenulum

Bruises or lacerations inside the mouth in these areas usually come from having a bottle or feeding spoon jammed into the baby's mouth. These types of injuries cannot be self-inflicted until the baby is old enough to sit up and fall forward. They are often accompanied by a history of inconsolable crying (see the section about oral injury in chapter 6).

Ear

Pinch marks on the earlobe are not uncommon, as is swelling of the external ear, caused from blows to that tissue. Repetitive injury will cause a characteristic "cauliflower ear." Children who have been pinched or pulled on the earlobe usually have a matching mark on each surface.

Neck

Any strange bruises or cuts on the neck are almost always due to being choked or strangled by a human hand, rope, dog collar, and so on. Similar marks may come from sudden traction on a shirt or bib.

Knee or Shin

These are the most common sites for accidental bruises, not only in the child who is learning to walk but also in older children, who may fall or bump into objects when playing.

Buttocks, Lower Back, and Lateral Thighs

Bruises in these areas are almost always related to punishment from paddling; multiple bruises in these areas are not *commonly* accidental. 🔖

Genitals and Inner Thighs

Pinch marks, cuts, and abrasions are sometimes found on the penis, frequently related to punishment in toilet training. Deep grooves on the penis may be inflicted when tying off the penis with a rubber band or string. 🔖 Multiple bruises in this area are not usually accidental. Parents or caregivers of children with accidental genital injuries will usually give a specific, detailed, unsolicited history, for example, "the zipper caught his scrotum." Because of the tenderness of the area and its tendency to bleed profusely, both the parents or caregivers and children are immediately aware of these injuries; children sustaining accidental genital trauma are usually brought immediately to the emergency room. Sexual abuse should also be considered when injuries are present in this area.

■ Common Patterns of Abuse

Loop Marks

One of the most commonly recognized abusive marks is a characteristic loop mark made from a flexible object such as a belt, electric cord, or clothesline. Multiple bruises or lesions of this type are diagnostic of abuse. There are no naturally occurring illnesses that cause this type of mark (see Figure 3.1). 🔖

Hand Marks

☐ Grab Marks or Fingertip Bruises

This common manifestation of abuse is notable by characteristic oval-shaped bruises that resemble fingertips. 🔖 Often these bruises are inflicted on children who are violently shaken. Other symptoms of shaken baby syndrome will most likely help support this theory (see the section about shaken baby syndrome in chapter 6). The most common sites for these marks are on the upper arm, shoulder, and extremities of children who cannot yet walk.

Sometimes a parent or caregiver will squeeze a child's cheeks in order to force food or medicine into the mouth or to forcefully attempt to gain the child's attention. This action characteristically leaves a thumb mark on one cheek with several fingertip marks on the other.

☐ Encirclement Bruises

These bruises occur when a child is grabbed around the chest or stomach. The characteristic pattern is one or two thumbprints on one side of the body, with as many as eight fingermarks on the other side.

☐ Slap Marks

Slap marks frequently leave two or three linear, parallel bruises similar to the outline of the fingers (see Figure 3.2). 🖳 For example, a teenage girl presents with three linear marks on her right cheek as well as a small laceration on the outer bruise, which was caused by the ring her father was wearing when he slapped her.

▨ Bite Marks

Bite marks produce pairs of elliptical, crescent-shaped bruises or lacerations, often containing individual tooth marks. 🖳 Sometimes the two crescents meet to form a complete circle. Bite marks inflicted during sexual intercourse may have a central area of bruising, a "suck mark," or a "thrust mark" (see Figure 3.3).

The most common areas where bites occur are the limbs, abdomen, and cheeks. Frequently a forensic dentist or forensic pathologist may be able to match the pattern of the bite to a mold of the perpetrator's teeth. Therefore, it is important that these contusions be well documented with photographs and diagrams.

☐ Differential Diagnoses

- *Adult versus child.* If the distance between the center of the canine teeth (the third tooth on each side) is greater than three centimeters, the bite is most likely that of an adult, or at least someone with permanent teeth (over 8 years of age). Also, these may differ between the upper and lower teeth.

- *Human versus animal.* Bites such as dog bites tear flesh, whereas human bites only compress the flesh, causing contusions.

▨ Gag Marks

A child whose mouth has been gagged will usually have bruises extending from the corners of the mouth. 🖳

Figure 1: Loop Marks

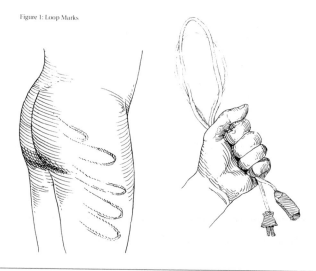

Figure 3.1. Loop Marks. (Illustration by Marsha Dohrmann. Reprinted with permission from Joyce K. Moore.)

Figure 3.2. Slap Mark. (Illustration by Marsha Dohrmann. Reprinted with permission from Joyce K. Moore.)

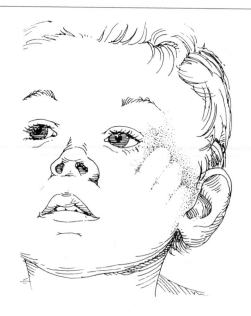

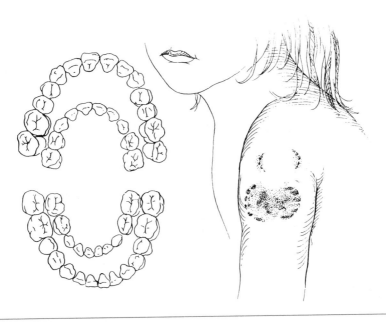

Figure 3.3. Bite Mark. (Illustration by Marsha Dohrmann. Reprinted with permission from Joyce K. Moore.)

Circumferential Marks

Circumferential tie marks around the ankles or wrists can be caused when a child is tied up. Depending on the material used, these marks are often in the form of rope burns or other friction burns, appearing as a large blister that circles the entire extremity. If the child has been tied to another object, the abrasions will only cover part of the ankle or wrist.

Strap Marks

Strap marks are usually one to two inches wide and are linear. In those caused by a belt, the eyelets or buckle can sometimes be discerned. Lash marks are thinner than strap marks. In both, the distal end of the strap usually hits the hardest, sometimes breaking the skin and leaving a loop-shaped mark. Long, linear scratches or bruises are often caused by switches such as tree branches. For example, a school social worker reports that an 8-year-old boy has eight linear marks on his back. He reports that his grandfather hit him with a strap for taking some change.

Marks Caused by Other Objects

Bizarre bruises with sharply defined borders are almost always inflicted. Often the object used can be identified by the shape of the contusion. For example, a hairbrush would leave many small puncture wounds, while a comb may leave many small, linear bruises (from its being dragged across the skin). For example, a 3-year-old child presents with a long, almost sticklike, bruise with an oval-shaped mark on one end. The mother later admits to using a wooden spoon to spank the child.

Hair Loss

Alopecia, or loss of hair, can signal several different problems in a child's condition. Parents or caregivers who use a child's hair as a convenient handle for seizing him or her will pull out patches of hair. This injury can result in a subgaleal hematoma, a separation between the scalp and the skull that fills with blood (see description and Figure 6.1 in chapter 6).

☐ Differential Diagnoses

- Trichotillomania, a psychological condition in which the child pulls out his own hair, may be confused with abuse and requires psychological treatment.

- Tinea capitis (ringworm) is a fungus that may cause circular patches of hair to fall out.

- Various nutritional deficiencies can cause the hair to fall out.

- Idiopathic hair loss has no apparent cause. This is always a possibility when no other abusive symptoms exist. In this condition, the scalp is smooth and hair follicles are very sparse or absent.

■ Neglect

A neglected child can often be identified by skin that is dirty and uncared for. Severe, untreated diaper rash, feces in the folds of skin and under the nails, or multiple insect, rat, or dog bites, when severe and prolonged, might be indicators of neglect if the parent refuses to respond to help and education. ♜ In failure-to-thrive situations, the infant's skin seems "baggy" and loose because underlying muscle tissue and fat have been used by the body for energy. Loss of hair may also be seen in failure-to-thrive situations. Children with an excessive amount of "play" bruises that are not attributed to a bleeding disorder may also be victims of neglect through lack of supervision.

Differential Diagnoses

☐ **Bleeding Disorders**

In the medical provider's assessment for abuse or neglect, he or she will consider the possibility of certain bleeding disorders that would make the child predisposed to bruising. A child whose blood does not coagulate properly will have an abnormal amount of blood released from injured vessels. This means that the child will not only bleed more profusely from an open wound but that he or she will also bleed more profusely under the skin, causing it to appear more bruised than it normally would. The following are examples of bleeding disorders.

- *Hemophilia.* An inherited disease in which blood fails to clot adequately and abnormal bleeding occurs.

- *Leukemia.* A disease in which there is a tremendous increase in the number of immature white blood cells that are unable to fight infection. There is also a marked decrease in the production of platelets and red blood cells, causing a child to bruise easily. What otherwise might be a relatively mild infection may prove fatal for someone with leukemia.

- *Idiopathic thrombocytopenic purpura (ITP).* A bleeding disorder characterized by a marked decrease in the number of blood platelets in the system, resulting in multiple bruises.

- *Lack or malabsorption of fat soluble vitamins, particularly vitamin K.* This is also known as "bleeding disorder of the newborn" in infants who do not receive a vitamin K injection following delivery. The frequent allegation that a child simply bruises easily can be determined legitimately by medical tests for this condition. It is important to remember, however, that bleeding disorders and abuse are not mutually exclusive; children with these medical conditions are just as likely to be abused as other children. Most likely, the medical provider will perform a bleeding function test for these disorders. Some of the most common tests are complete blood cell count (CBC) with platelets, prothrombin time (PT), partial thromboplastin time (PTT), and bleeding time.

- Other causes of abnormal bleeding are viral infections, which can sometimes produce anticoagulants that circulate in the blood and cause the child to bleed or bruise easily. There are also some medications that cause coagulation problems in children. One common drug is salicylate, or aspirin, which a parent or caregiver may add to a baby's bottle to relieve pain. Too much of this or similar drugs can cause a child to bruise easily. The medical provider will usually request a list of any medications that the child may be taking at that time.

☐ Dermatological Disorders

- *Ehlers-Danlos syndrome.* This is an inherited disorder of collagen fibers, in which the skin is velvety, hyperelastic, and fragile. Minor trauma may lead to bruises, hematomas, poor healing, and wide, shiny, "paper-thin" scars. Bleeding studies are normal.

- *Allergic skin conditions.* Skin conditions such as Erythema multiforme (unexplained red blotches that turn into bruises; the rash progresses if child is kept under observation) and urticaria pigmentosa (darkened areas on the skin, which erupt into "hives" when rubbed or irritated) are thought to have an allergic process.

- *Phytophotodermatitis.* This is a reaction to a phototoxin and occurs when the skin is touched by the juice of certain plants and then exposed to the sun. Plants that may produce this include lime, lemon, fig, parsnip, celery, and herbal preparations.

- *Contact dermatitis.* This can be caused by exposure to detergents, rubber substances, poison ivy, and other irritants.

☐ Naturally Occurring Cutaneous Marks Confused With Signs of Abuse

- *Mongolian spots.* Appearing as grayish blue, clearly defined spots on the buttocks, back, legs, upper arms, and shoulders, these birthmarks are those most commonly mistaken for abuse. 🖳 They are present at birth or shortly after and last from two to three years but can persist into adulthood. In one study, Mongolian spots were present in 10% of the Caucasian babies examined, 95% of the African American babies, 80% of Asian babies, and 70% of Hispanic and Native American babies (Cordova, 1981).

- *Maculae ceruleae.* These bluish spots appear on the skin concomitantly with head or pubic lice. They disappear when the lice are treated.

- *Salmon patches.* These pink marks appear commonly on the nape of the neck, on the eyelids, above the nose, and on the mid-forehead of newborns. A mark is sometimes referred to as an "angel's kiss" or a "stork bite."

- *Strawberry marks (hemangiomas).* These lesions are usually not present at birth but appear during the first four to six weeks of life.

☐ Folk Practices

- *Coin rubbing.* Vietnamese children sometimes present with linear bruises on the chest and back, which, although they resemble signs of abuse, are actually the result of the folk medicine practice *cao gio* (pronounced "cow zow"). ⌨ In this practice, used to relieve symptoms such as fevers, chills, and headaches, the skin is massaged with oil and stroked with the edge of a coin until bruising occurs. Normally, this practice should not cause undue concern about child abuse. Adherence to this practice when a child is seriously ill, with refusal to seek medical care, may raise a question of medical neglect.

• *Cupping.* This is a practice often seen in Asian or Mexican cultures in which small cups are heated and placed on the skin to draw out fever and pains. As the cups cool, they produce a suction vacuum, resulting in bruises and sometimes burns. ⌨

As part of the investigation into abusive treatment versus folk-healing practices, the worker may wish to consult with a cultural healer in addition to a medical provider.

Injuries to the skin will likely be the most common injury encountered by CPS workers. Understanding the various types of injuries, their possible causes, and other explanations will help facilitate better assessments as well as interventions.

References

Cordova, A. (1981). The Mongolian spot. *Clinical Pediatrics, 20,* 714–722.

Langois, N., & Gresham, G. (1991). The aging of bruises: A review and study of the color changes with time. *Forensic Science International, 50,* 227–238.

Schwartz, A., & Ricci, L. (1996). How accurately can bruises be aged in abused children? Literature review and synthesis. *Pediatrics, 97*(2), 254–257.

Sugar, N., Taylor, J., & Feldman, K. (1999). Bruises in infants and toddlers: Those who don't cruise rarely bruise. *Archives of Pediatric & Adolescent Medicine, 153,* 399–403.

4

Joyce K. Moore
Jean C. Smith

Abuse by Burns

Although burns are common causes of unintentional (accidental) injury, approximately 10% of pediatric burn cases are the result of child abuse. Boys are more commonly victims of both burn accidents and abuse, with a peak age of 2 to 3 years. Although abusive burns can occur in any shape or form, there are some particular patterns that occur more frequently, such as immersion burns, splash burns, and contact burns. Others include chemical, electrical, and microwave burns. It is important to know what to look for in the medical provider's diagnosis and treatment of the burn, as well as some common indicators of abuse.

■ Medical Terminology Used in Burn Injuries

In assessing a burn, the medical provider will usually make note of its severity, the extent of the body covered, and its exact location. Each of these determinations is documented in a customary way. It is useful for the worker to understand the significance of these findings.

Severity

The severity of burn injuries is categorized according to the number of layers of skin injured. 💻

- *Superficial* (formerly called a first-degree burn). 💻 This burn involves only the outer layer of the skin (the epidermis) and is characterized by erythema (redness), hyperemia (redness that disappears under pressure), tenderness, and swelling. Although not usually severe, these burns can be serious if they cover a large percentage of body area. An example of a superficial burn would be a sunburn.

- *Partial thickness* (formerly called a second-degree burn). 💻 This burn extends through the epidermis and into the dermis (the next layer of skin). It is characterized by vesicles (weeping blisters) on the skin's surface and pain secondary to nerve-ending damage. If no infection occurs, these injuries usually take from 14 to 21 days to heal. When severe, they can sometimes require surgery.

- *Full thickness* (formerly called third- and fourth-degree burns). The entire thickness of the skin (both epidermis and dermis, and including the hair follicles) is burned. The area looks white or charred and is not sensitive to touch or a pinprick because the blood vessels and nerve endings are destroyed. If bone or muscle is involved, the burn is equivalent to the formerly classified fourth-degree burn. These injuries require hospitalization and usually require skin grafting. These burns heal with scarring, creating a change in color and a "parchment" type of skin.

Extent

The extent of the burn is another important factor in determining its severity. For example, a superficial burn that covers a large part of the body may be more serious than a full thickness burn that covers a small part of the body. Medical providers express the extent of burns in percentages of total body surface area covered.

Burns are considered severe when they cover

- over 10% of the body in children under 2 years of age;
- over 15% of the body in children between 2 and 12 years of age;
- over 20% of the body in children of any age; and
- the face, hands, or genitalia.

Burns covering over 65% of the body are sometimes fatal, even when they are only superficial burns. The exact location of the burn will usually be documented in the medical provider's report by a diagram. These locations are important factors in determining the likelihood of abuse. Accidental burns are most likely to occur on the front of the head, neck, trunk, hands, and arms. Those found on the back of the head, neck, chest, extremities, and genitalia are rarely self-inflicted and are very likely abusive.

The Importance of the History

A detailed history is especially important in determining the etiology of a burn (Peck & Priolo-Capel, 2002). A scene investigation by the worker provides critical information. When acquiring the history and subsequently relating it to the medical provider, the worker should include the following information:

- Who was involved in the incident? What is the child's developmental maturity? (i.e., was the child mature enough to have done what was alleged?) For example, an infant not capable of climbing would not be able to get onto a countertop and sit on a hot electric burner, resulting in burns to the buttocks.

- When exactly did the act occur? If there was a delay in seeking treatment, why? (Medical providers can usually estimate the age of burns to tell if they have really "recently occurred.")

In cases of suspected immersion burns, the worker should ask the following questions:

- What was holding the hot water? (Some areas of skin may remain unburned because these areas have been held in contact with the wall of the tub. This pattern would not occur if the child were held in a pot of hot liquid on a stove burner.)

- How deep was the liquid in the container?

- What was the exact position of the child's body when the incident occurred?

- What was the estimated temperature of the liquid? (In burns reported to be due to hot tap water, the worker may ask for assistance from law enforcement in checking the setting on the water heater and the temperature of the tap water.)

In the case of splash burns, the worker should ask the following questions:

- How far did the liquid travel in the air before hitting the child? (Across the room? From the stove to the floor?)

- What was the estimated volume of the hot liquid? (Was this a full soup pot or a cup of hot tea?)

- What was the exact position of the child's body when the incident occurred?

- What clothing was the child wearing when the incident occurred? Were the clothes removed immediately?

- What exactly was the liquid that splashed the victim? Was it greasy?

In summary, any burns that occur with one or more of the following problems should have an investigation of possible maltreatment:

- A history incompatible with the physical findings

- A burn incompatible with the developmental age of the child

- Burns assessed as older than the historical account indicates

- Nutritional neglect

- Bruises, lacerations, and scars in addition to the burns
- Evidence of fractures (skeletal survey should be done on all children less than 2 years of age)
- Burns attributed to siblings (although these can occur accidentally)
- An adult not present at the incident who is seeking medical attention
- Treatment delay of 24 hours or more
- A previous history of burns

■ Immersion Burns

These are the most frequent types of abusive burns in children.

Temperature of Tap Water and Related Burn Times

The time for a child's skin to burn at specific water temperatures is actually extrapolated from studies done with adults in 1947. Current literature suggests that young children can sustain partial and full thickness burns after 10 seconds of exposure to 130°F, after 1 second at 140°F, and 0.5 seconds at 150°F (Jenny, 2001). While it was once common to preset new electric heaters at 150°F and gas heaters at 140°F, this is no longer true. Many states have enacted legislation that requires homeowners to lower preset temperatures on new heaters to 120–125°F. ☙ In homes in which the high temperature of the water seems to be a problem, medical providers can suggest that a family lower its preset temperature to the minimum. Many apartment dwellers have little choice about water temperature settings. The worker can help prevent nonintentional tap-water burns by assisting the family in their efforts to request adjustment of the hot water heater by the local gas or electric company.

Patterns

Immersion burns usually occur when parts of the body are forced into hot water, usually from being held under a running tap or placed in a filled tub. The restrained child cannot move in the liquid, thus the burns leave clear lines of demarcation on the skin.

☐ Hands and Feet

Hands and feet that have been forcefully held under water usually have symmetrical "stocking" or "glove" patterns, which are uniform in depth. ☙ Often the child will tripod onto his or her hands and feet to try to protect the rest of his or her body. The palms of the hands and soles of the feet have particularly thick skin, usually resistant to thermal damage.

Any full thickness burns to these areas should be suspected as abusive (see Figure 4.1).

☐ **Perineum**

Another common scald pattern is seen on the perineum, the area between the vagina and anus in the female, or the scrotum and anus in the male. These burns are often inflicted as a form of punishment for the child who is not yet toilet trained. In an effort to both clean and punish the child, the caregiver may hold him in a "jack-knifed" position (see Figure 4.2), in which his knees are held against his chest, forcing his perineum under hot running water or dunking him into a tub or pot of hot water.

There are several characteristics of nonaccidental immersion burns:

- *"Doughnut hole."* A child who has been forced into a porcelain or fiberglass tub will often have parts of his or her body, usually the buttocks, resting on the bottom of the tub. ☚ Because this area is in contact with the cool tub instead of the hot water, it will not burn, thus creating a patch of unburned skin in the center of the burn, much like a doughnut hole.

- *Parallel lines.* In this type of pattern, there is a uniform burn on all areas exposed to the liquid. A distinct line separates the skin area that has been exposed from that which has not. These lines can be made parallel by positioning the body into the estimated position of the child at the time of immersion. A careful examination of these patterns can often lead to the diagnosis of abuse.

Figure 4.1. Hand Immersion Burn: Glove Pattern. (Illustration by Marsha Dohrmann. Reprinted with permission from Joyce K. Moore.)

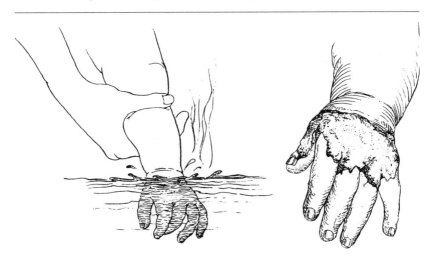

Figure 4.2. Baby Immersed. (Illustration by Marsha Dohrmann. Reprinted with permission from Joyce K. Moore.)

- *Flexion.* Often the burned area will have a "zebra-stripe" appearance, in which there are stripes of unburned skin in the middle of the burned area (see Figure 4.3). ☜ These "stripes" occur at the areas of flexion that are bent when the body comes into contact with the liquid. Because the skin in these areas is pressed against other areas of skin, it does not come into contact with the liquid and is thus spared burning.

Differential Diagnoses

☐ Accidental Immersions

It would not be unusual for a child who has fallen into a hot tub to raise herself onto her hands and feet in an effort to regain balance and to climb out of the water. Such an accident could create burns similar to those in forced immersion. However, there are some differences in these types of patterns:

- Accidental burns have no clear line demarcating the burned and unburned skin, and the burns will not be symmetrical on both hands or on both feet. Children will thrash around, creating uneven burn patterns on each limb.

- Accidental burns will not be as deep as forced burns, for an unrestrained child will usually be able to remove him or herself from the burning environment.

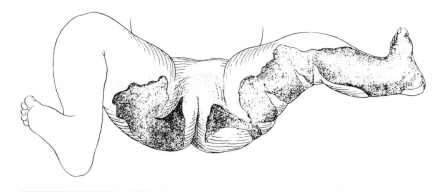

Figure 4.3. Flexion Burn Patterns: Doughnut Hole, Parallel Lines, Zebra Striping. (Illustration by Marsha Dohrmann. Reprinted with permission from Joyce K. Moore.)

- Any burns that involve just the perineum and possibly the feet, with no burning of the hands, should be questioned, for it is almost impossible for a child to fall into a tub in this position accidentally.

- A parent or caregiver who claims that he or she tested the water and "thought it was all right" should arouse suspicion. Adults find water to be uncomfortable at temperatures around 109°F, while temperatures must be above 130°F to cause full thickness burns in 10 seconds.

- Although accidental burns are not an uncommon occurrence in any household, frequent accidental burns can be indicators of neglect. Parents or caregivers who fail to watch their children in the kitchen or do not have protective screens around wood stoves or heaters may need to be educated. However, children in persistently high-risk and neglectful environments should be carefully considered for out-of-home placement. 🖳

Case Example

A 9-month-old child was admitted to the burn unit with a full thickness burn to the toes and sole of her foot. The burn "ran" up the back of the leg with an apparent "exit" at the back of the thigh. This is a pattern often seen after contact with an electrical current. The parents stated that the baby was sleeping with them on a futon in the living room. The baby was placed between the parents and the wall. The parents admitted that the electrical socket on that wall was missing the plastic protective plate and they thought the baby stuck her foot against the exposed wires. A home investigation by CPS revealed that the dwelling contained multiple exposed sockets and frayed electrical cords, thus a high-risk environment that is not currently safe for the child.

■ Splash Burns

In splash burns, a hot liquid is either thrown or poured onto the victim. The depth of the burn in these cases is usually not as deep as that seen in immersion burns. This is because the liquid usually cools as it falls through the air and runs off the skin before deeply damaging the skin (unless the hot liquid is retained by clothing against the skin). Usually there are several small, scattered, "satellite" burns seen. The area that comes into contact with the main mass of fluid is usually the area of deepest burn. 🖥️ Often the pattern is an "arrowhead" configuration (see Figure 4.4). By examining the burn pattern, it may be possible to estimate the direction from which the liquid came, as well as the position of the body during contact.

Accidental Splash Burns

When determining the etiology of splash burns, look closely at the area of the body covered by the burn. Self-induced accidental burns rarely can occur from behind. Accidental burns, such as those occurring from a hot liquid being pulled from the stove, are most likely to occur on the front of the head, neck, trunk, and arms. 🖥️

Other factors to look for are the extent of the burn and its compatibility with the history of the accident. If a parent or caregiver has spilled a cup of cof-

Figure 4.4. Arrowhead Burn Pattern. (Illustration by Marsha Dohrmann. Reprinted with permission from Joyce K. Moore.)

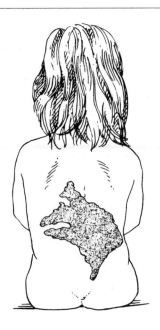

fee on a child, the burns should not cover a large percentage of the child's body. An average coffee cup simply does not hold enough liquid to cover a large area. If the child suffers from extensive burns on a large percentage of total surface body area, the history should be compatible in terms of the amount of liquid involved.

■ Contact Burns

Contact burns are the second most frequent cause of abusive burns. It is often easy to identify the object of contact from the shape of the burn.

Cigarette Burns

Cigarette burns are the contact burns most frequently seen in abusive situations. These burns measure about 8 to 10 millimeters in diameter and are often found in multiple occurrences on the trunk, external genitalia, and extremities, such as the palms of the hands and the soles of the feet. ⬛ Depending on the duration of contact, these can be anything from blisters to excavated wounds. Healed cigarette burns may appear as either hyperpigmented (darkened) or hypopigmented (with an absence of color) areas of the skin. Sometimes, however, they may leave no residual traces.

☐ Accidental Cigarette Burns

A child may brush against a cigarette that is being held in someone's hand. These burns are usually found on the child's face, arms, or trunk, depending on the height of the child and the height of the person holding the cigarette. An accidental burn is usually more elongated than round, with a higher degree of intensity on one side, due to the effect of brushing past the lighted tip. ⬛ Usually the history should verify this possibility.

Often the blisters produced by the skin disease impetigo are similar in appearance to cigarette burns. Impetigo blisters usually do not leave scars, whereas cigarette burns may. ⬛ The worker should remember that impetigo could occur as a result of cigarette burns if the wounds go untreated. Suspicious blisters will generally be cultured by the practitioner for bacteria that may be found with impetigo and then treated with antibiotics.

Burns by Objects

Some common instruments used in abusive situations are irons, stove burners, heater grates, radiators, electric hot plates, curling irons, and hair dryers. ⬛ A study of electric hair dryers showed that at high heat, dryers held stationary approximately three inches from the skin are capable of producing a full thickness burn in 1 to 10 seconds, dependent on the power level of the dryer. In most instances, dryers are kept in constant motion to avoid overheating the skin. In addition, the protective grid on many dryers is capable of producing a partial thickness burn within 1 to 2 seconds for as long as 2 minutes after the dryers are turned off (Prescott, 1990). In some burns, objects such as combs, keys, knives, or cigarette lighters are heated and "branded" into the skin. Like cigarette burns, there are some typical patterns that can help in determining the etiology of these types of burns.

Accidental Burns by Objects

First, look at the pattern of the burn. Could the child simply have brushed against or sat on the object? Accidental burns usually have irregular shapes and are deeper and clearer on one edge. Although some infants will not be able to move away from the burning object, most young children will do so reflexively, thus leaving an irregular pattern. During hot summer months children may present with superficial and partial thickness burns caused by vinyl upholstery, seat belts, infant backpack carriers, or seat belt buckles. These burns are often considered suspicious not only because they are so obvious but also because parents or caregivers usually cannot recall how they might have occurred. For example, on a day in which the outdoor temperature is 79°F, red vinyl can reach a temperature of 155°F, hot enough to cause a full thickness burn in 1 to 2 seconds. Some colors that are particularly heat prone, in order of increasing severity, are red, green, blue, and black. It may be helpful to recreate the position of the car seat to determine if the burned area could have come in contact with the heat prone parts of the seat.

Chemical, Electric, and Microwave Burns

Chemical Burns

Chemical burns are often deeper and more severe than scalding burns. This is because the burning process continues as long as the substance is in contact with the skin, as opposed to scalding burns, in which the water cools, evaporates, or eventually runs off of the body. Clothing impregnated by kerosene, acetic acid, and other mild irritants has been shown to produce lesions resembling superficial and partial thickness burns when the material remains in contact with the skin for a period of time.

Electrical Burns

The majority of children with electrical burns are under 5 years of age. Most injuries occur from the conduction of current through the saliva of a child who is sucking or mouthing an electric cord. A child who bites a live electric cord will usually have characteristic burns at the corners of the mouth.

These burns often present as deep injuries. An unusual type of abusive electrical burn is produced by a stun gun. These are reported as having a characteristic lesion of a pair of superficial circular burns about 5 millimeters in diameter located about 5 centimeters apart (Jenny, 2001).

Microwave Burns

Burns resulting from microwave ovens are very deep, affecting both the skin and the deep muscle layers, which have a greater water content and burn more quickly. Layers of fat are relatively spared during the burning. Often the tissue is actually charred in this situation.

Folk Practices

The aftereffects of several folk medicine and home treatments could be misinterpreted as abusive burns. It is helpful for the CPS worker to be aware of the most common of these practices and patterns. For example, home remedies using creams or ointments in the treatment of muscle strains can result in chemical burns.

A Mexican American practice called "cupping" (see chapter 3), in which a cup of ignited alcohol is placed over an affected part of the body, usually results in bruises but may also create burns.

Children in Southeast Asian families will sometimes present with burns or scars that look like cigarette burns. These are usually 0.5 to 1 centimeter in diameter and are located randomly around the lower rib cage or in a definite pattern around the umbilicus, or belly button. These burns are part of a folk medical therapy (called moxibustion) in which pieces of burning string are lowered onto the child's skin, in the belief this will cure abdominal pain or fever.

At least one case of a partial thickness burn, coupled with inhalation pneumonia, has been reported as a result of fabric dipped in kerosene and applied to the skin in an attempt to treat upper respiratory congestion (Nussinovitch, 1992).

Treatment and Placement Decisions

The child should receive immediate medical evaluation if

- the burn is over 10% of the body of an infant less than 2 years in age;
- the burn is over 15% of the body of a child between 2 and 12 years in age;
- the burn is over 20% of the body of a child of any age;

- there are facial or perineal and genital burns; or

- there are full thickness burns.

One of the first decisions a practitioner will make in the medical evaluation is whether or not to hospitalize the child. This usually occurs when a victim has partial or full thickness burns. Victims who are not hospitalized, and those who are returning home after hospitalization, will still need special care. In the worker's assessment of a child's posttreatment placement, consideration should be given to the ability of the parent or caregiver to perform the following treatments: 🐱

- *Dressing changes.* Can the parent or caregiver understand and perform the mechanics of the dressing changes? Is he or she psychologically fit to view and care for the wounds? Is the environment sanitary enough to avoid infection?

- *Emotional support.* Because burn injuries are exceptionally painful and debilitating, the victim needs a lot of support and reassurance at this time; the caregiver must be aware and sensitive to the burned child's special needs.

- *Subsequent treatment.* Treatment of the burned child continues long after acute care has healed the wounds. As the child grows and develops, he or she will need continuous evaluations and often surgeries to reconstruct the contractures of healing skin. Hospital burn units usually have social workers who will be able to assist in discharge planning for the child.

Encountering burns resulting from child abuse is perhaps one of the more difficult injuries for CPS workers to deal with in the course of conducting casework. The potential for scarring and other long-term damage does create an emotional reaction by all persons involved in the case. Thus, it is even more important that CPS workers objectively understand the injuries and work collaboratively with medical providers to ensure proper treatment for the child.

References

Jenny, C. (2001). Cutaneous manifestations. In R. Reece & S. Ludwig (Eds.), *Child abuse: Medical diagnosis and management* (2nd ed., pp. 23–45). Philadelphia: Lippincott Williams & Wilkins.

Nussinovitch, M. (1992). Chemical pneumonia and dermatitis caused by kerosene. *Clinical Pediatrics, 31,* 574.

Peck, M., & Priolo-Capel, D. (2002). Child abuse by burning: A review of the literature and an algorithm for medical investigations. *The Journal of Trauma, 53,* 1013–1022.

Prescott, P. (1990). Hair dryer burns in children. *Pediatrics, 86,* 692–697.

5

Joyce K. Moore

Jean C. Smith

Abusive Fractures

Estimates of fractures occurring in children who are physically abused vary from 11% to 55% depending on the child's age and the radiographic imaging techniques used (Cooperman & Merten, 2001). In 1946, Dr. John Caffey described infants with unexplained long bone fractures and subdural hematomas. Later, in 1962, Dr. C. Henry Kempe used these early diagnostic imaging findings in developing the concept of the battered child syndrome. Radiology can confirm the presence of fractures, identify other "hidden" fractures, provide an estimate of when fractures occurred, and give possible causes.

Children less than 2 years old have most of the abusive fractures in child abuse situations. From 55% to 70% (Cooperman & Merten, 2001) of all abusive fractures occur in infants that are less than 1 year old. Only about 2% of *accidental* fractures are found in infants less than 18 months old (Cooperman & Merten, 2001). In some instances, the discovery of a fracture is the first indication to consider the possibility of child abuse. In assessing whether or not a fracture is the result of child abuse, the worker must work closely with the medical team to combine the details of the entire history with the radiographic and other medical findings (see chapter 2).

■ When to Suspect Abuse

When investigating a case for child abuse, it is important to consider discrepancies between the type and age of the fracture(s) and the history given. It is important for the worker to obtain a detailed history of the injury including the exact date and time of the occurrence and the way the incident occurred, and to possibly visit the site where the injury happened. Radiographic and imaging techniques will help confirm or disprove this history. In infants, some fractures have particular radiographic findings that a diagnosis of abusive trauma may be made with little other supporting history or clinical findings. The worker should be suspicious of abuse when any of the following occur:

- Fractures are "accidentally" discovered during an examination. For example, rib fractures that are identified when a child with suspected pneumonia has a chest X-ray.
- The fracture is more severe than the history given.
- Multiple fractures are found in different parts of the skeleton without a history of major trauma such as an auto accident.
- Multiple fractures in various stages of healing exist.
- Skeletal trauma is accompanied by other injuries, for example, burns or bruises to other parts of the body.

Case Example

An 18-month-old child brought to the emergency room with a persistent cough and fever has a routine chest X-ray that reveals lateral rib fractures. Careful examination of the skin identifies bruising of the scalp and ear on the left side of the head. A skeletal survey also identifies a healing fracture of the right femur.

The absence of bruising or swelling at the fracture site is irrelevant in deciding whether or not a fracture is nonaccidental.

The CPS worker should be aware that in particular cases of suspected physical abuse, a skeletal survey should be done to identify subtle but highly specific bone abnormalities necessary in the diagnosis of abusive fractures. The skeletal survey is a specific set of radiographs and *not* a "baby-gram" (a radiograph of the infant's entire body in one or two X-rays). Standards have been published by the American College of Radiology and the American Academy of Pediatrics (AAP) Section on Radiology in order to use the most appropriate and optimum imaging techniques necessary to clarify findings and document them in the most accurate fashion (AAP, 2000).

The AAP's position statement on diagnostic skeletal imaging is as follows: "The skeletal survey is mandatory in all cases of suspected physical abuse in children less than 2 years of age. A screening skeletal survey beyond 5 years of age has little value. Patients in the 2-year to 5-year age group must be handled individually, based on the specific clinical indicators of abuse. At any age, when clinical findings point to a specific site of injury, the customary protocol for imaging that region should be used. Application of these guidelines to selected cases of neglect and sexual abuse is appropriate when associated physical maltreatment is suspected."

A medical provider skilled at interpreting X-rays, such as a pediatric radiologist, can use all these imaging findings to diagnose the type of fracture, determine where it exists, and estimate its age. The aging of fractures is usually written in the radiology report as acute (less than a week), healing (1 to 4 weeks old), and old or chronic (untreated, healed with callus). The medical provider may request additional radiographs or special imaging techniques to assist in these determinations. Note that in healthy children and infants, fractures—both abusive and nonabusive—will usually heal over time so that no radiographic findings remain. For these reasons, the medical provider in certain instances may request the worker's assistance in obtaining previous X-rays taken at other medical facilities.

Case Example

A 16-day-old infant presents with a fever of 102 degrees. An evaluation for systemic infection, including blood and urine cultures, was done at a regional hospital. Reportedly, a chest X-ray at this hospital was read as normal. The infant was transferred to a university hospital for further workup. After admission, the infant began having seizures. Because a cause for the seizures could not be determined, trauma was considered and a skeletal survey was obtained two weeks after admission. The skeletal survey revealed two healing posterior rib fractures. Therefore, the CPS worker was asked to obtain the chest film from the regional hospital for comparison to the university hospital X-rays in order to aid in the determination of the time of occurrence of the rib fractures.

■ Medical Terminology

Bones of Infants and Children

A medical provider's first step in investigating a fracture is determining its location and its type. This determination can often help uncover the etiology of the fracture. Nonmedical professionals may wish to refer to a skeletal diagram to determine the location of a particular bone. It should be noted that some bones have two names. For example, a "collar bone" is also called a clavicle, and a "shoulder blade" is also called a scapula. Long bones refer to bones of the legs and arms.

Long bones are divided into three distinct sections. The diaphysis refers to the shaft or midportion of the bone. The epiphysis refers to the end of the bone. In a growing child, these ends are separated from the diaphysis by a layer of cartilage, called the epiphyseal plate, or metaphysis. As the bone grows, this cartilage slowly produces more and more compact bone, causing the bone to lengthen. This growth plate is one of the weakest areas of the child's bone and is a common area of injury in child abuse. The outer covering of the bone, the periosteum, contains blood vessels and special cells that help in repair following an injury. The distal portion of the bone refers to the end farthest from the person's trunk, while the proximal end refers to that closest to the trunk. Posterior means toward the rear. Lateral pertains to the side, while bilateral pertains to both sides.

Types of Fractures

The list of names for particular types of fractures is very detailed; however, the CPS worker should be familiar with some of the major terms that medical providers use in describing a break.

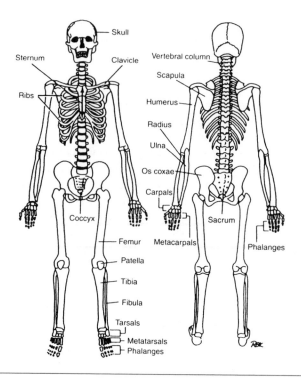

Figure 5.1. Human Skeleton. (From Bruck-Kan, 1979. Reprinted with permission from the author.)

- *Closed fracture.* A fracture of the bone with no skin wound.

- *Complicated fracture.* A fracture in which the broken bone has injured some internal organ.

- *Compound fracture.* A fracture in which the bone is broken and protruding through the skin.

- *Compression fracture.* A collapse of the bone along the direction of force. (An example would be a compression fracture of a vertebral—back or spine—bone from slamming the child down on their buttocks in the sitting position.)

- *Displaced fracture.* A fracture in which the broken ends are not in alignment. These fractures require "reduction" or realignment so that the bone can heal properly. A "closed" reduction is done by the medical provider gently pulling and repositioning the bone without a surgical incision in the skin. An "open" reduction is realigning the bone directly after a surgical incision is made in the skin and tissue over the bone.

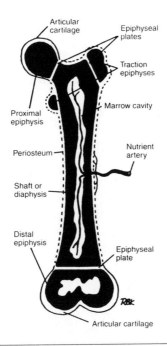

Figure 5.2. Long Bone. (From Bruck-Kan, 1979. Reprinted with permission from the author.)

- *Greenstick fracture.* A fracture in which the bone is partially bent and partially broken, as when a greenstick breaks.

- *Hairline fracture.* A minor fracture in which all the portions of the bone are in perfect alignment. Also called a linear fracture when present in the skull.

- *Impacted fracture.* A fracture in which the bone is broken and one end is wedged into the interior of the other end. Also called a buckle fracture.

- *Metaphyseal fracture.* A chip of the growing end of a bone pulled off by a ligament. This fracture usually comes from shaking (see Figure 5.3). ⌨

- *Pathologic fracture.* A fracture of a diseased or weakened bone, produced by a force that would not have fractured a healthy bone.

- *Spiral fracture.* A slanting, diagonal fracture. ⌨

- *Transverse fracture.* A fracture in which the fracture line is at right angles to the long axis of the bone. ⌨

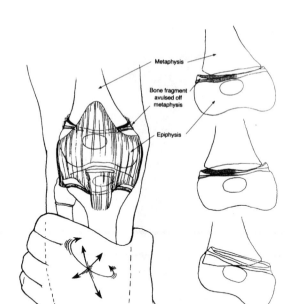

Figure 5.3. Metaphyseal Avulsion Fracture. (Illustration by Marsha Dohrmann. Reprinted with permission from Joyce K. Moore.)

■ Specific Mechanisms of Abuse and Their Consequences

Table 5.1 has been constructed from Leonard Swischuk's chapter in *Radiology of the Skeletal System* (1981) and continues to be relevant today.

■ Dating the Fracture

Dating a fracture is one of the most important steps in determining the veracity of the caregiver history. Whenever the date of the history does not coincide with the age of the fracture, the worker should be suspicious of abuse. In determining the date of a fracture, the medical provider will examine any soft tissue damage, such as bruises or lacerations, the visibility of the fracture line on an X-ray, the stage of the callus (the new bone forming around the fracture), and the changes in the periosteal new bone (the outer covering of the bone, which helps in repair). In very young children,

Table 5.1. Types of Fractures

Mechanism	Area Injured	Type of Fracture
Direct blow	Extremities	Transverse, diaphyseal injuries
	Clavicle	Midshaft fracture
	Face	Facial, jaw fractures
	Abdomen	Injuries to internal organs
	Chest	Rib fractures, internal injuries
Twisting force	Long bones	Spiral fracture
		Metaphyseal fractures
Shaking	Skull	(See chapter 6 in this book.)
	Long bones	Metaphyseal fractures
	Spine	Various injuries
Squeezing	Chest	Bilateral fractures of ribs

signs of old fractures can sometimes disappear entirely after six months to a year. Subtle or hairline fractures may be difficult to discern on an X-ray, because the bone has not yet had time to form a callus. Here are some general guidelines for determining the age of fractures.

- *0 to 10 days:* No signs of callus present, only swelling and the fracture itself visible.

- *10 days to 8 weeks:* Callus formation, epiphyseal thickening, periosteal thickening in the injured area.

- *8 to 12 weeks:* Periosteum begins to blend back into old bone.

■ Different X-rays and the Appropriateness of Their Uses

Skeletal radiography (or an X-ray) is the main "tool" that a medical provider uses to determine the location, age, and cause of a suspected fracture. Although these procedures are usually benign, they should not be done unless indicated. The medical provider will avoid exposing the child to unnecessary amounts of radiation by keeping records of his X-rays and using specific, pediatric-appropriate techniques. If it is necessary to take a child to another medical provider, be sure to request that all of the medical records, including X-rays or copies of X-rays, be sent to the new medical provider.

Skeletal Survey

The skeletal survey is an X-ray procedure in which the entire skeleton, including the skull, thoracic cage, spine, and extremities, is radiographed to determine the presence of fractures in any part of the body.

The general rule to keep in mind is that the less the child is able to tell about where he or she hurts, the greater the value of the skeletal survey. There are possible situations in which a skeletal survey is not recommended, such as cases of suspected sexual abuse in which no signs of physical abuse are recognized, or soft tissue injuries to older children who are quite capable of reporting physical injuries. See the AAP's recommendations on diagnostic skeletal imaging above.

Bone Scan

The bone scan is also referred to as a radionuclide skeletal scintography and is a process in which radioactive substances are injected into the bloodstream. The scintillations, or "heat," from these radionuclides are then photographed in those areas of new bone growth. The advantage of this method is that it can detect fractures within 24 hours after they occur, whereas conventional X-rays may take as long as 8 to 10 days for detection. This process is especially helpful in determining rib fractures and periosteal (bone lining) injuries. It is not a good method, however, for reviewing metaphyseal fractures, because these occur at a site where there is a lot of growing bone, injured or not. This method also lacks sensitivity in detecting skull and vertebral fractures. Bone scans are typically quite expensive in small hospitals, where they are used infrequently.

Areas of the Body Commonly Associated With Abuse

Extremities

Extremities are where most of the fractures in abused children occur. These are most likely to be in the long bones of the arms and legs and are not as common in the hands and feet. These fractures commonly present as transverse or spiral fractures of the diaphysis and as metaphyseal fractures. Spiral fractures in a child who cannot yet walk should raise suspicion. Metaphyseal fractures are highly associated with twisting or jerking forces and are extremely uncommon in documented accidental injury, including motor vehicle accidents.

☐ Differential Diagnoses

- *Birthing trauma.* Clavicular and humeral (both shaft and epiphyseal) fractures are occasionally found in newborn babies, especially those from breech deliveries. If an infant over 10 days of age shows fractures with no signs of healing, they should be considered as occurring after birth.

- *Little League elbow.* Frequently, epiphyseal separations occur when a child continually flexes his elbow in the action of throwing a ball.

The age of the child and the history can usually exclude this possibility.

- Infants receiving passive exercises for therapeutic reasons have been known to sustain fractures of the extremities when a caregiver administers them improperly. This problem should present itself in the history and deserves immediate attention.

Ribs and Sternum

Rib fractures are another common injury caused by abuse, with almost 90% of these fractures occurring in children under 2 years of age (Cooperman & Merten, 2001). Usually, the rib cage is pliant under mild pressure. Therefore, any fractures of this area should be considered the product of major unintentional trauma or abuse. ▄€

While rib fractures can be caused by direct blows, squeezing is a well-documented mechanism of posterior and lateral rib fractures (Kleinman, 1998). The assailant's palms are usually laterally placed, with thumbs in front and fingers at the back. Compression is from front to back, with initial fractures occurring next to the spine and additional fractures occurring laterally as the pressure increases (see Figure 5.4).

Because the compression forces are more or less uniform during shaking, the fractures are often multiple and bilateral. Direct blows in older children may result in rib fractures at the point of impact.

Figure 5.4. Hard Compression of Ribs. (Illustration by Marsha Dohrmann. Reprinted with permission from Joyce K. Moore.)

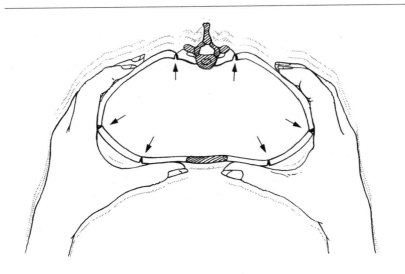

Fractures of the sternum (breastbone) are rarely reported in abused infants and children, but when present, they are diagnostic of abuse.

☐ Differential Diagnosis

Children may present with rib fractures that are said to be the result of CPR. It has been found, however, that although these injuries do occur in adults, children do not receive rib fractures from CPR, and such fractures should be considered as being caused by another form of injury.

■ Skull Fractures

These fractures are a common manifestation of child abuse and can be very serious. Chapter 6 covers this topic in detail.

■ Vertebral Fractures

Although they are not as common as fractures of the extremities or skull, vertebral fractures are another type of injury sometimes seen in abuse. These can occur from forced bending of the spine, or hyperflexion, a process that can cause the discs between the vertebrae to painfully pinch into the spinal cord. These abuses are seen most often in children under 2 years old and are usually associated with other injuries to the limbs. As described above, the vertebrae can be fractured by compression from forcefully slamming a child onto his or her buttocks while in the sitting position. In some cases, vertebral injuries may be caused by shaken baby syndrome due to hyperflexion and hyperextension of the spinal column. In this instance, symptoms of neurologic injury such as vomiting, weight loss, irritability, and slowed development may be present. Often, however, no neurologic signs of injury exist, and the vertebral lesions go unrecognized.

☐ Differential Diagnoses

In addition to considering accidental trauma as a cause of fractures, the medical provider may test for various organic abnormalities, such as genetic problems or bone diseases, as possible causes for the radiological findings.

- *Congenital syphilis.* This disease causes bone irregularities similar to trauma, not only as a result of the disease itself but also as a result of a weakening of the bone, which makes it more susceptible to damage.

- *Infantile cortical hyperostosis (Caffey's disease).* This skeletal abnormality typically presents itself in infants up to 2 to 3 months old with red, painful, swollen extremities. One diagnostic feature is that 95% of the bone abnormalities caused by this disease involve the mandible or jaw.

- *Leukemia.* A severe disease of the blood-forming organs, including the bone marrow, and is associated with progressive anemia, internal hemorrhage, and exhaustion.

- *Menkes kinky hair syndrome.* This syndrome, resulting from a deficiency in copper metabolism, results in symmetrical problems in the shaft (diaphysis) and the ends (metaphysis) of the bone. Often associated with failure to thrive, Menkes kinky hair syndrome is also associated with seizures, psychomotor retardation, and progressive neurologic degeneration. Its name is derived from the characteristic sparse, kinky hair that appears on the scalp a few months after birth.

- *Osteogenesis imperfecta* (OI). Of all the various conditions suggested by caregivers and their legal representatives to explain inflicted fractures, this is the most frequently cited. ☙ It is an inherited disorder of connective tissue that leads to abnormal bone formation and increased fragility. Various types of OI have other clinical features, such as short stature, blue sclera, wormian bones in the skull, hearing loss, etc. While severe cases may manifest themselves in the newborn period with extensive fractures, others may not be apparent for months or even for years. Connective tissue biopsy may be instrumental in confirming the diagnosis of OI in some cases. This, however, is rarely necessary.

  When entertaining the possibility of OI in a case of suspected child abuse, the pediatrician, orthopedist, geneticist, and radiologist must work together in a coordinated effort to arrive at the proper diagnosis. In the presence of unexplained fractures or fractures typical for child abuse, the possibility of OI is unlikely without the presence of some other associated clinical feature of OI such as a family history of frequent fractures with minor injuries, poor dentition, hearing difficulties, short stature, and a bluish-grey tint to the whites of the eyes. The key to distinction is the correlation of clinical history, physical examination, family history, and radiologic findings.

- *Osteomyelitis.* Bacterial bone infections can produce skeletal changes that resemble fractures.

- *Osteopenia of prematurity.* Premature infants, particularly those who have had associated respiratory problems requiring various therapies including treatment with certain medications (such as fursomide) and special feeding and nutritional requirements may be predisposed to weakened bones and increased risk of fractures with normal handling.

- *Rickets.* Although fractures are not a common result of infantile nutritional rickets, this deficiency can cause other irregularities in the bones similar to those caused by trauma such as metaphyseal irregularity, periosteal reaction, and new bone formation.

- *Scurvy.* Resulting from vitamin C deficiency, scurvy can cause irregularities and fractures of the bones. It is generalized, meaning it affects all of the bones of the body, and is usually accompanied by bruising and swelling of the extremities. Scurvy is extremely rare before the age of 6 months.

Case Example

Joseph, a premature baby, has bones that have not completely mineralized (hardened). Since Joseph also has immature lungs and respiratory problems, some of the medications used to reduce fluids in his lungs will leach minerals out of his bones. This decreased mineralization of the bones can result in fractures with normal handling while he is in the hospital or in his parents' care.

It is important to remember that these diseases are all quite infrequent. Despite these other diagnoses, nonaccidental trauma or child abuse accounts for 11% to 55% of the skeletal trauma seen in children. Keep in mind the significance of the age of the child in these statistics. Over 80% of abusive fractures occur in children below the age of 18 months, while only 2% of the accidental fractures occur in this age group (Cooperman & Merten, 2001).

- Other rare conditions/diseases:

  - *Drug-induced toxicity.* Correct diagnosis is based on history of drug therapy or exposure.
  - *Neuromuscular defects.* Particularly those associated with muscular contractures of the extremities. Children with these defects may suffer fractures during routine handling or physical therapy. It should be kept in mind, however, that these children are also at an increased risk of child abuse due to their disability and thus a thorough assessment should be done.

Fractures resulting from child abuse indicate a violent episode that clearly announces the need for proper intervention by CPS to protect children. The first step in the intervention process is conducting a full assessment to understand how the child was injured and then implementing a plan to protect the child from future harm. Understanding the injuries a child sustained is an important component of that assessment.

References

American Academy of Pediatrics, Section on Radiology. (2000). Diagnostic imaging of child abuse. *Pediatrics, 105*, 1345–1348.

Cooperman, D., & Merten, D. (2001). Skeletal manifestations of child abuse. In R. M. Reece & S. Ludwig (Eds.), *Child abuse: Medical diagnosis and management* (2nd ed., pp. 123–156). Philadelphia: Lippincott Williams & Wilkins.

Kleinman, P. (1998). *Diagnostic imaging of child abuse.* St. Louis, MO: Mosby.

Swischuk, L. (1981). Radiology of the skeletal system. In N. Ellerstein (Ed.), *Child abuse and neglect: A medical reference* (pp. 253–274). New York: John Wiley.

6

Kathryn M. Wells

Injuries to the Head, Eyes, Ears, Nose, and Mouth

Child abuse is the most common cause of head injury in children younger than 1 year of age (Billmire & Myers, 1995). Trauma to the head and associated areas is present in about 50% of abused children (Willging, Bower, & Cotton, 1992). Abusive head trauma is currently the most common cause of mortality from child abuse as well as the leading cause of trauma-related death among children (Duhaime et al., 1992; Gotschall, 1993). In addition, it accounts for lesser degrees of brain injury including severe neurologic, developmental and behavioral sequelae, even in those infants appearing normal two months following the injury. Although hard to quantify because of underrecognition and underreporting, inflicted head injuries are believed to account for about 25% of hospital admissions for child physical abuse. In addition, these children's injuries are disproportionately more severe than injuries in children that suffer accidental injuries, frequently because of failure of the caregiver to seek timely medical care or the lack of a complete history given to the medical provider (Duhaime et al., 1992). Children under 2 years of age are at the greatest risk for this type of trauma. It is estimated that abusive head trauma is the cause of 80% of deaths in children less than 2 years of age (Sirotnak, Grigsby, & Krugman, 2004).

Abusive head injuries arise from a variety of mechanisms including direct impact from a blow or throw, penetrating trauma, asphyxiation or hypoxia (lack of oxygen), or shaking, with or without impact causing acceleration, deceleration, and rotational forces on the skull. The constellation of injuries associated with this type of trauma is sometimes referred to as shaken baby syndrome or shaken impact syndrome. Primary brain injuries occur at the moment of the injury while secondary injuries result from lack of oxygen to the brain resulting in hypoxemia–ischemia (lack of oxygen to the tissues causing tissue damage) and the resultant cerebral edema (swelling).

Whenever there is suspected trauma to the head or face, a medical provider should examine the child immediately. It is important to remember that "infants who do not cruise, rarely bruise" (Sugar, Taylor, & Feldman, 1999, p. 399). Therefore, bruises are rarely seen in children less than 9 months of age and should always be considered concerning. External soft tissue injuries of the head and face are generally contact injuries and should also be evaluated by a medical provider, because facial or scalp soft tissue injuries in very young children have been linked to subtle intracranial injuries (Greenes & Schutzman, 1998; Gruskin & Schutzman, 1999; Jenny, Hymel, Ritzen, Reinert, & Hay, 1999). Child abuse should be seriously considered when there are severe infant head injuries in the absence of significant history for accidental trauma. A complete medical examination should include an evaluation for injuries to the skull, brain, eyes, ears, nose, and mouth.

■ Cranial Injuries

The Scalp

The scalp consists of the skin and soft tissues that cover the skull. Trauma to the scalp can cause alopecia (loss of hair), lacerations, bruising, or hematomas. Children who have been pulled or yanked by the hair may have several markers of this type of abuse. ⌨ In addition, blunt impact may be evidenced by subgaleal hematomas (bleeding underneath the scalp), edema (swelling), or bruises on the scalp. Often, these injuries are obscured by the child's hair, and careful assessment may include removal of the hair for better examination. Deep scalp injuries are often first identified during an autopsy. However, external signs of abusive head trauma may be minimal, even in life-threatening or fatal head injury cases.

Alopecia may result from a multitude of causes. Traumatic alopecia is the loss of hair due to some traumatic event such as excessive hair pulling. In these situations, the hair is often spiraled at the ends where it was stretched and broken off. The scalp may or may not be tender at these sites. Other medical causes of alopecia include infections, drug ingestion, or metabolic illness.

Subgaleal hematomas occur when the scalp separates from the skull, causing blood to pool underneath the skin, creating a soft, "boggy" area (see Figure 6.1). This bleeding or hemorrhage causes a hematoma. This injury is usually associated with blunt impact injuries but can also arise from hair pulling (Hamlin, 1968). When this injury occurs in the frontal region of the skull, it may result in "raccoon eyes" (or bruising below the eyes) from the blood tracking down into the soft tissue spaces around the eyes. ⌨ This injury may not become noticeable for 1 or 2 days following its occurrence and may take several weeks to resolve.

The Spinal Cord and Neck

Frequently no signs of a neurologic injury exist and, therefore, spinal lesions often go unrecognized. The child may, however, present with sudden death,

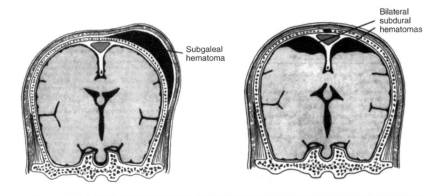

Figure 6.1. A Subgaleal Hematoma (right) and Subdural Hematomas (left).

neurologic deficit, paralysis, or other signs of neurologic injury such as vomiting, weight loss, irritability, or slowed development.

Injuries to the spinal cord can occur during a shaking event because of the lack of strength in an infant's neck and the relative large size and weight of an infant's head (Case, Graham, & Wood, 1998). These injuries are rare and are felt to occur as a result of the mechanical tolerances of the spinal ligaments being greater than that of the spinal cord and result in subsequent injury to the cord during a traumatic event (Pang & Wilberger, 1982). Therefore, spinal injury may be seen without fracture of the vertebrae or the surrounding ligaments (Feldman, Weinberger, Milstein, & Flinger, 1997). There have also been reports of injuries to an infant's spinal cord when the child's head was grabbed and the body shaken (Parrish, 1996; Piatt & Steinberg, 1995).

Although uncommon, vertebral fractures, either fractures of the spinous processes along the spine or the vertebral body itself, may also be seen in abuse. These injuries are probably more common than realized because they are often not symptomatic (Kleinman, 1987). Spinous process may be caused by forced bending (hyperextension or hyperflexion) or twisting (torsion) of the spine while vertebral body fractures may result from excessive force being applied downward onto the child's spinal column (such as slamming a child into a car seat). These injuries have also been associated with the rapid acceleration and deceleration forces caused by an infant being shaken without support of the head, causing severe flexion and extension of the infant's neck. Again, this occurs because the child's head is large and heavy compared to the rest of the child and the neck muscles are comparatively weak. However, a neck injury does not need to be present to support a shaking history.

The Skull

The skull is made of eight separate cranial bones that ultimately fuse together, forming immobile joints called sutures. In the newborn infant, the bones of the skull have not yet fused together or completely calcified. The infant skull has two "soft spots" or *fontanelles*, which are the spaces created where several skull bones come together (the *anterior fontanelle* is located on the top of the head and the *posterior fontanelle* is located at the apex of the skull). The anterior fontanelle may stay open until the child is 15 months old but the posterior fontanelle usually closes in the first few months of life (see Figure 6.2).

If the infant brain sustains an injury, it may swell or the area around the brain may bleed, causing increased pressure inside the skull. This pressure may cause the sutures to separate or the fontanelles to bulge. There are other problems that can cause a bulging fontanelle, all suggesting an intracranial pathology, such as meningitis or hydrocephalus. Therefore, this symptom should always prompt an urgent evaluation of the infant by a medical provider.

Skull fractures constitute the second most common form of skeletal injury in abuse (Merten, Cooperman, & Thompson, 1994). These injuries are caused by a direct impact to the head and may be detected by radiographic evaluation of the skull. However, a skull fracture cannot be dated by the radiologist.

Description of the fracture includes the name of the bone(s) involved and the type of fracture. Linear skull fractures and fractures of the parietal bone are the most common skull fractures seen in both abusive and accidental injuries (Leventhal, Thomas, Rosenfield, & Markowitz, 1993). The child may or may not have evidence of external trauma such as bruising or swelling overlying the fracture. Abuse should be suspected when there is no clear history of accidental trauma or when the fractures are multiple, extensive, or accompanied by other injury. Further, abuse should also be suspected if

Figure 6.2. Fontanelles of the Infant Skull (left) and Fontanelles of the Adult Skull (right). (From Bruck-Kan, 1979. Reprinted with permission from the author.)

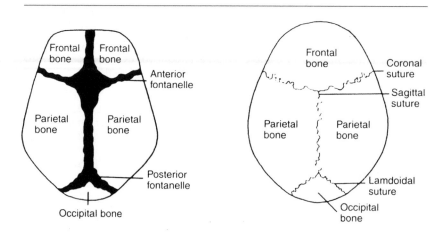

the fracture is nonparietal or nonlinear or if the child is very young. Skull fractures do not predict brain injury. In addition, the absence of a skull fracture does not exclude the possibility of a significant underlying brain injury.

As with all childhood injuries, the best and sometimes only indicator of the etiology or cause of an injury is the compatibility between the history and the physical findings. Child abuse should be suspected when life-threatening or fatal injuries result from uncorroborated short falls. Past studies have indicated that, except in the cases of epidural hemorrhage, children who fall from heights of less than 90 cm (3 feet) rarely sustain serious head injury (Helfer, Slovis, & Black, 1977). Therefore, reports that serious injuries resulted from falls from beds, sofas, or cribs should be viewed with skepticism. It is also important to correlate the history with the child's developmental maturity. For example, a history given for a skull fracture in a 2-week-old infant that the child rolled off a changing table is unlikely given that rolling is not developmentally accomplished until 6 to 8 weeks of life.

Injury to the Brain

Prognosis of a head injury relates to the intracranial component. Brain injury can be caused by either direct impact trauma or indirect impact from acceleration, deceleration, and rotational forces during a shaking or impact injury. This type of trauma is responsible for most of the morbidity and mortality associated with severe inflicted head injury. The immaturity of the infant skull and brain make them more susceptible to trauma. Because the infant brain floats in a relatively larger space of cerebrospinal fluid than the adult brain, it has room to move around and sustain injury. Brain injury should be suspected in any infant presenting with altered consciousness of unknown etiology.

☐ Epidural Hematoma

The epidural space is located between the skull and the dura membrane and bleeding into this area causes an epidural hematoma or hemorrhage. This is caused by a contact injury that is frequently the result of accidental trauma but has also been seen in abused children (Merten & Osborne, 1984). There may be delayed clinical deterioration with this injury. Because these injuries are usually due to the tearing of an artery that traverses this space, they are considered surgical emergencies as they may be life threatening due to rapid and severe bleeding.

☐ Subdural Hematoma

The subdural space is located between the dura and the arachnoid membranes. Bleeding into this space causes a hematoma and is called a subdural hematoma or hemorrhage (see Figure 6.1). The injury can result from a

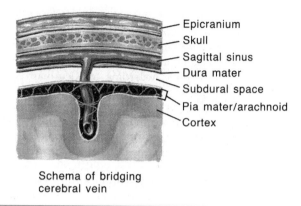

Schema of bridging
cerebral vein

Figure 6.3. Brain Meninges. (From Kessler & Hyden, 1991: 1, 15. Netter illustration used with permission from Icon Learning Systems, a division of MediMedia USA, Inc. All rights reserved.)

contact injury similar to what occurs in an epidural hematoma. A subdural hematoma may also occur as a result of a noncontact injury from severe acceleration or deceleration with or without rotational injury when there is tearing of the bridging veins that extend from the surface of the brain to the dura. These fragile cerebral veins are poorly supported and can be easily damaged when the head is shaken or slammed into a surface. Once they are damaged, they release blood into the cavity called the subdural space. The blood pools underneath the dura, creating a hematoma, which then exerts pressure on the brain tissue. This bleeding may extend along the surface of the brain and into the posterior interhemispheric fissure (the space between the cerebral hemispheres). There may be accompanying cerebral edema and/or skull fractures. However, the absence of external cranial soft tissue injuries or skull fractures neither excludes cranial impact nor confirms shaking alone as the mechanism for the injury.

Acute subdural hematomas occur rapidly following an incident of trauma while *chronic* subdural hematomas evolve over time as they represent areas of older blood in the subdural space that has begun to break down. These may be discovered during a routine physical examination when the infant's head is found to be larger than expected, prompting a CT scan (computed tomography scan) or an MRI (magnetic resonance imaging). It is possible that the event that caused the original injury was not reported to medical providers or the symptoms caused by the injury were subtle and felt to be related to another cause such as illness or gastroesophageal reflux. Sometimes both acute and chronic subdural hematomas are detected at the same time. All of these injuries can cause permanent brain damage, seizures, developmental and learning disabilities, and death. They are frequently accompanied by lethargy, breathing difficulty, convulsions, decreased level of consciousness, vomiting, and irritability. When accompanied by retinal hemorrhages, and long bone fractures, abuse should be strongly suspected.

☐ Subarachnoid Hematoma

The subarachnoid space is located between the arachnoid membrane and the surface of the brain. A subarachnoid hematoma may result from many different mechanisms that may or may not be associated with abuse.

☐ Parenchymal Injury

The parenchyma refers to the tissue located within the brain tissue. Injuries here may or may not be related to abuse. These injuries include contusions, lacerations, concussion, axonal injuries, infarctions, encephalomalacia, shearing tears, cerebral edema, and herniation.

Brain contusions are bruises of the brain tissue itself and typically are caused by contact injuries. These injuries occur as a result of compression on the surface of the brain resulting from impact to the cranium. Lacerations may occur in this manner also. An isolated noncontact injury may also cause a contusion (Ommaya, Grubb, & Naumann, 1971). When contusions are located on the same side as the impact point to the head, they are called coup injuries and when they are located on the opposite side they are called contre-coup injuries.

Primary diffuse brain injuries are noncontact injuries and include concussion, diffuse axonal injuries, prolonged coma, and tissue-tear hemorrhages. *Concussion* is the beginning of the clinical continuum of diffuse brain injury and is felt to require rotational cranial acceleration (Ommaya & Gennerelli, 1974). More severe primary diffuse brain injury may appear clinically as immediate loss of consciousness with prolonged coma and without mass lesions. This is often associated with *diffuse axonal injury*, which is the result of traumatic injury to the axons of the brain. The subsequent swelling of these axons and their decreased function contributes to respiratory depression and ultimately anoxia (lack of oxygen to the brain). There may be associated tissue-tear hemorrhages, which, if the infant survives, may later appear as infarctions, shearing tears, and encephalomalacia. These injuries are the result of a lack of blood to the brain, causing necrosis or death of the brain tissue.

Cerebral edema may be the result of any injury to the brain and refers to swelling of the cerebrum. ▣ This can occur unilaterally (on one side) or bilaterally (on both sides) in the brain. It is the most difficult to manage and frequently life-threatening consequence of head trauma.

☐ Intraventricular Injury

The ventricles are the very central spaces in the brain through which the cerebrospinal fluid flows. Bleeding into this area, known as intraventricular hemorrhage, may arise from newborn problems, such as prematurity, vascular malformations, bleeding disorders, trauma (accidental or inflicted), or as a complication of surgery.

☐ Shaken Baby Syndrome/Shaken Impact Syndrome

Shaken baby syndrome (SBS) and shaken impact syndrome (SIS) are terms that are used to describe the constellation of symptoms that occur as a result of severe acceleration/deceleration/rotational force on an infant's head. 🖳 This syndrome is a frequently described mechanism of head injury in abused children and involves infants who are held by the arms or trunk and violently shaken. There may or may not be impact with either a hard or soft surface in addition to the shaking. An example may be a child who is shaken, then thrown into or against a crib or other surface, striking the back of the head and thus undergoing a large, brief deceleration. This child may have both injuries from impact in addition to the severe acceleration and deceleration. Commonly, infants with this identified form of injury are less than 2 years of age and are often less than 6 months of age. In fact, it is estimated that 80% of deaths from head trauma among children under age 2 are nonaccidental. Because these children frequently have no obvious external signs of injury, they are often initially misdiagnosed. Additionally, shaking or cranial impact is not usually an isolated event but rather is frequently proceeded by other abuse and accompanied by multiple other social risk factors, suggesting risk to siblings.

Presenting symptoms are often irritability, poor feeding, and lethargy. The child may present for medical care with a history of apnea (not breathing adequately), seizures, visual impairment, or as an unexplained infant death. There may be bruising of the head, thorax, or extremities, but usually there are no external signs of trauma. The history given at the time of presentation is often vague, not consistent with the injuries, or not present at all. Frequently the history then changes as more information about the child's injuries is presented.

The most common manifestations of this type of abuse are *subdural hematomas, interhemispheric blood, retinal hemorrhages,* and *bone injuries* such as rib fractures and long bone metaphyseal fractures. 🖳 Other findings may include subarachnoid hemorrhages, bilateral chronic subdural hematomas, cerebral edema, profound neurological impairment, seizures, injuries of the spinal cord, cranial contusions, and skull fractures. Shaking leads to apnea, which frequently triggers a "cascade of events" including hypoxia (lack of oxygen) and results in swelling of the brain tissue. The duration of hypoxia correlates with the severity of the brain injury and ultimately the outcome (Johnson, Boal, & Baule, 1995).

Limited long-term outcome studies reveal very frequent and severe neurological, developmental, and/or behavioral sequelae in victims of SBS, even among infants who appeared clinically normal 2 months post injury (Bonnier, Nassogne, & Evrard, 1995).

Medical Assessment of Head Injuries

All *growth parameters* should be obtained and compared. Measurement of head circumference that is over the 90th percentile for age and/or a child whose head is growing faster then expected often prompts the need for evaluation of possible intracranial abnormality, including injury (see Figures 11.2 and 11.4 in chapter 11).

A complete *physical examination* including close evaluation of the skin and nervous system should be performed. Special attention should be focused on the eyes and, if possible, a pediatric ophthalmologist should be consulted to do a complete eye examination, including indirect ophthalmoscopy.

Several *laboratory studies* are usually obtained including blood counts (assessing for anemia), bleeding studies (assessing for bleeding tendencies), liver function tests (assessing for liver damage), amylase and lipase (assessing for damage to the pancreas), and a urinalysis (assessing for damage to the bladder or kidneys). If there is concern for the possibility of infection such as meningitis causing the presenting symptoms, a lumbar spinal tap may be done. In this procedure a small amount of fluid that surrounds the brain and the spinal cord (cerebrospinal fluid) is withdrawn from the lower portion of the spine and evaluated for signs of infection. The presence of blood in this fluid may signal that bleeding has occurred.

Radiographic studies play a significant role in assessing children that present for evaluation of possible head trauma, particularly infants that present with suspected trauma, altered consciousness, retinal hemorrhages, long bone or rib fractures, or excessive bruising. A *CT scan* of the head is one of the most useful radiologic techniques for detecting acute injuries inside the skull and is therefore recommended for initial management. This study can detect hemorrhages that may exist in any of the locations inside the cranium. It may also detect fractures of the skull or widening of the sutures caused by brain swelling or bleeding. It assists in identifying the location, extent, and severity of the injury. After identifying a subdural hematoma by CT, the medical provider may need to "tap" the area of pooled blood with a needle, thus releasing some of the pressure from the brain. This fluid is then sent for cultures and other studies. An abdominal CT may also need to be considered, depending on the age of the infant as the child may have sustained trauma of unknown extent and damage to other organs.

MRIs as well as serial CTs provide increased accuracy in diagnosis. The MRI is useful in demonstrating small injuries as well as assisting in the differentiation of different stages of resolution. It may also assist in evaluation for vascular lesions that may cause hemorrhage.

A complete *skeletal survey* should always be done in a child less than 2 years of age suspected of having abusive head trauma as it may identify skull fractures as well as subclinical fractures of other bones. Special attention needs to be given to the skull, the ends of the long bones, and the ribs. The examination may need to be repeated in two to four weeks to assess for healing injuries that may not have been identified initially. The age of skull fractures cannot be estimated accurately, but the general timing can sometimes be determined for other fractures.

☐   **Differential Diagnoses**

- *Benign subdural fluid collection of infancy, or an effusion.* This is a condition that appears at birth. The appearance of this condition on CT and MRI scans differs from subdural hematoma. In addition, this condition is not accompanied by any signs of intracranial injury other than increased head circumference.

- *Tinea capitis (ringworm).* This is a fungal infection of the scalp that may produce round areas of baldness (and may appear on other parts of the body). Diagnosis is usually made clinically and may include demonstration of florescence of the area under a Wood's lamp.

- *Caput succedaneums.* Scalp hematomas that appear as swellings on newborn infants after passage through a birth canal or delivery assisted by the use of forceps or vacuum suction. This will disappear within the first few weeks after birth.

- *Cephalhematoma.* Caused by bleeding into the layer of fibrous tissue that immediately overlies the skull, called the periosteum, often during childbirth. This will also disappear within the first few weeks of life.

- *Accidental injury.* This is frequently given as the explanation for an abusive head injury. Skull fractures result when a child receives a direct impact injury to the head. A common history given for head injuries is that the child fell from a bed, changing table, or sofa. Although accidents such as falls may cause minor head injuries, child abuse should be suspected when serious injury results from unwitnessed accidents such as falls. Serious head injuries are extremely rare when children fall from short heights such as cribs, beds, or couches (Lyons & Oates, 1993). Past studies have suggested that children who fall from heights of 90 centimeters (about 41 inches) or less very rarely sustain serious head injury. Further, death is unlikely to result from injuries sustained in a fall of less than 20 feet unless it has resulted in an epidural hematoma (Chadwick, Chin, Salerno, Landsverk, & Kitchen, 1991; Helfer et al., 1977). Stairway falls have also not been shown to result in life-threatening injury as they are essentially a series of short falls (Joffe & Ludwig, 1988). Also, it is important to consider the child's developmental maturity and whether the child is capable of performing what the parent or caregiver has reported.

- *Meningitis.* This is an infection of the fluid that bathes the brain and spinal cord.

- *Bleeding tendencies.* Bleeding disorders such as hemophilia and von Willebrand's disease can cause subdural hematomas but are ruled out with the initial medical evaluation of these injuries.

Prognosis in Abusive Head Injuries

The developmental and neurologic outcomes in children that are victims of abusive head trauma are typically poor. Approximately one-third of these children will die, one-third will suffer disability, and of the remaining one-third that appear normal for the short term, another one-half will develop late findings of the injury such as microcephaly (small head), hydrocephalus (fluid around the brain), seizures, developmental delay, learning disabilities, and psychological and/or behavioral disabilities. Diffuse cerebral edema is life threatening. Infarction due to lack of blood and oxygen to the brain can cause necrosis (death) of the brain tissue.

Posttraumatic hypopituitarism, injury to the part of the brain that secretes hormones affecting growth, can result in delayed growth of the child and may be detected through laboratory tests.

Eye Injuries

Eye injuries from both accidental and nonaccidental causes are common in childhood. It is conceivable that any ocular injury could be the result of child physical abuse. The face is involved in up to 45% of child abuse cases with the eyes being affected up to 61% of the time (Levin, 1990). The injuries may result from direct blows to the eyes or from trauma such as results from the acceleration and deceleration forces involved in shaking.

As with all cases of suspected child physical abuse, a complete history accompanied by a thorough medical evaluation is required to differentiate abuse from accident. A complete medical evaluation should include measurement of visual acuity and field of vision of both of the eyes. A detailed evaluation of the external surface of the eye as well as its mobility and the movement of the pupil should be performed. The medical provider may also use a direct ophthalmoscope to visualize the retina in the back of the eye. Referral to an ophthalmologist may be necessary for further diagnostic testing including indirect ophthalmoscopy.

Direct blows to the eye may cause the lens to detach and become dislocated in the eye. This injury acutely affects the child's ability to focus and may cause the formation of a cataract (opacity of the lens). A *subconjunctival hemorrhage* can also be caused by direct trauma to the eye. This results from the breaking of a small blood vessel in the conjunctiva (the mucous membrane that forms the inner surface of the eyelid and covers the front part of the eyeball itself), causing the eyeball to appear red or dark and bruised. This injury can also be the result of increased intrathoracic pressure in a child who is coughing excessively. These lesions usually clear within 2 weeks and go through the usual stages of resolution of color from dark red through yellow.

Direct trauma that causes injury to the tissue around eyes, generating black eyes (*periorbital ecchymosis*), creates difficulty when it comes to estimating the time since the injury. Because the skin around the eye is loosely attached to the underlying tissues, large amounts of blood may accumulate, preventing the determination of how long ago the child was injured. Bruising in this area may look darker for its age than injury on other parts of the body. Injury to both eyes should raise suspicion as accidental injuries generally occur on one side of the face, but it should be noted that an injury to the forehead can cause tracking of the blood into the tissue around the eyes giving the false impression of bilateral eye injury (often referred to as "raccoon eyes"). Allergic conditions can produce the appearance of bruising underneath the eyes ("allergic shiners") but this is not actual bruising.

Chemical burns of the eye always constitute an emergency and should be evaluated and treated immediately. The eye should be flushed with water as soon as possible and the child should be taken to the emergency department of the nearest hospital. It is important not to overlook the possibility of intentional infliction of chemical injuries or lack of appropriate supervision as a form of child abuse.

Corneal abrasions occur when the cornea (the transparent layer in the front of the eye) sustains lacerations or abrasions as a result of direct trauma.

A *hyphema* refers to a collection of blood in the anterior chamber of the eye (the area in front of the lens) resulting from the rupture of blood vessels in that area. This injury occurs as a result of direct trauma to the eye and requires immediate medical attention.

Retinal Hemorrhage

A thorough eye examination is essential in the evaluation of suspected abusive head trauma as injuries to the retina, the delicate innermost layer of the eye, are frequently discovered (Elner, Elner, Arnall, & Albert, 1990). Although retinal hemorrhages are not always present in cases of abusive head trauma, the literature suggests that approximately 80% of children with abusive head trauma also have evidence of retinal hemorrhages (Green,

Lieberman, Milroy, & Parsons, 1996). Infants who have suffered abusive head trauma such as shaking often present with retinal hemorrhages. Therefore, the presence of this finding should always prompt further evaluation for injuries often associated with abusive head trauma. The presence of retinal hemorrhages in conjunction with fractures, cerebral injury, or bruises is a strong indicator that abuse has occurred.

A medical provider with the highest available level of expertise should be employed for examination of the eyes of an infant believed to have sustained abusive head trauma. This should consist of an ophthalmologist or, if possible, a pediatric ophthalmologist. Injuries to the retina are described both by their location and by their extent, because these factors are very helpful in determining the cause of the hemorrhages. Although few hemorrhages located in the posterior pole may result from accidental injury, extensive, multilayer hemorrhages extending out to the periphery are suggestive of abusive head trauma. Additionally, hemorrhages into the vitreous part of the eye (the gelatinous central portion of the eyeball) represent more severe ocular injury and are linked to deeper intracranial injury as well as more severe cranial trauma (Green et al., 1996). Retinal hemorrhages cannot be used to date an injury (Levin, 1990).

Although retinal hemorrhages are felt to be a hallmark of abusive head trauma, other ocular injuries may be present in cases of abusive head trauma (Rao, Smith, Choi, Xu, & Kornblum, 1988). Retinal detachment and optic nerve hemorrhages have been reported in these cases (Lambert, Johnson, & Hoyt, 1986).

It is unusual to find retinal hemorrhages as a result of conditions other than abusive head trauma. A thorough medical evaluation can rule out other rare causes of retinal hemorrhages. The differential diagnoses for retinal hemorrhages include birth trauma, accidental trauma, a bleeding disorder, or a prolonged increase in intracranial pressure. Retinal hemorrhages from these causes typically appear different than those caused by abusive trauma.

Newborn infants with retinal hemorrhages related to the birth process do not have other intracranial injuries similar to those of abused children (Smith, Alexander, Judisch, Sato, & Kao, 1992). Moreover, these hemorrhages are usually mild and resolve within a few days. The more extensive hemorrhages from birth usually resolve by 6 weeks (Levin, 2000).

Injuries to the retina are rare in severe head trauma due to accidents and do not occur in cases of mild to moderate head trauma (Buys, Levin, Enzenauer, Elder, & Morin, 1992). Retinal hemorrhages can result from severe accidental trauma such as a significant motor vehicle accident or a fall from a high window (Duhaime et al., 1992). However, the retinal hemorrhages in these circumstances are often different in appearance than those from nonaccidental trauma and are the result of extraordinary force (Johnson, Braun, & Friendly, 1993).

Retinal hemorrhages rarely can occur as a result of nontraumatic causes such as coagulopathy (bleeding disorder), meningitis, severe hypertension, endocarditis (infection of the lining of the heart), vasculitis (inflammation of the blood vessels), sepsis, and carbon monoxide poisoning (Singer, Bolte, Christian, & Selbst, 1994). These can all be ruled out by medical evaluation.

Finally, retinal hemorrhages do not result from cardiopulmonary resuscitation in children with a normal coagulation profile and platelet count (Odom et al., 1997). When retinal hemorrhages are noted in a child that has undergone cardiopulmonary resuscitation, it should be assumed that the child sustained some type of trauma before receiving CPR.

■ Ear Injuries

Ears are other areas of the head that may reveal injury in an abused child and therefore should be carefully examined. These injuries can be the result of direct blows, grabs, or penetrating trauma. Direct blows to the ear may result in bruising of the pinna (outer ear), abrasions, scarring, perforation of the eardrum, or hemotympanum (a collection of blood in the inner ear) (Leavitt, Pincus, & Bukachevsky, 1992). ☂ Pinching or pulling of the ear may also cause characteristic bruising on the front and back of the pinna (Welbury & Murphy, 1998). There may also be bruising of the scalp around the edge of the ear as a result of a blow to the side of the head and ear. These injuries should always be considered suspicious since the area around the ear is relatively protected from accidental injury by a triangle formed from the top of the head to the shoulder and the neck.

Lacerations of the external auditory meatus (the passage leading from the outside into the internal ear), eardrum, middle ear, or inner ear can only be achieved by penetrating trauma such as the insertion of a sharp, pointed object. Although these injuries may be the result of an adult or child's innocent attempt to clean the ear with cotton swabs, repeated penetrating injuries are rarely accidental and should be considered suspicious. An isolated perforation of the eardrum can occur as a result of infection in the middle ear. The family will usually report the child's ear pain and subsequent drainage of purulent material (pus) from the ear canal. Children with chronically untreated ear infections should be considered possible victims of neglect.

"Tin ear syndrome" refers to a presentation characterized by unilateral ear bruising, retinal hemorrhages, and ipsilateral cerebral edema (which is on the same side as the ear bruising) (Hanigan, Peterson, & Njus, 1987). This combination of findings may be the result of blunt injuries to the ears in conjunction with severe rotational acceleration of the head (shaken baby syndrome). The resultant brain injury may be highly lethal.

■ Nasal Injuries

Injuries of the nose are occasionally seen in victims of child physical abuse. Blunt trauma to the nose can cause bruising, abrasions, bleeding, or nasal bone fractures (Willging et al., 1992). Fractures of the nose are infrequent in pre-adolescent years and should prompt suspicions of nonaccidental trauma.

Penetrating trauma of the nose can cause injury to the nasal septum (the partition that divides the nasal cavity into two sections). Destruction of the columella refers to the part of the septum closest to the tip of the nose. These injuries can be the result of the insertion of foreign bodies into the nose by a curious, normally developing child or by an angry caregiver as a punishment.

As with all types of potentially abusive injuries, history and developmental age are important in determining the accidental or nonaccidental nature of the injury. Also, foreign bodies found in more than one site (e.g., nose, ear canals, urogenital area, or rectum) should raise stronger suspicions of abuse.

■ Oral Injuries

The physical significance in both feeding and communication make the mouth an easy target for physical abuse. Injuries to this area include bruises, burns, lesions, "split lips," broken or misplaced teeth, frenulum tears, and jaw fractures. A history of injury to the mouth is important in determining the nature of the injuries.

Bruising, burns, abrasions, or lacerations of the lips or inside the mouth should always raise strong suspicions of child abuse and should prompt further evaluations for other manifestations of physical abuse (Grace & Grace, 1987). ■ Bruises or scars on the external corners of the mouth suggest that the child may have been gagged. ■

Frenulum tears are highly suspicious for abuse and should therefore always be carefully assessed for when suspecting nonaccidental trauma. ■ The frenula are the small folds of skin that connect the lips to the gums and connect the tongue to the floor of the mouth. Injuries to these parts of the mouth can occur from a direct blow to the face or from the forceful jamming of a spoon or bottle into a resistant child's mouth. They can also be accompanied by bruising of the lips and palate (the roof of the mouth).

Erythema (redness) and petechiae (small bruises) at the junction of the hard and soft palates or the floor of the mouth may suggest that the child was made to perform fellatio (oral stimulation of the male genitalia). Other signs of sexual abuse may include evidence of sexually transmitted diseases in the mouth or throat (Jessee, 1995).

Traumatic injury to the deciduous (baby) teeth of young children can be quite common and may or may not be abusive in nature. An *avulsion* refers to a tooth that has been totally removed from the socket. 🗩 This injury requires a moderate to severe amount of force. Treatment of this type of injury should be sought immediately to avoid loss of the tooth. *Fractures* of the teeth can occur as a result of accidental falls or from teeth being struck by or striking a hard object. Immediate treatment by a dentist should be sought in an attempt to preserve the teeth. *Intrusions* occur when teeth are forced into the supporting bony structure. Deciduous teeth are more easily intruded than permanent ones. Usually these teeth will re-erupt within three to twelve months but should still be evaluated by a dentist. Teeth that are loosened in the mouth but have not come out of the socket are referred to as *luxated*. Both deciduous and permanent teeth can be easily luxated and the severity of the blow need not be severe to cause such injuries.

Fractures of the upper jaw (maxilla) are relatively rare in children and are the result of significant trauma. Fractures of the lower jaw (mandible) are much more common but are still the result of trauma. Both injuries require immediate evaluation and treatment by an oral or plastic surgeon in order to avoid disfigurement.

The history of any mouth or jaw injury and the efforts of the caregiver to obtain appropriately timed care both play a factor in the assessment of these injuries.

Dental neglect should be considered when extensive dental caries (cavities) and oral infections persist despite the elimination of barriers (financial or transportation-related) to care.

■ Treatment

Any cases in which abusive trauma to the head, eyes, ears, nose, and mouth are suspected require immediate referral; the earlier they are detected, the better the chances of the child's survival. Nevertheless, about one-third of abusive head trauma injuries will result in death. Treatments for individual injuries will vary with each particular case.

References

Billmire, M. E., & Myers, P. A. (1995). Serious head injury in infants: Accident or abuse? *Pediatrics, 75,* 340–342.

Bonnier C., Nassogne M. C., & Evrard, P. (1995). Outcome and prognosis of whiplash shaken infant syndrome: Late consequences after a symptom-free interval. *Developmental Medicine and Child Neurology, 37,* 943–956.

Bruck-Kan, R. (1979). *Introduction to human anatomy.* New York: Harper & Row.

Buys, Y., Levin, A., Enzenauer, R., Elder, J., & Morin, D. (1992). Retinal findings after head trauma in young infants and young children. *Ophthalmology, 99,* 1718–1723.

Case, M., Graham, M., & Wood, J. (1998, September). *Spinal cord injury in child abuse by shaking.* Paper presented at the Second National Conference on Shaken Baby Syndrome, Salt Lake City, Utah.

Chadwick, D. L., Chin, S., Salerno, C., Landsverk, J., & Kitchen, L. (1991). Deaths from falls in children: How far is fatal? *Journal of Trauma, 31,* 1353–1355.

Duhaime, A. C., Alario, A. J., Lewander, W. J., Schut, L., Sutton, L. N., Seidl, T., Nudelman, S., Budenz, D., Hertle, R., Tsiaras, W., & Loporchio, S. (1992). Head injury in very young children: Mechanism, injury types, and ophthalmic findings in 100 patients younger than 2 years of age. *Pediatrics, 90,* 179–185.

Elner, S. G., Elner, V. M., Arnall, M., & Albert, D. M. (1990). Ocular and associated systemic findings in suspected child abuse: A necropsy study. *Archives of Ophthalmology, 108,* 1094–1101.

Feldman, K. W., Weinberger, E., Milstein, J. M., & Flinger, C. L. (1997). Cervical spine MRI in abused infants. *Child Abuse and Neglect, 21*(2), 199–205.

Gotschall, C. S. (1993). Epidemiology of childhood injury. In M. R. Eichenberger (Ed.), *Pediatric trauma: Prevention, acute care, rehabilitation* (pp. 16–19). St. Louis, MO: Mosby Yearbook.

Grace, A., & Grace, S. (1987). Child abuse within the ear, nose and throat. *Otolaryngology, 16,* 108–111.

Green, M. A., Lieberman, G., Milroy, C. M., & Parsons, M. A. (1996). Ocular and cerebral trauma in nonaccidental injury in infancy: Underlying mechanisms and implications for paediatric practice. *British Journal of Ophthalmology, 80,* 282–287.

Greenes, D. S., & Schutzman, S. A. (1998). Occult intracranial injury in infants. *Annals of Emergency Medicine, 32,* 680–686.

Gruskin, K. D., & Schutzman, S. A. (1999). Head trauma in children younger than 2 years: Are there predictors for complications? *Archives of Pediatrics and Adolescent Medicine, 153,* 15–20.

Hamlin, H. (1968). Subgaleal hematoma caused by hair pull. *Journal of the American Medical Association, 205*(5), 314.

Hanigan, W. C., Peterson, R. A., & Njus, G. (1987). Tin ear syndrome: Rotational acceleration in pediatric head injuries. *Pediatrics, 80,* 618–622.

Helfer, R. E., Slovis, T. L., & Black, M. (1977). Injuries resulting when small children fall out of bed. *Pediatrics, 60*(4), 533–535.

Jenny, C., Hymel, K. P., Ritzen, A., Reinert, S. E., & Hay, T. C. (1999). Analysis of missed cases of abusive head trauma. *Journal of the American Medical Association, 281*(7), 621–626.

Jessee, S. A. (1995). Orofacial manifestations of child abuse and neglect. *American Family Physician, 52,* 1829–1834.

Joffe, M., & Ludwig, S. (1988). Stairway injuries to children. *Pediatrics, 82,* 457–461.

Johnson, D. L., Boal, D., & Baule, R. (1995). Role of apnea in nonaccidental head injury. *Pediatric Neurosurgery, 23,* 305–310.

Johnson, D. L., Braun, D., & Friendly, D. (1993). Accidental head trauma and retinal hemorrhage. *Neurosurgery, 33,* 231–235.

Kessler, D. B., & Hyden, P. (1991). Physical, sexual, and emotional abuse of children. *Clinical Symposia/CIBA-GEIGY, 43*(1), 15.

Kleinman, P. K. (1987). Spinal trauma. In P. K. Kleinman (Ed.), *Diagnostic imaging of child abuse* (pp. 91–102). Baltimore: Williams & Wilkins.

Lambert, S. R., Johnson, T. E., & Hoyt, C. S. (1986). Optic nerve sheath and retinal hemorrhages associated with shaken baby syndrome. *Archives of Ophthalmology, 104,* 1509–1512.

Leavitt, E. B., Pincus, R. L., & Bukachevsky, R. (1992). Otolaryngologic manifestations of child abuse. *Archives of Otololaryngology—Head & Neck Surgery, 118,* 629–631.

Leventhal, J. M., Thomas, S. A., Rosenfield, N. S., & Markowitz, R. I. (1993). Fractures in young children: Distinguishing child abuse from intentional injuries. *American Journal of Diseases in Children, 147*(1), 87–92.

Levin A. (1990). Ocular manifestations of child abuse. *Ophthalmology Clinics of North America, 3,* 249–264.

Levin, A. (2000). Retinal hemorrhages and child abuse. In T. J. David (Ed.), *Recent advances in pediatrics* (no. 18, pp. 151–219). London: Churchill Livingstone.

Lyons, T. J., & Oates, K. (1993). Falling out of bed: A relatively benign occurrence. *Pediatrics, 92,* 125–127.

Merten, D. F., Cooperman, D. R., & Thompson, G. H. (1994). Skeletal manifestations of child abuse. In R. M. Reese (Ed.), *Child abuse: Medical diagnosis and management* (pp. 23–53). Malvern, PA: Lea & Febiger.

Merten, D. F., & Osborne, D. R. S. (1984). Craniocerebral trauma in the child abuse syndrome: Radiological observations. *Pediatric Radiology, 14,* 272–277.

Odom, A., Christ, E., Kerr, N., Byrd, K., Cochran, J., Barr, F., Bugnitz, M., Ring, J. C., Storgion, S., Walling, R., Stidham, G., & Quasney, M. W. (1997). Prevalence of retinal hemorrhages in pediatric patients after in-hospital cardiopulmonary resuscitation: A prospective study. *Pediatrics, 99*(6), E31–35.

Ommaya, A. K., & Gennerelli, T. A. (1974). Cerebral concussion and traumatic unconsciousness. *Brain, 97,* 633–654.

Ommaya, A. K., Grubb, R. L., & Naumann, R. A. (1971). Coup and contre-coup injury: Observations on the mechanics of visible brain injuries in rhesus monkeys. *Journal of Neurosurgery, 35,* 503–516.

Pang, D., & Wilberger, J. E., Jr. (1982). Spinal cord injury without radiographic abnormalities in children. *Journal of Neurosurgery, 57,* 114–129.

Parrish, R. (1996, January). Isolated spinal cord injury in child abuse [Letter]. *Pediatric Trauma Forensic Newsletter,* 1.

Piatt, J., & Steinberg, M. (1995). Isolated spinal cord injury as a presentation of child abuse. *Pediatrics, 96,* 780–782.

Rao, N., Smith, R. E., Choi, J. H., Xu, X. H., & Kornblum, R. N. (1988). Autopsy findings in the eyes of fourteen fatally abused children. *Forensic Science International, 39*(3), 293–299.

Singer, J., Bolte, R., Christian, C., & Selbst, S. M. (1994). Retinal hemorrhage. *Pediatric Emergency Care, 10*(5), 303–305.

Sirotnak, A, Grigsby, T, & Krugman, R. (2004). Physical abuse of children. *Pediatrics in Review, 25*(8), 264–277.

Smith, W. L., Alexander, R. C., Judisch, G. F., Sato, Y., & Kao, S. C. (1992). Magnetic resonance imaging evaluation of neonates with retinal hemorrhages. *Pediatrics, 89*(2), 332–333.

Sugar, N. F., Taylor, J. A., & Feldman, K. W. (1999). Bruises in infants and toddlers: Those who don't cruise rarely bruise. *Archives of Pediatrics and Adolescent Medicine, 153*(4), 399–403.

Welbury, R. R., & Murphy, J. M. (1998). The dental practitioner's role in protecting children from abuse: The orofacial signs of abuse. *British Dental Journal, 184,* 61–65.

Willging, J. P., Bower, C. M., & Cotton, R. T. (1992). Physical abuse of children: A retrospective review and an otolaryngology perspective. *Archives of Otololaryngology—Head & Neck Surgery, 118*(6), 584–590.

7

Kathryn M. Wells

Abdominal and Thoracic Injuries

Injuries to thoracic (chest) and abdominal organs due to child abuse are frequently underreported. However, it is known that chest and abdominal wounds that result from child abuse are the most lethal and children with these injuries often die before detection and treatment (Ludwig, 2001).

Trauma to the thoracic area is less common than trauma to the abdominal organs. Although it is estimated that less than 1% of child abuse cases involve visceral injuries, when present, they have a 50% mortality rate (Cooper et al., 1988). Therefore, any child who is suspected to have sustained internal injury should *immediately* be taken for emergency treatment. These injuries require a high index of suspicion for detection. The high mortality rate with these injuries relates to the severity and nature of the injuries often sustained and the organs affected (they often bleed rapidly), delay in medical care, delay in the correct diagnosis because of incomplete or absent history for the injury, and the young and noncommunicative nature of the victim. Additionally, these injuries are further complicated by the following features: children who suffer these injuries rarely anticipate the blow and are therefore unable to protect themselves from it; the force covers a larger percentage of body area because of the child's small size; symptoms may not be immediately present; there is usually a lack of a single imaging study or laboratory test for diagnosis; and there is often a delay in recognition of these injuries in children who present with other forms of abuse such as head injuries or multiple fractures.

■ When to Suspect Internal Injuries

Any time there is a history of blows (such as punching or kicking) to the abdomen, chest, or lower back, the suspicion of internal injuries should be raised. There is frequently no evidence of bruising because the forces are transmitted internally and rarely leave external signs. Therefore, bruising in these locations should always raise concern and prompt immediate medical evaluation. 🖥️

The presentation of the child depends on the type and severity of the injuries, the length of the time since the injury, and the rate of bleeding caused by the injury. Although there are usually no external signs of injury, the following list details some of the most common indicators that a problem exists.

- Pain in the abdomen, chest, or any internal area
- Abdominal tenderness
- Decreased bowel sounds
- External bruising of the chest or stomach
- Distended or swollen abdomen
- Tense abdominal muscles upon palpation
- Labored breathing
- Pain in the chest while breathing
- Nausea and/or vomiting
- Fever
- Lethargy
- Cardiovascular failure and collapse, shock, or cardiac arrest

Many times children with these injuries present with other signs of trauma or in an altered mental status (even unconscious) without any external signs of trauma. Upon further evaluation the child may be noted to have a distended abdomen, decreased bowel sounds, and abdominal pain on palpation (if conscious). Further evaluation is performed such as an abdominal CT scan or ultrasound and the child is then found to have sustained an abdominal injury. Further questioning of the caregiver may reveal several hours' to days' worth of history of "not feeling well," lethargy, poor appetite, and possibly vomiting. Unfortunately, many of these children present to care so late that they don't survive the initial presentation; some even die before surgery can be undertaken.

Abdominal Injuries

Major blunt abdominal trauma is second to head injuries as a cause of death in inflicted child abuse (Huyer, 1994). One study revealed an 11% incidence of abusive injuries (Ledbetter, Hatch, Feldman, Flinger, & Tapper, 1988) with 40% to 50% mortality (O'Neill, Meacham, Griffin, & Sawyers, 1973). However, this may be an underestimate, since it is believed that many of these cases go undetected. Accidentally injured children with severe abdominal injuries have a mortality rate of 21% (Ledbetter et al., 1988).

Most commonly, children who sustain severe nonaccidental abdominal trauma are between the ages of 6 months and 3 years (Cobb, Vinocur,

Wagner, & Weintraub, 1986) and are most typically around 2 years of age. They may have other old pattern injuries typical for child abuse at presentation (Huyer, 1994).

Blunt trauma accounts for most abusive abdominal injuries, although deceleration forces may cause injury to these organs as well. The literature indicates that violent forces are required to cause a life-threatening abdominal injury. Punches to the abdomen may be especially harmful when directed toward the midline of the body, in which case the organs such as the pancreas, liver, spleen, and small intestine are pressed against the spine. Rapid deceleration injuries may occur when a child is thrown against a wall, causing shearing of the attachments of the organs or of their vascular supply. Bruising of the abdomen in these cases is a rare finding because the force is transmitted back through the intra-abdominal structures. The onset of symptoms usually ranges from one hour to two and a half days with presentation including vomiting (often green, or bilious), abdominal pain, and tenderness (Huyer, 1994).

Abdominal injuries may include injuries to any of the following organs: liver, pancreas, spleen, stomach, small intestine (duodenum, jejunum, and ileum), large intestine, and rarely the kidneys.

Figure 7.1. Digestive System. (From Bruck-Kan, 1979. Reprinted with permission from the author.)

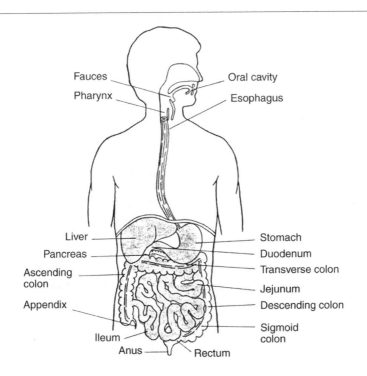

☐ Liver

The liver, the largest solid organ in the body, filters the blood as it comes from the intestines. It is located in the right upper abdomen but the left lobe of the liver actually crosses the midline to overlie the spine. Of the various abdominal injuries among battered children, injuries to this organ are among the most common (Cooper, 1992). These injuries, which may be referred to as hepatic injuries, are also the most serious and life threatening of the intra-abdominal injuries because of the highly vascular nature of the organ predisposing to severe bleeding. Some injuries may cause bleeding of the liver underneath the capsule (subcapsular hematoma) while others may actually lacerate, or tear, the tissue causing the accumulation of blood in the peritoneal cavity. ☐

☐ Pancreas

This gland, situated in a fixed position behind the stomach and in front of the spine, produces secretions that aid in digestion. Injuries to the pancreas are also quite commonly found in cases of child abuse (Sternowsky & Schaefer, 1985). This organ is usually injured by a crushing action, which may produce pancreatitis, inflammation of the pancreas, or a pancreatic pseudocyst, a cystlike nodule in the pancreas. Injuries to this organ can also be the result of accidental injury including bicycle handlebar trauma and motor vehicle crashes. Pancreatitis may present as abdominal pain, vomiting, and fever, with the onset of symptoms usually being gradual.

☐ Spleen

This organ, located in the upper left abdomen, is involved in producing and filtering blood. Splenic injuries are one of the most common forms of injury found in accidental trauma (e.g., from motor vehicle accidents or bicycle falls). These injuries are less common in nonaccidental trauma as this organ is partially protected by the overlying ribs. However, an injury to the spleen in a child who is not ambulatory or without adequate history should raise concerns of child abuse until proven otherwise. Splenic injury causes internal bleeding, which can be life threatening.

☐ Stomach

Stomach perforation has been reported as a result of child physical abuse (Case & Nanduri, 1983; Siemens & Fulton, 1977). Stomach rupture may be complicated by peritonitis (infestation of the abdominal cavity) that follows the soiling of the peritoneal cavity with gastric contents (Schechner & Ehrlich, 1974). Mortality is usually very high in these cases.

☐ **Small Intestine**

The small intestine, a digestive organ attached to the stomach, is composed of three regions: the duodenum, the jejunum, and the ileum. Injuries to this organ are common among abusive abdominal injuries. Although they may occur anywhere along the bowel, injuries of the intestine related to child abuse most commonly occur in the duodenum (Nijs, Vanclooster, de Gheldere, & Garmijn, 1997; Tracy, O'Connor, & Weber, 1993) and the jejunum. These injuries are also the most difficult to diagnose. There may be areas of bleeding located in the bowel wall referred to as intramural hematomas or tears often referred to as transections or perforations. In cases of abuse, perforations are most commonly seen in the jejunum (60%), then the duodenum (30%) and finally the ileum (10%) (Huyer, 1994).

☐ **Peritoneum**

This membrane lines the abdominal cavity. Any rupture of this membrane can cause peritonitis (inflammation and infection of the abdominal cavity).

☐ **Kidney**

The kidney filters toxins from the blood and produces urine. Injuries to the kidneys often involve blows to the lower back and are frequently accompanied by pain in that area. These injuries may occur as a result of abusive and nonabusive trauma. These injuries are relatively rare since the kidneys are protected quite well by the surrounding tissues.

☐ **Anal-Rectal Injury**

Although injuries to this area usually involve sexual abuse, there have been reports of anal and rectal injuries as the result of insertion of foreign objects into the rectum by forceful application of enemas or thermometers. These injuries can present with pain and/or rectal bleeding or bruising (see chapter 10 for more information).

☐ **Retroperitoneal Hematomas**

The retroperitoneum refers to the area behind the peritoneum. Injuries to this area are rare and difficult to diagnose. They are mainly found when there are indications of ongoing blood loss and other possible sites are ruled out. Frequently, injuries are not found until autopsy examination.

☐ **Abdominal Vascular Injury**

The abdominal vasculature refers to the blood vessels that feed the abdominal organs and range from the aorta and the inferior vena cava to the mesenteric vessels, which traverse through fibrous tissue called the mesentery. Injuries to these organs suggest extreme force and result in high rates of morbidity and mortality due to internal bleeding.

☐   **Differential Diagnoses**

In abdominal injury, there are other accidental explanations that may explain the injury (Ludwig, 1993; Reece & Grodin, 1985). Some differential diagnoses that may explain abdominal injury are the following:

- Motor vehicle accidents (especially if the child was wearing a lap belt, which is often referred to as the *lap belt complex* and is a collection of injuries from the rapid deceleration of a child against a seat belt [Asbun, Irani, Roe, & Bloch, 1990; Glassman, Johnson, & Holt, 1992])

- Infections

- Handlebar injuries (where the child is injured when they crash on their bicycles and the handlebars impale the abdomen)

- Falls occasionally are the source of intra-abdominal injury but care must be taken in obtaining the history, assessing for the body position or contact with an object during the fall. Falls down stairs can cause minimal injury (Joffe & Ludwig, 1988) but should not be accepted as an explanation for severe life-threatening abdominal injuries.

▨   **Thoracic (Chest) Injuries**

Abusive chest injuries are less common than abdominal injuries. This is in part because of the protection of these organs by the rib cage as well as probably underrecognition and underdiagnosis. Injuries to the chest are often very difficult to diagnose and require a high index of suspicion. Similar to abdominal injuries, chest injuries result from direct trauma as well as deceleration forces and require the use of substantial force. Also similar to abdominal trauma, there is often no indication of bruising, but if present, bruising may indicate significant underlying injury. In fact, in infants and toddlers with bruising, the incidence of chest wall or back bruising is extremely low, representing less than 2% of the bruises (Sugar, Taylor, & Feldman, 1999). Therefore, bruising in this location is rarely related to accidental trauma and should always prompt further evaluation. Thoracic injuries may include several different types of injuries, including the ones listed below.

☐   **Hypopharynx and Esophagus**

Injuries of the hypopharynx and esophagus have been noted in child abuse (McDowel & Fielding, 1984; Morzaria, Walton, & MacMillan, 1998). When a child presents with blood coming from the hypopharynx, an injury of the back of the throat or the esophagus should be considered. Injury of the hypopharynx may be caused by objects or the parent forcing a finger into the back of the child's throat. These injuries may be accidental (such as a child who falls with an object in her mouth) or nonaccidental (such as a caregiver forcing an object into a child's mouth out of frustration). Pharyngeal injuries are often discovered as a result of the identification of other thoracic (chest) abnormalities (Reece, Arnold, & Splain, 1996). For example, the esophagus can be injured as a result of blunt force trauma as well as from ingestion of forced caustics resulting in erosive injury (Ablin & Reinhart, 1990).

☐ Rib Fractures

Rib fractures are the most common incidences of thoracic trauma (Kleinman, 1987) and may also be a marker for intra-abdominal, intrathoracic or intracranial trauma (Ng & Hall, 1998). In fact, rib fractures, particularly posterior rib fractures, are felt to be highly specific for abuse (Kleinman & Schlesinger, 1997).

Differential diagnoses for rib fractures may include the following, all of which require medical evaluation for diagnosis:

- Accidental injury

- Poor nutrition

- Metabolic disease

- Rickets

- Osteogenesis imperfecta

CPR is not felt to be a cause for rib fractures in children, especially posterior fractures (Evers & DeGaeta, 1985; Spevak, Kleinman, Belanger, Primafk, & Richmond, 1994).

A child who has sustained rib fractures will be in pain and will likely have periods of frequent crying, irritability, and possibly difficult breathing evidenced by a change in the respiratory pattern with short, shallow respirations.

☐ Hemothorax/Pneumothorax

Chest injuries are dangerous because broken ribs can puncture or damage the space around the lungs (the pleural cavity), causing leakage of air (pneumothorax) or blood (hemothorax) into the space.

☐ Lungs

Pulmonary contusions are any bruises to the lungs. These injuries are felt to be rarely identified in inflicted injury (McEniery, Hanson, Grigor, &

Horowitz, 1991), which may be related to their difficult diagnosis. A lung contusion (bruise) may underlie an area of chest wall trauma and may only be diagnosed at the time of an autopsy or, rarely, by a chest CT.

☐ Heart

Injuries to the heart consist of bruising or contusions and are the result of a direct blow to the chest, a blast injury, compression of the heart between the sternum and the spine, acceleration/deceleration injury, and penetration by fractured ribs. These injuries may cause electrical conduction abnormalities (arrhythmias) as well as damage to the cardiac muscle itself. These are also rarely found in pediatric accidental and nonaccidental trauma (Marino & Langston, 1982). They may occur in accidental trauma following a large amount of force (e.g., a motor vehicle accident or being kicked by a horse) but are not the result of CPR (Cohle, Hawley, Berg, Kiesel, & Pless, 1995).

■ Assessment

Children who are thought to have sustained abusive thoracic or abdominal trauma need to be evaluated by medical personnel immediately. An initial medical assessment will be done to ensure the child's clinical stability. The medical provider will obtain a detailed history of any possible injury to the chest or abdomen, if possible. Because accurate history of the actual cause of the injury may not be forthcoming, the medical team will also work to clarify when the symptoms began and the nature and course of the symptoms. The medical provider will then complete a thorough physical examination, which will include serial examination of vital signs, examination for external signs of trauma, and careful assessment for evidence of underlying injury. Then additional evaluation may be obtained as deemed appropriate.

Laboratory Evaluation

Laboratory evaluation may assist in assessing for signs of underlying trauma. The medical provider will usually obtain a complete blood count (CBC—to assess for signs of bleeding, infection, or nutritional deficiency), bleeding studies (prothrombin time [PT], partial thromboplastin time [PTT], and bleeding time—to assess for bleeding tendencies), chemistry panels (to assess for metabolic abnormalities), liver function tests (AST, ALT—to assess for liver injury), a urinalysis (to screen for kidney or bladder injury or infection), and serum amylase and lipase (to detect enzymes that may be elevated in pancreatic injury).

Radiographic Evaluation

Several radiographic studies may be useful in the evaluation of abusive abdominal and thoracic trauma. Plain chest radiographs may reveal rib fractures, pneumothorax, hemothorax, or pneumopericardium, and plain abdominal radiographs may reveal evidence of intestinal obstruction or perforation as well as foreign bodies or surrounding bony injury. A chest CT may reveal a pulmonary or cardiac contusion or rib fractures while an abdominal CT may assist in identifying solid organ (liver, spleen, pancreas, kidney) injuries as well as some hollow viscous (duodenum, jejunum) injuries such as bowel wall hematomas. An upper GI series and barium enema may be helpful in further assessing the visceral abdominal organs (esophagus, stomach, duodenum, jejunum, and colon). Other evaluations may include abdominal ultrasound (the use of ultrasound to produce images of organs or tissues, which can be done in the emergency department), urography (radiography of the urinary tract), angiography (radiography of the blood vessels), radionuclide scans, and intravenous pyelography.

Treatment

Any cases in which abdominal or thoracic trauma are suspected require immediate referral; the earlier they are detected, the better the chances of the child's survival. Nevertheless, it is estimated that many of these injuries will result in death. Treatments for individual injuries will vary with each particular case; almost all will require a hospital stay. Children who experience shock due to blood loss may also experience a compromised central nervous system, which requires extensive medical support and treatment. Some children may also require surgical intervention.

References

Ablin, D. S., & Reinhart, M. A. (1990). Esophageal perforation with mediastinal abscess in child abuse. *Pediatric Radiology, 20,* 524–525.

Asbun, H. J., Irani, H., Roe, E. J., & Bloch, J. H. (1990). Intra-abdominal seat-belt injury. *Journal of Trauma, 30,* 189–193.

Bruck-Kan, R. (1979). *Introduction to human anatomy.* New York: Harper & Row.

Case, M. E., & Nanduri, R. (1983). Laceration of the stomach by blunt trauma in a child: A case of child abuse. *Journal of Forensic Science, 28,* 496–501.

Cobb, L. M., Vinocur, C. D., Wagner, C. W., & Weintraub, W. H. (1986). Intestinal perforation due to blunt trauma in children in an era of increased nonoperative treatment. *Journal of Trauma, 26,* 461–463.

Cohle, S. D., Hawley, D. A., Berg, K. K., Kiesel, E. L., & Pless, J. E. (1995). Homicidal cardiac lacerations in children. *Journal of Forensic Science, 40,* 212–218.

Cooper, A. (1992). Thoracoabdominal trauma. In S. Ludwig & A. Kornberg (Eds.), *Child abuse: A medical reference* (2nd ed., pp. 131–150). New York: Churchill Livingstone.

Cooper, A., Floyd, T., Barlow, B., Niemirska, M., Ludwig, S., Seidl, T., O'Neill, J., Ziegler, M., Ross, A., Gandhi, R., & Catherman, R. (1988). Major blunt trauma due to child abuse. *Journal of Trauma, 28,* 1483–1487.

Evers, K., & DeGaeta, L. R. (1985). Abdominal trauma. *Emergency Medicine Clinics of North America, 3,* 525–539.

Glassman, S. D., Johnson, J. R., & Holt, R. T. (1992). Seatbelt injuries in children. *Journal of Trauma, 33,* 882–886.

Huyer, D. (1994). Abdominal injuries in child abuse. *The APSAC Advisor, 7*(24), 5–7.

Joffe, M., & Ludwig, S. (1988). Stairway injuries in children. *Pediatrics, 82,* 457.

Kleinman, P. K. (1987). *Diagnostic imaging in child abuse.* Baltimore: Williams & Wilkins.

Kleinman, P. K., & Schlesinger, A. E. (1997). Mechanical factors associated with posterior rib fractures in abused infants. *Pediatric Radiology, 27,* 87–91.

Ledbetter, D. J., Hatch, E. I., Feldman, K. W., Flinger, C. L., & Tapper, D. (1988). Diagnostic and surgical implications of child abuse. *Archives of Surgery, 123,* 1101–1105.

Ludwig, D. (2001). *Child abuse: Medical diagnosis and management.* Baltimore: Lippincott Williams & Wilkins.

Ludwig, S. (1993). Pediatric abdominal trauma. *Topics in Emergency Medicine, 15,* 40.

Marino, T. A., & Langston, C. (1982). Cardiac trauma and the conduction system: A case study of an 18-month-old child. *Archives of Pathology & Laboratory Medicine, 106,* 173–174.

McDowel, H. P., & Fielding D. W. (1984). Traumatic perforation of the hypopharynx: An unusual form. *Archives of Disease in Childhood, 59,* 888–889.

McEniery, J., Hanson, R., Grigor, W., & Horowitz, A. (1991). Lung injury resulting from a nonaccidental crush injury to the chest. *Pediatric Emergency Care, 7,* 166–168.

Morzaria, S., Walton, M. J., & MacMillan, A. (1998). Inflicted esophageal perforation. *Journal of Pediatric Surgery, 33,* 871–873.

Ng, C. S., & Hall, C. M. (1998). Costochondral junction fractures and intra-abdominal trauma in non-accidental injury (child abuse). *Pediatric Radiology, 28,* 671–676.

Nijs, S., Vanclooster, P., de Gheldere, C., & Garmijn, K. (1997). Duodenal transaction in a battered child: A case report. *Acta Chirurgica Belgica, 97,* 192–193.

O'Neill, J., Meacham, W., Griffin, P., & Sawyers, J. (1973). Patterns of injury in the battered child syndrome. *Journal of Trauma, 13,* 332–339.

Reece, R. M., Arnold, J., & Splain, J. (1996). Pharyngeal perforation as a manifestation of child abuse. *Child Maltreatment, 1,* 364–367.

Reece, R. M., & Grodin, M. A. (1985). Recognition of nonaccidental injury. *Pediatric Clinics of North America, 32,* 41–60.

Schechner, S. A., & Ehrlich, F. E. (1974). Case reports: Gastric perforation and child abuse. *Journal of Trauma, 14,* 723–725.

Siemens, R. A., & Fulton, R. L. (1977). Gastric rupture as a result of blunt trauma. *American Surgeon, 43,* 229–233.

Spevak, M. R., Kleinman, P. K., Belanger, P. L., Primafk, D., & Richmond, J. M. (1994). Cardiopulmonary resuscitation and rib fractures in infants: A postmortem radiologic-pathologic study. *Journal of the American Medical Association, 272,* 617–618.

Sternowsky, H. J., & Schaefer, E. (1985). Traumatic pancreatitis with peripheral osteolysis suggesting child abuse [German]. *Monatsschr Kinderheilkd, 133,* 178–180.

Sugar, N. F., Taylor, J. A., & Feldman, K. W. (1999). Bruises in infants and toddlers: Those who don't cruise rarely bruise. *Archives of Pediatrics and Adolescent Medicine, 153,* 399–403.

Tracy, T. Jr., O'Connor, T. P., & Weber, T. R. (1993). Battered children with duodenal avulsion and transection. *American Surgeon, 59,* 342–345.

8

Joyce K. Moore
Jean C. Smith

Child Abuse by Poisoning

Dr. C. Henry Kempe first referred to poisoning as a form of child abuse in 1962. Since that date, workers in both the medical and CPS fields have become increasingly aware of this and other less obvious forms of maltreatment. In 1993, the American Association of Poison Control Centers reported 5,400 toxin exposures in children as being due to "malicious intent" on the part of a caregiver (Litovitz, Clark, & Soloway, 1994). Literature reviews have shown hundreds of published cases of children poisoned by alcohol, illicit drugs, prescription drugs, over-the-counter medications, folk remedies, and common household substances (Bays & Feldman, 2001).

For purposes of identification and intervention, poisoning as a form of child maltreatment may be divided into four distinct categories: (1) impulsive acts under stress, (2) bizarre child-rearing practices, (3) neglect (lack of supervision), and (4) pediatric condition falsification (Munchausen's syndrome by proxy). With increased reporting, the patterns of these four categories have become more clearly defined.

■ Impulsive Acts Under Stress

It is not surprising that the same stressful environment that might provoke a parent or caregiver to hit a child might also provoke him or her to give drugs to a child. Drug administration with the intent to sedate is probably the most common reason for nonaccidental poisoning. Sedatives such as alcohol, barbiturates, or antihistamines are most commonly used in this practice. Parents may use drugs that have been prescribed for themselves or they may use those prescribed by a pediatrician, which are usually for the elimination of colic symptoms.

Case Example

A father is taking care of his two children, ages 2 and 4, who have severe colds. In an effort to quiet the children, he forces them to drink a huge dose of adult prescription cough syrup. Tragically, the next morning, both children are found dead.

When this problem is recognized early and when the family is capable of learning the hazards of medicating children improperly, the results of appropriate intervention are usually good. When parents or caregivers are under continually high stress, are unable to change their behavior, or are drug abusers themselves, removing the child from the home should be considered.

■ Bizarre Child-Rearing Practices

Parents or caregivers who poison their children by adhering to bizarre child-rearing practices fall into two categories: those who are well intentioned yet uneducated, and those who intentionally use poisoning as a form of punishment.

Nonintentional Poisoning

Some parents or caregivers may accidentally poison their children by giving them toxic doses of vitamins, minerals, herbs, or "roots," in an attempt to cure an illness or to ward off disease. Alternatively, a parent might feed a baby an improperly diluted formula, resulting in either water or salt intoxication. Although these mistakes are forms of neglect that should be reported, they are often successfully treated with education, support, and a close monitoring of the situation.

Poisoning as a Form of Punishment

Parents or caregivers may wish to punish children by forcing them to ingest toxic amounts of chemicals or food. Others may give their children drugs to initiate them into the drug culture. Both practices can cause severe damage to the child, both physically and psychologically. If the CPS worker is aware that a child has been repetitively forced to ingest any substance as a form of punishment, or if a child suffers adverse effects from even one episode, the CPS worker should have the child examined by a medical provider. The following list includes substances reported in this type of abuse:

- *Table salt.* Frequently used as a punishment for bed-wetting, the forced ingestion of table salt is the most common form of nonaccidental poisoning. The resulting hypernatremia (excess sodium in the blood) causes dehydration, seizures, and vomiting.

- *Water intoxication.* The second most frequently reported form of abuse, also a common punishment for enuresis (involuntary urination), is the forced ingestion of water. The resulting hyponatremia (a decreased amount of sodium in the blood) is among the most common pediatric electrolytic disorders. This condition can lead to seizures, convulsions, confusion, lethargy, and comas. Other causes for this condition are metabolic disorders and inappropriate use of baby formula.

- *Hot peppers or "Texas Pete."* The forced ingestion of hot peppers and their derivatives can damage the mucous membranes of the mouth and stomach as well as injure the nervous system. These can also become clogged in the child's throat, leading to problems in breathing.

- *Ground black pepper.* The powdered consistency of ground black pepper can cause it to become clogged in the throat or lungs, leading to apnea, or a cessation of breathing.

- *Laxatives.* Excessive ingestion of laxatives and the resulting diarrhea may lead to severe dehydration, fever, and bloody stools.

- *Household products.* Various substances reported in this type of abuse are lye derivatives (toilet bowl cleaner), hydrocarbons (lighter fluid), detergents, and oil.

- *Drugs.* Drugs reported in abusive ingestion include anticoagulants (blood thinners), insulin, barbiturates, quaaludes, antidepressants, sedatives, tranquilizers, and painkillers.

Case Examples

A 5-year-old child was forced by her father to drink an estimated one-half gallon of water at one time. She was brought to the hospital emergency room in an unresponsive state and resuscitative efforts were unsuccessful. The father explained that he had made her drink the water because "she had eaten some bad sherbet." The father was subsequently convicted of manslaughter.

A toddler was admitted to the hospital with difficulty swallowing. Examination of the mouth and upper throat revealed chemical-type burns. In a subsequent interview, the child said that his mother made him "eat the white powder from a box." Investigation of the household by CPS revealed white powdered drain cleaner (lye) in a box.

■ Neglect (Lack of Supervision)

Most accidental poisonings are the result of improper storage of household chemicals, such as bleach, charcoal, lighter fluid, furniture polish, or kerosene. In most cases, the parents or caregivers are concerned and seek medical attention promptly. These cases can usually be managed by educating the parents or caregivers on home safety. ⬛ Repeated accidental poisoning may indicate outright neglect or stress within the family. Other signals, such as the child's uncleanliness, malnourishment, or lack of medical care may also indicate neglect. These cases should be assessed for neglect and possible physical abuse.

■ Pediatric Condition Falsification (or Munchausen's Syndrome by Proxy)

This increasingly reported form of abuse is one of the most misleading and hard to diagnose. See chapter 9 for a complete discussion of this parenting disorder.

■ Assessment and Management

In the assessment and management of suspected poisoning, the medical provider and CPS worker must work together in gathering and documenting a complete medical and social history. The former should include all previous poisoning episodes. The social history should include

- Parent/caregiver occupation(s)

- Unusual illnesses/hospital admissions of siblings

- History of previous illness of parents/caregivers or family (psychiatric, drug/alcohol abuse, underlying disease)

- A list of all drugs available to the parents and in the child's surroundings

Case Example

A 1-year-old infant was transported by EMS to the emergency department on two occasions for the sudden onset of apnea (cessation of breathing). Following the second successful resuscitation, a toxicology screen was performed and revealed a narcotic, Dilaudid, which is primarily used as a pain reliever for advanced-stage cancer patients. Prior to the second event, it was documented by law enforcement that the mother had spent the afternoon shopping, leaving the infant in the father's care. The father reported giving the baby a bottle of formula and law enforcement was able to recover the used bottle. Neither parent was a medical provider; however, they managed a medical placement agency, thus having access to a number of medical practitioners (and, presumably, the drug that was used).

Keep in mind that no "toxicology screen" is truly comprehensive. Toxicology testing in a particular institution usually reflects the incidence with which a toxin is encountered in that geographical area. Therefore, the social history is imperative to the selection of appropriate tests (Cross, 1992).

References

Bays, J., & Feldman, K. (2001). Child abuse by poisoning. In R. M. Reece & S. Ludwig (Eds.), *Child abuse: Medical diagnosis and management* (2nd ed., pp. 405–441). Philadelphia: Lippincott Williams & Wilkins.

Cross, R. (1992). Toxicology testing: What you get may not be what you requested (or needed). *Bulletin of Laboratory Medicine, University of North Carolina Hospitals, 126,* 1.

Litovitz, T., Clark, L., & Soloway, R. (1994). The 1993 annual report of the American Association of Poison Control Centers toxic exposures surveillance system. *American Journal of Emergency Medicine, 12,* 546–584.

9

Joyce K. Moore

Jean C. Smith

Pediatric Condition Falsification

Pediatric condition falsification (PCF), more commonly known as Munchausen's syndrome by proxy, is an abusive parenting disorder that has been identified by both medical and nonmedical professionals. The syndrome derives its original name from the eighteenth-century author Baron Karl Frederick von Munchausen, who wrote a book of wild, exaggerated tales of his life's adventures. In 1951, the term "Munchausen's syndrome" was used to describe adults who produced false medical histories and fabricated physical symptoms and laboratory findings, causing themselves needless medical tests and evaluations, sometimes even surgery. ⌨

Consequently, in 1977, Dr. Roy Meadow created the term "Munchausen's syndrome by proxy" to describe a form of child abuse in which the parent or caregiver relates fictitious illnesses in a child by either inducing or fabricating signs or symptoms of the illnesses. As a result, the child is subjected to extensive medical tests and hospitalizations. The American Professional Society on the Abuse of Children (APSAC) now recommends that the medical diagnosis of the child be called pediatric condition falsification (Schreier, 2002). Current criteria for PCF include

- an illness fabricated—symptoms are faked or induced by the parent or caregiver;

- the child is taken to doctors repeatedly and often to several different doctors with the parent hiding his or her role in the causation of the child's illness/symptoms;

- the symptoms subside when the child is separated from the perpetuating caregiver; and

- the caregiver is diagnosed as acting out of a need to assume the sick role by proxy or as another form of attention-seeking behavior (Meadow, 2002).

It is estimated that 9% to 30% of all recognized PCF cases have resulted in mortality. All of these deaths occurred in children under 3 years of age.

Case Example

A 6-month-old infant was repeatedly brought to the hospital by a parent for seizures and apnea spells. Electroencephalograms (EEGs) and medical examinations were normal on multiple occasions. No seizures or apnea were ever noted by health care personnel. On a number of occasions, immediately after discharge from the hospital or after a clinic visit, the child was brought to the hospital by ambulance for another spell. The child was hospitalized in a special room with a constantly recording EEG and a videotape of the child. On two occasions, the EEG showed abnormalities while the parent held the child out of range of the camera. The EEG machine broke and was removed from the room while the videotape machine was left running, unknown to the parent. Later the same day, the parent came out of the room and called the nurse because the baby had "stopped breathing." A review of the videotape showed that the parent had held a pillow over the baby's face prior to calling the nurse.

■ Characteristics of PCF

▨ The Victim

Boys and girls stand an equal chance of becoming victims of PCF. Although infants and toddlers are at the age of highest victimization and mortality, cases have been reported in older children. A child may develop an actual illness as a result of his or her subjection to the parent's or caregiver's treatment or as a result of the invasive investigation by the medical staff. The legitimate existence of a disease should not exclude the child from the possible diagnosis of PCF. Older children may "buy into" the perpetrator's creation of the illness and begin to see themselves as truly ill even when they are separated from the influence and actions of the perpetrator.

▨ The Parent or Caregiver

In all of the cases of PCF documented in the literature prior to 1990, the perpetrator had been the mother or foster mother of the victim. The father is often distant and uninvolved with the family. Often he appears completely unaware that the problem exists. Usually, the mother is

- intelligent and articulate, with a friendly, socially adept personality;

- capable of forming a close but "shallow" rapport with the hospital staff;

- extremely close and attentive of the child, claiming that he will eat or take his medication "only for her" (Being attentive to a child and actively participating in medical treatment are certainly normal and desirable parental behaviors. In the absence of other characteristics, these behaviors alone should not prompt consideration of PCF.);

- isolated and emotionally distant from her husband, family, and friends; and

- medically knowledgeable, to some degree, but not necessarily formally medically trained.

Although psychological and psychiatric treatment is always recommended for these mothers, the treatment in documented cases has been lengthy and variable in success. Review of these cases has shown that safety of the child is contingent on the parent acknowledging her role in the production of symptoms (Parnell & Day, 1998).

A handful of father perpetrators have now been identified in the literature (Meadow, 1998). The initial published case of a father as perpetrator involved an infant admitted six times for reported apnea, reported apnea with seizures, and finally reported blood in the mouth and stool in addition to the previous complaints. On the last admission, apneic spells and tremors occurred for the first time during hospitalization. On the third day after admission, the father was discovered pressing the infant's face against the crib mattress. This case illustrates a phenomenon previously noted in mother perpetrator cases: the escalation of reported and/or produced symptoms over time. However, this particular father did not fit the profile previously described for mothers. The parents were young, unwed and unemployed; the father was not overly friendly to the staff, at times accusing them of not knowing what was going on with his infant; and he expressed frustration at the lack of answers. Whether the prevalence of father figures as perpetrators of PCF is more common than previously suspected and whether the characteristics of father perpetrators are different are currently unanswered questions.

Additional Clinical Signs of PCF

- The history and physical findings do not coincide.

- The unusual symptoms, signs, or observations of the child do not make clinical sense.

- The differential diagnoses consist of disorders less common than PCF.

- The child fails to tolerate or respond to current medical therapy without clear cause.

- A parent or caregiver is less concerned than the medical provider, even sometimes comforting the medical staff.

- A parent or caregiver welcomes or requests medical tests of her child, even when the tests may be painful.

Among the common presentations of PCF are seizures, apnea, diarrhea and vomiting with the method of production being lying, drug poisoning, suffocation, or induced vomiting. But it is important to realize that the combinations and types of simulation and/or production of clinical symptoms are limitless. Recent reports have included the production of behavioral and psychiatric symptoms.

■ General Guidelines for Detection

Deception is the hallmark of PCF. Medical providers are trained to rely on parental history when evaluating and treating children. It is the medical expectation that histories will be given truthfully. Thus, the medical provider's training often obscures and delays the detection of PCF. Once suspected, the diagnosis of PCF is generally made by one or a combination of three methods: review of all medical records; trial separation of the child from the caregiver; or directly observed or documented creation of the symptoms or illness. ⌨

Review of Medical Records

It is important for the worker to obtain all medical records, including such things as primary care provider records, hospital records (including nurses' daily progress notes), ER records, urgent care records, county health department records, EMT transport reports, and any consulting specialist records. Because there may be records in multiple sites, cities, and states, this can be a time-consuming task. Because the caregiver may not divulge all of the performed medical encounters, contacting all medical facilities in the region may be necessary. The Medicaid register and other health insurance information may be of help in identifying other sources of medical care. Optimally, all records should then be reviewed by an independent medical professional (who is not involved in providing any direct care to the child or family) with experience in the recognition of PCF.

Case Example

Joshua was a 9-year-old boy with an extensive history of behavioral problems, including anger, depression, and aggression and reported asthma, a "brain tumor," seizures, and gastroesophageal reflux. At one point he was on a total of 15 different medications at the same time. His mother gave a history of many of the medical diagnoses being made in another distant state. Workers took several months to identify where he had received medical care, provide appropriate releases, and obtain these records. It was only through the review of these records that it was determined that the mother was creating a history in order to obtain a toxic combination of medications for her son, which was contributing to his behavioral problems.

Trial Separation of the Child From the Caregiver

In the history, it is important to look carefully at temporal links between the presence of the caregiver and the child's symptoms and illness events. If it seems that the symptoms only exist in the caregiver's presence, a trial separation should be considered. It may be necessary to arrange the separation through a court order. Any visits between the child and caregiver must be carefully supervised by experienced staff in constant attendance. No food, drink, or medicines should be brought in by family. During this time period, the caregiver should also be closely monitored as this is a period of increased emotional distress (and potential self-destructive behaviors) for the caregiver. Other children remaining in the home must also be monitored as the caregiver may transfer falsification attempts to them.

Directly Observed or Documented Creation of Symptoms or Illness

Documentation of symptom production can be obtained by covert video surveillance of the child or by laboratory confirmation of drugs or foreign substances in specimens obtained from the child.

Many large hospitals have established a protocol and the physical capability to visually monitor a child without caregiver knowledge. The caregiver is allowed to stay with the child and provide care as she or he would provide in the home. This type of observation has proven to be useful in identifying the production of symptoms such as seizures, apnea episodes, vomiting, and lethargy, as these conditions often cannot be verified by laboratory tests and the parent or caregiver description of occurrences is taken at face value. The worker should become familiar with protocols and facilities within their state, locale, or region as the legal requirements for this type of surveillance may vary in different settings.

Drug screens can be performed to look for the presence of medications that could produce observed or described symptoms (see chapter 8). Drug levels should be done to determine therapeutic versus toxic (overdose) levels of prescribed medications. If blood is found in specimens, it should be analyzed to ensure that it is the child's blood. If PCF is suspected, the medical provider caring for the child should ensure that the laboratory preserves specimens from the child for further future analysis as additional information about possible drugs and toxins becomes available.

Management

In the decisions regarding placement of the child, CPS workers and the medical team will need to closely consider each particular case. Often an initial removal of the child will allow time to assess the parents or caregivers and to appraise the success of initial intervention. It is recommended that children not return to the home if the mother is unresponsive to treatment or if she denies the problem entirely. Placement in the home of the mother but under the father's supervision is not considered a safe alternative.

Once PCF is strongly suspected or detected, the worker must identify a primary medical care provider for the child who is familiar with PCF. This medical provider will see that the child's true medical needs are being met and will monitor consultations with specialists to determine that such consultations are truly indicated.

■ Obstacles in the Detection and Management of PCF

Lack of Knowledge

One of the largest roadblocks to both the recognition and management of these cases is the public's lack of knowledge of PCF. Both the medical provider and CPS worker will need to educate others, such as attorneys and the courts, about this form of child abuse.

Disbelief

Often the parents will befriend the medical staff, CPS staff, attorneys, and members of the court system. Their attempts to charm people into believing their innocence are often successful, and thus a hindrance in the management of PCF. The courts often rely heavily on psychiatric evaluations of the caregiver. In the past, these have proven fairly ineffectual in diagnosing specific psychiatric conditions in PCF perpetrators.

Doctor Shopping

In their constant search for sympathy from the medical profession, caregivers will often "doctor shop," moving from hospital to hospital, sometimes even leaving the state to do so. Doctor shopping, however, disrupts or terminates effective and consistent intervention. This also frequently produces additional confusion about the child's true diagnosis because new medical providers accept the caregiver's history of symptoms and then order additional unneeded diagnostic procedures and treatments.

In summary, a medical provider skilled in the detection of PCF and the CPS worker must often serve as the catalyst to assist other members of the medical community and the judicial system in recognizing the potential signs of PCF and in ensuring that the appropriate diagnostic interventions are successfully carried out for the safety of the child. "The single largest impediment to making a diagnosis of MSBP [PCF] is the failure to include it in the differential diagnosis" (Rosenberg, 2001).

References

Meadow, R. (1998). Munchausen syndrome by proxy abuse perpetrated by men. *Archives of Diseases of Children, 78,* 210–216.

Meadow, R. (2002). Different interpretations of Munchausen syndrome by proxy. *Child Abuse and Neglect, 26,* 501–508.

Parnell, T., & Day, D. (1998). *Munchausen by proxy syndrome: Misunderstood child abuse.* Thousand Oaks, CA: Sage.

Rosenberg, D. (2001). Munchausen syndrome by proxy. In R. Reece & S. Ludwig (Eds.), *Child abuse: Medical diagnosis and management* (2nd ed., pp. 363–383). Philadelphia: Lippincott Williams & Wilkins.

Schreier, H. (2002). Munchausen syndrome by proxy defined. *Pediatrics, 110,* 985–988.

10

Andrew P. Sirotnak
Joyce K. Moore
Jean C. Smith

Child Sexual Abuse

In most states the legal definition for the molestation of a child is an act of a person (adult or child), which forces, coerces, or threatens a child to have any form of sexual contact or to engage in any type of sexual activity at his or her direction. This includes inappropriate touching (clothed or unclothed), penetration using an object, forcing sexual activity between children, or asking a child to view, to read, or to pose for pornographic materials. 💬

Most children being evaluated for sexual abuse will not have significant physical findings on examination. However, a thorough physical and genital exam is necessary. A practitioner with expertise and specialized skills should do these examinations with children and adolescents. Many parents and caregivers do not realize that the pediatric genital exam is very different from that performed on adults. In fact, only in rare cases will the experienced examiner perform an internal exam or use a speculum.

As with all medical evaluations, the complete history is one of the most important components of a medical examination for sexual abuse. This history includes the presenting problem and symptoms, past medical history, developmental history, and family history. The history guides the examination, the type of laboratory studies to be done, consideration of the differential diagnoses, and the final diagnosis. The physical examination is most helpful when it is complete, that is, a "head-to-toe" exam. A complete physical—rather than just a genital exam—helps to "normalize" the experience for children who are typically familiar with routine well-child exams. The purposes of a medical exam are the following:

- Identify conditions requiring urgent treatment.

- Examine the whole body for any abnormalities and assess pubertal development.

- Obtain physical evidence if present.

- Reassure the child and the family of physical intactness and healing.

- Facilitate the child or adolescent's regaining control of his or her body.
- Formulate a plan for treatment recommendations.

■ When to Seek an Exam for Sexual Abuse

The first important decision, which the worker must make, is determining when to request a medical examination for the child. If the reported abuse occurred within the past 72 hours, the child should be examined immediately for the purpose of collecting data or specimens crucial in legal proceedings, and because wounds can heal very rapidly. In other cases, the immediate exam is not as urgent as beginning the history and preparing the family and child for the exam. The worker can use these general guidelines in making the decision whether to seek an immediate exam.

- If the abuse occurred or may have occurred within the past 72 hours and there is a disclosure or allegation of possible oral-genital or genital-genital contact, the child should be seen immediately. Preferably, the child should not bathe, change clothes, brush teeth, gargle, or use the bathroom before the examination.
- Clothing worn by the child, bedding, and towels at the scene may be the most important sources for laboratory confirmation of assault. A study of the results of sexual assault kits performed on prepubertal victims show that after 24 hours all forensic evidence was obtained from clothing and linens (Christian et al., 2000).
- If the child has vaginal pain, bleeding, or discharge from the urethra, vagina, or rectum; painful urination (dysuria); or complaints of pain when walking or sitting, the child should be examined immediately.
- Children who have been abused weeks or months previously should be examined as soon as it is practical.
- Siblings of suspected victims of sexual abuse should also be examined as soon as practical.
- Children with repeated complaints of abdominal pain or vaginal inflammation with no other symptoms should be considered as possible abuse victims and should be examined as soon as it is practical.

A 5-year-old child who tells her parent that she was fondled several days ago by a babysitter would not need an immediate medical exam; however, she would need a forensic interview as soon as possible. A common report might be the preverbal or very young child who returns from a parent weekend visit and a guardian thinks the genital area is red or irritated—both nonspecific findings. This might be caused from poor hygiene, infectious or nonspecific vaginitis, nonabusive trauma, or nothing alarming at all. If the family history is concerning for sexual abuse risks (prior sexual abuse, behavior changes, other family victims of sexual abuse), the family might be counseled by either a CPS worker or medical provider to have a medical examination by a primary care provider. Finally, a child or adolescent with clear disclosure of sexual abuse within the past 48 to 72 hours and with penetrating trauma or contact with ejaculation or with signs of trauma present (e.g., bruising, bleeding, blood in urine or stool, pain with walking, urination) should be seen emergently by a medical provider.

■ Behavioral Changes Indicating Abuse

The first indicators of sexual abuse may not be physical signs but behavioral changes or abnormalities. Unfortunately, at times, adults around the child may misinterpret these behaviors as disobedience or rebellion by the child or adolescent. Examples may include any of the following types of behavior:

- A 3-year-old girl shows signs of some trauma, does not want to be with a certain relative care provider, has nightmares, and regresses in her toilet training by wetting the bed.
- A 5-year-old boy aggressively attempts to undress and fondle peers and uses sexually explicit language in the preschool bathroom.
- A 6-year-old draws sexually graphic pictures in her art book and withdraws from normal play activity.

Normal Sexual Development

Before the worker can identify any behavior as abnormal, it is important to become familiar with the normal sexual development, related behaviors, interactions, and feelings of the growing child (American Academy of Pediatrics [AAP], 2001; Friedrich, Fisher, Broughton, Houston, & Shafran, 1998; Friedrich, Grambsch, Broughton, Kuiper, & Beilke, 1991; Haka-Ikse & Mian, 1993; Ryan & Blum, 1994; Schoentjes, Deboutte, & Friedrich, 1999). The following summary gives not only normal behaviors in childhood development but also common abnormal behaviors, which may indicate abuse. It is important to remember that no child will follow these developmental stages exactly. Some may mature more quickly, others more slowly, and others may have different behaviors occurring naturally from the influences of their particular environments. Deviations in behavior do not necessarily indicate a serious problem or sexual abuse in particular, but they should be assessed in the context of the history, physical findings, and the child's family environment (Hillman & Solek-Tefft, 1988).

☐   **Infancy (Birth to 1 Year)**

This stage includes three phases of psychosexual development:

1. *Pair bonding.* Sometimes called the oral stage of development, in the early phase the child derives pleasure and security from sucking, body contact, cuddling, rocking movements, clinging, and touching. Genital touching may occur naturally here, as infants enjoy touching all parts of their body randomly.

2. *Genital play.* Genital self-touching usually occurs between the ages of 6 and 12 months as a part of the child's exploration of his own body. Although it usually begins during the third year, masturbation might occur in the first two years. Infants may thrust their pelvises when being cuddled or falling asleep. This behavior should diminish over time. It is important that the parents or caregivers do not punish infants for self-stimulation or masturbation.

3. *Identification of gender.* During this stage of development the child is learning how her own body is similar to her same sex parent. This gender identification does not necessarily determine later sexual preference.

An infant's behavioral and physical symptoms of sexual abuse include the following:

- Displacing of fear and anxiety through excessive crying and fretful behavior
- Physical ailments such as vomiting, feeding problems, bowel disturbances, and sleep problems
- Failure to thrive

☐   **Toddler and Early Childhood (2 to 5 Years)**

Toilet training, with all of the pressures and anxieties involved, usually occurs during this stage. Common sexual behaviors observed in 3-year-olds include handling of their own genitals, kissing parents and other children, cuddling, and a beginning awareness of genital differences between males and females.

As children enter early childhood they typically show directed genital play and specific sexual sensations and feelings are first manifested. Common sexual behavior at age 4 includes kissing, cuddling, touching, and mild masturbation. The child may show an increased curiosity about sex. At this stage, they may purposely display their genitals to peers. They are often fascinated by excretion. At the same time, children begin to develop a need for increased privacy, especially in the bathroom.

Five-year-olds are usually more serious, self-contained, and better able to imitate adult behavior. Open genital display decreases, as well as bathroom fascination. Children play interpersonal games, including "family," "marriage," "doctor," and "store."

Behavioral and physical symptoms of sexual abuse of children ages 2 to 5 include the following:

- Fear of a particular person or place
- Regression to earlier forms of behavior such as bed-wetting, stranger anxiety, separation anxiety, thumb sucking, baby talk, whining, and clinging
- Victimization of others
- Fear of being abandoned if the caregiver cannot come to the child's assistance or momentarily leaves the child alone
- Feelings of strong shame or guilt
- Excessive masturbation
- Sexually inappropriate or graphic language, drawings, or behaviors that demonstrate knowledge of sexual acts
- Enuresis (wetting the bed or clothes) or encopresis (soiling of stool)

☐ **Latency (6 to 9 Years)**

Six-year-olds have an increased awareness of and interest in the anatomical differences between sexes. They may ask practical questions about sex, such as how a baby comes out of the mother's stomach and if it hurts the mother in the process.

Seven-year-olds are still quite interested in the topic of birth. Children are often discreet about their bodies and more anxious about being touched. Children may talk and joke about boyfriends and girlfriends. Occasional masturbation is common. Intense or frequent masturbation may signal anxiety, distress, or sexual abuse.

At the ages of 8 and 9, children display increased secretive behavior among peers and an increased interest in socialization. Specific sexual interest remains diffuse, and sexual behavior is often absent or discreet.

Behavioral and physical symptoms of sexual abuse of children ages 6 to 9 include the following:

- Nightmares and other sleep disturbances
- Fear that the attack will recur
- Phobias concerning specific school or community activities or specific people
- Withdrawal from family and friends

- Regression to earlier behaviors

- Eating disturbances

- Sexually inappropriate or graphic language, drawings, or behaviors that demonstrate knowledge of sexual acts

- Enuresis (wetting the bed or clothes) or encopresis (soiling of stool)

- Recurrent physical ailments or somatic complaints such as abdominal pain, headaches, and urinary or bowel difficulties

☐ Preadolescence (10 to 12 Years)

Initial signs of puberty and the development of secondary sexual characteristics either have occurred or are beginning. Strong friendships as well as developing romantic interests with peers occur at this stage. Boys and girls may engage in playful tickling or hitting, which, although it may have some degree of sexuality, does not seem directly motivated by sexual concerns.

Behavioral and physical symptoms of sexual abuse of children ages 10 to 12 include the following:

- Depression

- Nightmares and other sleep disturbances

- Poor school performance

- Promiscuity

- Use of illegal drugs or alcohol

- Fear that the attack will recur

- Eating disturbances

- Regression to earlier behaviors

- Withdrawal from family and friends

- Aggression

- Recurrent physical ailments or somatic complaints such as abdominal pain, headaches, and urinary or bowel difficulties

☐ Early Adolescence (13 to 15 Years)

This stage is characterized by two major changes: pubertal maturation and interest in peer group involvement. Girls usually begin menstruation by this period and boys experience ejaculation through dreams (nocturnal emissions) or masturbation. Both girls and boys experience strong sexual feelings, including sexual dreams and fantasies. Interest in adult movies and reading material develops. Masturbation is common at this stage.

Behavioral and physical symptoms of sexual abuse of children ages 13 to 15 include the following:

- Running away from home
- Severe depression
- Early marriage
- Promiscuity, which may include prostitution
- Early pregnancy
- Use of illegal drugs or alcohol
- Suicidal thoughts or gestures
- School truancy
- Poor school performance
- Pronounced fear that the attack will recur
- Grief over the loss of one's virginity
- Anger and rage about being forced into a situation beyond one's control
- Withdrawal from family and friends
- Pseudomature behaviors
- Anger and rage about attempted routine disciplinary action, such as being grounded, by a parent or caregiver
- Recurrent physical ailments or somatic complaints such as abdominal pain, headaches, and urinary, menstrual, or bowel difficulties
- Sexually transmitted diseases

☐ Adolescence (16 to 20 Years)

Adolescent boys and girls begin assuming adult roles at this stage. Their desire to be independent may cause conflicts and family problems. They may purposely violate sexual restrictions to gain distance from family problems and to release tension. Serious problems of unchecked sexuality may occur at this stage, such as pregnancy, abortion, or sexually transmitted diseases. In this stage, sexual abuse is similar to rape in that it can occur in individuals who have had consensual sexual activity or intercourse.

The Child Sexual Abuse Accommodation Syndrome

From his experiences working with sexually abused children, Dr. Roland Summit recognized five common characteristics among childhood sexual abuse victims. In 1983 he categorized these into what he calls the Child Abuse Accommodation Syndrome and this typology continues to be the most common way of understanding sexual abuse today.

☐ Secrecy

In order for prolonged sexual abuse to occur, the perpetrator must establish some form of secrecy with the child. Often this secrecy relies on threats or illogical explanations of why the child should not tell of the abuse. No matter how sincere or gentle these explanations may seem, their implied danger and secrecy make it clear to the child that the acts are something bad or dangerous. Many children never tell their secret. Often, when it is uncovered, adults fail to comprehend the fear that has caused the child to remain silent for so long. They react with anger and disbelief, wondering why the child did not tell sooner or why the child wanted to keep it a secret for so long.

☐ Helplessness

In their consideration of abuse, many adults fail to realize the helpless position of the child who often depends on the perpetrator for food, shelter, and basic family security. Adults may assume that the child who does not complain is, in a sense, consenting to the relationship when in reality the child has no choice. They expect him to cry for help, struggle to escape, and resist. With most children, however, this is not the case. Even when the perpetrator is not a caregiver, the child may feel powerless to refuse an adult's requests.

☐ Entrapment and Accommodation

Sexual molestation is often not a one-time occurrence. Frequently, these inappropriate relationships develop into addictive, compulsive patterns that continue until the child either leaves home or the situation is discovered. In order to deal with this continuous fear and subjection, most children have no choice but to submit to their situations. "The only healthy option left for the child is to learn to accept the situations and to survive. . . . The healthy, normal, emotionally resilient child will learn to accommodate to the reality of continuing sexual abuse" (Summit, 1983, p. 184). Often this accommodation involves self-punishment and self-blame, depression, and guilt. The child may create imaginary companions or even develop multiple personalities. Some children become aggressive and show outward rage. Others may turn to substance abuse. All of these behaviors are part of the child's "survival skills." They can only be overcome if the child can finally gain trust in a secure environment that provides consistent acceptance and care.

☐   **Delayed, Conflicted, and Unconvincing Disclosure**

As the abused child begins to mature into adolescence, he or she experiences a new sense of independence. At this point, the accommodation behaviors break down. Sometimes a family conflict or discovery by another person may trigger the breakdown. As the child's self-made walls of protection begin to crumble, the victim begins to rebel against the family's protectiveness. The child may choose friends the family does not like, drink, abuse drugs, break the law, or run away. Unfortunately, it is often not until the child reaches this stage of rebelliousness that the child reveals the abuse. Under these conditions, however, the disclosures often go unheeded. "Authorities are alienated by the pattern of delinquency and rebellious anger. . . . Most adults . . . tend to identify with the problems of parents in trying to cope with a rebellious teenager" (Summit, 1983, p. 186). Mothers, as well, typically react with disbelief and denial. The paradox of the disclosure of sexual abuse is that it is not until the child has become rebellious that the child has the courage to tell the secret.

☐   **Retraction**

Once children have told that they have been molested, the fears and threats underlying the secrecy become true. The mother may reject the child; the identified perpetrator calls the child a liar. The person providing economic support may be arrested or have to move out of the home. Under these circumstances, many children reverse their story, denying that it ever happened and "admitting" that it was made up.

Case Example

A 6-year-old girl was groomed by a perpetrator by promising rewards for allowing sexual touching and prompting the child to keep their "special game" a secret. This progressed to threats of harm or violence and she kept the secret out of fear, was trapped in recurrent victimization, and developed behavior symptoms, which her parent did not recognize as secondary to trauma. A delayed, spontaneous disclosure occurred, during an adult's discussion about safety with the child. After she disclosed and investigation ensued, a conflict developed in the family and the emotional response from the nonprotective, angry, equally traumatized parent led to a retraction by the child. She denied that the abuse occurred in order to bring normalcy back to the family.

■   **Presenting the Child for Examination**

When requesting an examination for child sexual abuse, the following history provided to the medical provider is helpful. Any information about the alleged or disclosed assault obtained by CPS, police, a witness, a parent, a caregiver, or a guardian may be helpful. It is important to inform the examiners of any information that is available. Gather information to respond to the following questions:

- What history has been provided by the child or guardian that raises concern about sexual abuse? Has the child or guardian reported genital or anal pain? Has there been any genital or anal bleeding or discharge? Has there been any difficulty or pain reported with urination or defecation? Has someone seen a rash, bruises, or other trauma to the genital, anal, or surrounding areas? Has there also been a physical assault to the child? Has the child's behavior been abnormal?

- In what way was the child sexually abused? What type of contact has been alleged or disclosed? (Oral-genital, genital-genital, or genital-anal contact; digital, genital, or object penetration of any part of body?) Was there ejaculation? Was a condom used? Was there any evidence at the site of the assault gathered by police such as blood, semen, lubricants, illegal drugs, or alcohol? Did the child or adolescent report having been given anything to eat or drink that made him sleepy or incoherent?

- What did the child say in a forensic interview with CPS, a therapist, or police?

- When was the last suspected incidence? Is this an acute assault within the last 48 to 72 hours or is this a remote or chronic event? Has the child been sexually abused in the past? When, how, and by whom? If there is a history of sexual abuse, has the child and/or family been in counseling for this abuse? With whom, and has therapy been helpful? Are there new disclosures or concerns discovered during therapy?

- Is there anyone in the family's living environment who currently has or previously had a sexually transmitted disease? Has anyone in the child's family or living environment been sexually abused?

- Has the child ever been examined for any type of child abuse or neglect?

- Is the parent or caregiver applying any ointments or creams to the child's genitals and is this a prescribed or required medication?

- Is the child toilet trained? Does the child wipe herself or need assistance? What is the bath and hygiene routine in the child's family, living environment, and childcare setting?

- If there is concern of an offending parent, caregiver, or companion of parent, is the other parent protective and supportive of the child? Is there any concern of false allegation through the parent or caregiver or coaching of the child? Is there a custody dispute complicating or precipitating the investigation or concern of sexual abuse?

- Were there any witnesses to the abuse?

When a child presents vaginal or anal irritation as a reason for suspected abuse, the worker should help the medical provider investigate for other possibilities that might cause the problem and should discuss with the parent these other causes of irritation, which follow:

- Could the child be allergic to any new bathing soaps, bubble baths, or clothing detergents?

- Has the child recently had any other infections or illnesses? Has she been taking any antibiotics?

- If there is genital discharge, how would it be described (e.g., color, bloody, foul smelling, copious)?

- Is there any recent enuresis or encopresis?

- How often is the child bathed?

- Does the child wear any type of clothing, such as tight jeans, plastic-covered or paper diapers, noncotton underwear, sanitary pads, or panty shields, that might cause irritation?

■ The Physical Exam: General

The timing of the physical examination should be considered in the context of acute physical assault in the past 72 hours in which acute trauma might be present or forensic evidence might need collection, or in the context of nonacute or chronic abuse in which documentation of healed trauma might be helpful. Regardless of the timing or nature of the sexual abuse, remember that the guardian and even the child might be anxious about either the health of the child or the exam itself. A child may want or need to know that his body is healthy in order to heal emotionally. Some cultures may emphasize the concepts of virginity or a healthy passage to adulthood prior to sexual activity. Finally, be cautiously aware of the parent or guardian who needs the exam in order to confirm or rule out abuse, to believe the child, or to prove that someone has hurt the child. A parent pursuing unnecessary examinations can be just as emotionally damaging to a child as an unbelieving or unsupportive parent.

During the physical exam, children may want to have the CPS worker, the mother, or another person who has a close relationship with them to remain in the examining room. The CPS worker's presence may not only help calm children but may also allow the worker to hear firsthand the medical provider's interview and any immediate findings. Depending on the age and gender of the child, the presence of the opposite gender parent during the exam might be uncomfortable for the child. It is never appropriate to have a suspected offending parent or caregiver present for a sexual abuse evaluation or examination of a child.

Remember that a child may have been already interviewed prior to a medical exam and it is always better not to re-interview a child multiple times. The examiner may need to ask specific questions about the alleged sexual abuse but it is always preferable and helpful if this information is provided beforehand. For example, a medical provider may hear from a detective that the disclosure is "penile-vaginal penetration." Much more helpful would be details, if available, of when the abuse happened, how many times it happened, its last occurrence, and if there was contact with blood or body fluid. Such information guides the medical examination and testing for STDs.

Do not expect to always leave the examination knowing for certain if a child has been sexually abused. The majority of sexually abused children have normal findings on their genital exams. A normal physical exam and negative laboratory results do not rule out the possibility of sexual abuse. The child's delayed disclosure may have allowed for healing of past trauma if it was present, or the child may have been sexually abused in such a manner as to not leave physical trauma (fondling, oral contact, exploitation). *The child's disclosure in the context of the medical examination, interview, or therapy becomes the most important aspect of the overall evaluation for sexual abuse.*

The medical provider should begin with a general physical examination of the child, looking for other signs of physical trauma or abuse and assessing overall growth and health. Remember that sexual abuse can occur along with physical abuse and neglect. The medical provider should also strive to make the genital exam as nontraumatic as possible by taking plenty of time to explain each step and to ask "where it hurts," "where the owie is on your body," or "what do you call this part of your body." In cases in which the child seems excessively fearful of the exam or has already been severely traumatized, or if acute trauma is present that needs urgent examination and treatment, the medical provider may need to sedate the child, which should be done in a controlled setting such as an emergency department or operating room.

Genital Examination: Tanner Staging

During the physical exam the medical provider will assess the child's physical sexual maturity. Because children may develop at different ages, medical providers refer to a scale that ranks the stage of the child's puberty development on a scale of 1 to 5. These stages of puberty development of breasts in girls, scrotum and penis in males, and pubic hair growth in both are called Tanner stages (Giardino, Finkel, Giardino, Seidl, & Ludwig, 1992; see Table 10.1 and Figures 10.1, 10.2, and 10.3).

Examination Techniques

Most of the genital assessment involves a careful, external examination. The young female is often most comfortable when on the exam table or seated

Table 10.1. Tanner Stages: Classification of Sexual Maturity in Females and Males

Stage	Pubic Hair	Breast Development in Females	Scrotum and Penis Development in Males
1	None	Preadolescent	Preadolescent
2	Sparse, long, slightly pigmented, develops at base of penis and edges of labia	Breast and papilla (nipple) elevated as a small mound; areola (pigmented area around nipple) diameter increases	Slight penis and scrotum enlargement and scrotum color is pink or reddened, not darkened; some texture changing
3	Darker, beginning to curl and an increased amount	Breast and areola enlarged (budding), without contour separation	Penis slightly enlarges; testes increase size; scrotum darkens slightly
4	Coarse, curly, more abundant but less than a mature adult	Areola and nipple form secondary, separate mound	Larger, darker thickened scrotum; penis larger; glans larger in breadth
5	Adult distribution and amount of dark curly hair; female triangle; spreads to medial surface of thighs	Mature nipple projects from areola, which is part of breast contour	Adult appearance of penis; testes sized like an adult's; darkened, thickened scrotum

in someone's lap, lying on her back with her heels drawn up to the buttocks and knees apart (the "frog leg" position). Another position is the "knee-chest" position, in which the child rests her head on her folded arms and supports her weight on her bent knees. This position is helpful for the examiner to visualize the posterior parts of the hymen tissue and the anus. It is, however, difficult at times to sustain, and some children may have been assaulted in this position (from behind). Careful monitoring of the child's affect and emotional state by the examiner and the support person is important. Finally, the "dorsal lithotomy" position, which may be used for adolescent exams, describes the position using stirrups, which is familiar as the adult pelvic position.

There are various techniques (separation and traction) for holding the genital labia apart to visualize the hymen and surrounding areas. In the assessment, the medical provider will examine the vagina as well as the anus for signs of old and new trauma and for hygiene. The condition of the hymen as well as the size of the hymenal ring and the vaginal introitus (the vaginal opening) will be evaluated. Frequently, the positions of specific findings will be referred to in a medical report by positions on the face of a clock (see Figure 10.4).

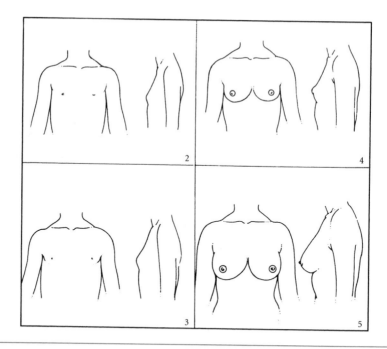

Figure 10.1. Tanner Stages: Breast Development. Illustration by Paul Singh-Roy. (From Giardino, Finkel, Giardino, Siedl, & Ludwig, 1992: 40. Copyright 1992 by Sage Publications. Reprinted with permission from Sage and the artist.)

☐ Female Genitalia Anatomy

The structures of the female genitalia are shown in Figure 10.5 and described below.

- *Clitoris.* The highly sensitive, erectile organ of the female vulva.

- *Hymenal membrane.* The mucous membrane that partially surrounds the vaginal opening. See below for detail.

- *Labia minora and labia majora.* Folds of skin or "lips" that surround the hymen and the vaginal opening. The labia minora are the smaller, more internal folds that directly surround the hymen and vaginal opening. In young girls these are completely hidden by the larger, more external labia majora.

- *Perineum.* The region between the vulva and anus in a female or the scrotum and anus in the male.

- *Vaginal introitus.* The hymenal or vaginal opening, or the small canal through which the penis enters during intercourse and through which the adolescent menstruates. In children or adolescents who

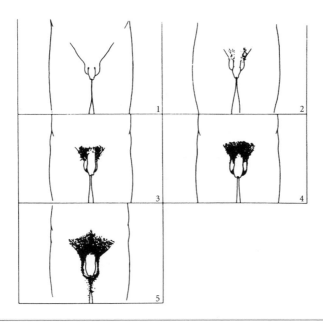

Figure 10.2. Tanner Stages: Male Public Hair. Illustration by Paul Singh-Roy. (From Giardino, Finkel, Giardino, Siedl, & Ludwig, 1992: 37. Copyright 1992 by Sage Publications. Reprinted with permission from Sage and the artist.)

Figure 10.3. Tanner Stages: Female Pubic Hair. Illustration by Paul Singh-Roy. (From Giardino, Finkel, Giardino, Siedl, & Ludwig, 1992: 37. Copyright 1992 by Sage Publications. Reprinted with permission from Sage and the artist.)

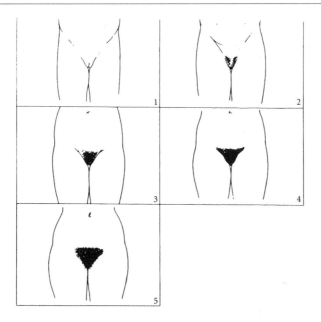

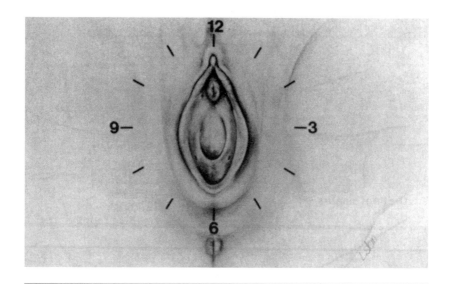

Figure 10.4. Clock Orientation with Patient in Frog Leg Supine Position. (From Giardino, Finkel, Giardino, Siedl, & Ludwig, 1992: 37. Copyright 1992 by Sage Publications. Reprinted with permission.)

Figure 10.5. External Structures of the Female. (From Giardino, Finkel, Giardino, Siedl, & Ludwig, 1992: 37. Copyright 1992 by Sage Publications. Adapted with permission.)

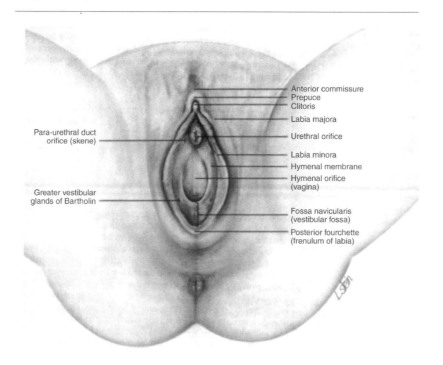

have not had penetration or sexual intercourse, the vaginal introitus is partially covered by the hymen, which usually has a central opening.

- *Vulva.* The female external genitalia.

- *Urethral orifice.* The opening through which the child urinates.

- *Fossa navicularis.* The concave space between the posterior fourchette and the posterior attachment of the hymen to the vaginal wall.

- *Posterior fourchette.* The point at which the labia minora meet posteriorly.

The medical provider may need to examine the vagina for foreign bodies or bleeding by using an otoscope, for magnification externally. The otoscope is a small instrument commonly used to examine the ears. In older children, the medical provider may choose to use a small speculum, *not* the same size as used with adult women, or a vaginoscope. Both are internal instruments and are used *only* if there is internal trauma suspected and this may require sedation of the child. The majority of child sexual abuse exams do not require either a speculum or finger inserted into the child's vagina so the exam is very different from a routine health care or an acute rape exam for an adolescent or adult.

A more commonly used instrument is the colposcope, which provides a magnified view of the genitalia (Muram, Arheart, & Jennings, 1999). Although this instrument was originally used to examine the cervix for the diagnosis of cancer, it is now also used as a magnification tool in identification of genital anomalies or variations and of trauma. One of the most advantageous aspects of colposcopic examination is that the instrument can be equipped with a 35 mm or digital camera that provides photographic documentation of the exam. The worker should remember that the examiner should explain to both the guardian and possibly the child why photos may be taken, where they will be stored, and that this is a part of the special exam for sexual abuse. Remember that children may have been sexually exploited by the taking of pornographic pictures and watching the child for change in affect or behavior is important. The medical provider may explain to the child that "this is part of a doctor's exam and no one is ever allowed to take photos of your private body parts." Again, the colposcope is a specialized light and does not touch or go into the child. A complete exam for a prepubertal child for suspected sexual abuse does not necessarily require the use of a colposcope, but most experienced child sexual abuse examiners at child advocacy centers or sexual assault centers now routinely use them.

Another technique that may be used for detecting small lesions on the posterior fourchette is the use of a dye called toluidine blue. When the dye is swabbed onto the perianal area, small, previously unnoticed lesions appear as darker, deeply stained regions (McCauley, Gorman, & Guzinski, 1986).

One of the important areas that the medical provider will examine is the hymen, the mucous membrane that partially covers the entrance to the vagina. Normal hymens can have different shapes or configurations (Berenson, 1995; Gardner, 1992; Heger, Emans, & Muram, 2000; McCann, Wells, Simon, & Voris, 1990).

The most common shapes are "annular," "crescentic," and "redundant" (see Figure 10.5). Other normal variations can occur although these are less common: "septate," "imperforate" (without an opening), "punctate" (with a pinpoint opening), or "cribriform" (several pinpoint openings). These words may be used in the medical report of the exam. Studies indicate that although variations in the anatomy of the hymen occur, all female infants are born with hymens (Jenny, Kuhns, & Arakawa, 1987).

The medical provider will look for any unusual injuries or scars. An important aspect of the exam is differentiating what may be a naturally occurring variation of the hymen and surrounding tissue from those findings caused by sexual abuse or accidental trauma (Berenson et al., 1999). Tags are normally occurring pieces of tissue often seen on the hymen and are not a result of trauma. The medical provider may refer to hymenal clefts (dips or elongated openings) or hymenal bumps. Although these can be indicators of abuse, both are also found in nonabused girls. But if the clefts in the hymen extend to the vaginal wall, then this is called a transection and this is caused by penetration through the hymen. Likewise, if the bumps are mounds of scar tissue instead of the softer, fattylike tissue seen in healthy, nonabused girls, then this also indicates direct trauma to the hymen. An attenuation of the hymen refers to a small "rim" or border that represents an actual decrease in the amount of hymenal tissue: this is caused by penetrating trauma.

Labial adhesions are also seen in nonabused girls. The labia are adhered together by thin, sensitive tissue, usually posteriorly. This area may get irritated by the pooling of urine. Some adhesions may rarely be seen after trauma so a history of labial trauma is important to obtain, especially if a primary care medical provider has not seen these present before. Treatment may involve topical estrogen cream to thin the tissue or surgical cutting of the adhesions if they are either very large or affect hygiene (Muram, 1999).

Another area the medical provider will examine is the vaginal introitus, or vaginal opening. As with the hymen, he or she will look for any signs of physical trauma, such as fresh tears or scars. Tears occurring from attempted or completed penile penetration often occur in the posterior part of the hymen or introitus, between the 3 and the 9 o'clock position, most often in the midline 6 o'clock position.

The medical provider will examine the width of the hymenal ring and vaginal opening. Some literature has suggested that transverse measurements (across the width of the opening) exceeding 4 millimeters in children who are less than 10 years of age are highly suggestive of abuse; however, this standard is no longer considered valid. Studies of nonabused girls of different ages have reported the range of hymenal opening sizes for girls of different ages and with different examination positions and techniques. It may be useful for the medical provider to use data such as this in assessing whether or not a particular hymenal opening is abnormal. However, use of such a limited and highly variable examination finding (the size can vary with age and patient size, as well as examiner technique) has not been supported by the latest medical literature. It also gives a false sense of reliability in the finding, as many children are sexually abused in ways that do not traumatize the hymen or even involve penetration. *The measurement of hymenal opening size should never be used as a sole indicator to diagnose or rule out sexual abuse* (Berenson et al., 2002).

The most important fact to understand about the examination for sexual abuse is that *the absence of genital trauma does not mean that sexual abuse has not occurred.* Most people imagine sexual abuse of a child by an adult as a brutal and violent act involving forcible penetration of the vagina or rectum. This, however, is not commonly the case. Even penile penetration may not cause bruising or severe cuts that lead to permanent scarring (McCann, Voris, & Simon, 1992). Additionally, rapid and significant healing of injuries to the hymen and genitalia can occur. Finally, delayed disclosure of sexual abuse is common and acute trauma may have healed and symptoms resolved before an exam occurs (Adams, Harper, Knudson, & Revilla, 1994; Emans, Woods, Flagg, & Freeman, 1987; Heger, Ticson, Velasquez, & Bernier, 2002; McCann & Voris, 1993).

In every examination the medical provider will look for and possibly test for sexually transmitted diseases (STDs) with cultures if indicated and will test for pregnancy when appropriate. Often bloodwork is needed for bloodborne STDs. Chemistry tests may be needed as baseline function tests—for example, liver enzymes—as medications for HIV may have side effects that are monitored by these tests.

In summary, a competent and thorough exam by an experienced medical provider will (1) document the history as provided by the CPS worker or law enforcement and the child; (2) describe the general physical and emotional health of the child; (3) provide a clear and detailed anatomic description of the genital and anal areas and note the position, techniques, and magnification used; and (4) clearly state that the exam finding is either confirmatory of the history for sexual abuse or that the exam is normal in appearance but does not rule out abuse given the history provided (AAP, 1999; DeJong & Finkel, 1990; Bays & Chadwick, 1993; Atabaki & Paradise, 1999; Finkel & DeJong, 2001). Finally, in some cases, the exam may actually lead to a diagnosis of false allegation of acute assault (an adolescent with no acute trauma) or to a diagnosis of another medical condition that resembled trauma.

☐   **Male Genitalia Anatomy**

The structures of the male genitalia are shown in Figure 10.6 and are described below.

- *Glans.* The cone shaped head of the penis, which contains the urethral orifice, or the opening through which the child urinates.

- *Testes.* The reproductive glands located under the penis, also know as testicles. The testes are enclosed in a sac-like pouch of skin called the scrotum.

Redness, bruises, "hickeys," and cuts on the shaft or glans of a penis may indicate forceful sucking by a perpetrator committing fellatio or from pinching or blunt trauma of the penis. Chafing or irritation may also occur from excessive handling or masturbation of the penis. Boys should be tested for sexually transmitted disease if there is any discharge from the urethral opening in order to identify the organism causing the problem.

Differential Diagnoses for Genital Trauma

In all children, an accidental type of injury is often very painful and frightening. In such situations most parents or caregivers will not hesitate to bring

Figure 10.6. External Structures of the Male, Circumcised. (From Giardino, Finkel, Giardino, Siedl, & Ludwig, 1992: 37. Copyright 1992 by Sage Publications. Adapted with permission.)

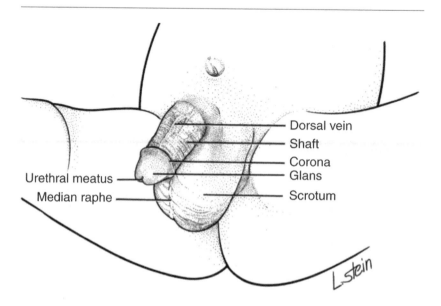

the child immediately to a medical provider or the emergency room, providing unsolicited, detailed explanations of the injuries.

Straddle injuries resulting from horseback riding, gymnastics, playing on monkey bars, rope climbing in gym class, sitting on or falling on bicycle bars, or sometimes climbing naked over the side of a tub are not uncommon. These injuries do not cause trauma to the internal hymen tissue or the anus. Accidental penetrating trauma to these areas is uncommon but does occur and has a clear history and usually no delay in care, as it is painful and may cause bleeding. For example, a toddler falls backward and straddles a plastic toy protruding in the tub at bath time (Bond, Dowd, Landsman, & Rimsza, 1995). Little boys may present with injuries from a scrotum that has been caught in hastily zipped trousers. In these cases, just as in all cases of suspected abuse, the developmental maturity of the child, the time elapsed before treatment, and the compatibility of the history and injury should be considered. Physically and psychologically healthy, normal children almost never purposely cause trauma to these body parts themselves.

Anus and Rectum

Digital or penile penetration of the anus is another frequent form of sexual abuse. Current literature suggests that boys and girls are at similar risk for this type of abuse. In a study of sexually abused boys, it was found that actual or attempted anal-penile penetration was the complaint in 62% of the victims. The degree of injury in anal penetration depends on many factors, including the size of the penetrating object, the amount of force used in the incident, the use (or not) of lubricant, and the frequency of penetration. Once the abuse has stopped, the gross physical signs of trauma can regress fairly quickly within days or weeks, even following long-lasting abuse (McCann & Voris, 1993). The doctor may refer to the anal region by the following terms.

- *Anus.* The external opening of the large intestine.
- *Anal verge.* The skin surrounding the anus.
- *Anal sphincter.* The circular muscle that closes the anus.
- *Perianal region.* The region around and close to the anus.
- *Rectal canal.* The end portion of the large intestine that leads to the anus.

Depending on the size of the child, injury following penetration may vary from bruises and small superficial cuts (fissures) to actual tears of the perianal skin, rectal canal, or anal sphincter. Fissures or lacerations around the anus may be caused by fingernails, a penis, or foreign bodies inserted into the anus. These small cuts and abrasions sometimes may leave scars, which can be seen by the medical provider. Penile penetration may cause anal hematomas (deeper bruising), swelling, or masses of blood in the anal tissue. When these injuries heal they may leave anal tags, small flaps or "tags" of skin within the anus. Anal tags may also occur naturally in the midline 12 and 6 o'clock positions and may not be a confirmatory indicator of abuse. Children who have suffered repeated episodes of anal penetration may also have thickening of the anal tissue and flattening or smoothing out of the rugae folds of the usually puckered, starburst-appearing anal tissue (see Figure 10.7).

Another indicator of penetration is anal dilatation, an expansion or stretching of the anus. Immediately following abuse, the anal sphincter may spasm, causing the opening to become very small and tight. In cases of repeated penetration, the anal sphincter may lose its tone, or capability to close properly. In the relaxed state, the anus may appear excessively large, causing the child to unintentionally soil his underclothing and leading to itching, irritation, and improper hygiene. Reflex anal dilatation, or an opening of the anus after stimulation of the surrounding skin, has been reported as a sign of sexual abuse. However, this is controversial as some medical researchers have reported seeing this in cases of chronic constipation, so its finding on physical examination alone is not indicative of sexual abuse.

☐ Differential Diagnoses

- Occasionally children may suffer accidental trauma to the anus, more commonly the buttocks and not the anus, perhaps through

Figure 10.7. Male Genitalia Trauma.

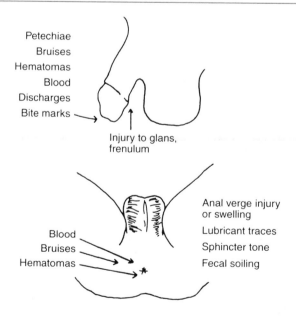

Petechiae
Bruises
Hematomas
Blood
Discharges
Bite marks

Injury to glans, frenulum

Blood
Bruises
Hematomas

Anal verge injury or swelling
Lubricant traces
Sphincter tone
Fecal soiling

play or from sitting on sharp objects. The history should clearly reveal this unusual form of trauma and sexual abuse must be ruled out by history (Kadish, Schunk, & Britton, 1998).

- Adolescents may self-stimulate the anus during masturbation and may also practice anal intercourse as birth control.

- Severe constipation with the passage of very large bowel movements can create fissures in the anus. Parents and occasionally the child may give a clear history of this problem, which usually causes great discomfort.

- Children with severe diarrhea may present with swelling, redness, or chapping in the perianal area.

- As in vulvovaginal irritations, lack of proper hygiene is a frequent cause of irritation and itching in the anal region. Occasionally children may contract a parasite known as "pinworms." These small white worms live in the upper part of the large intestine. The female creeps out of the anus and lays her eggs on the surrounding skin. These movements cause itching, which the child usually scratches, causing irritation, redness, or swelling. A doctor may check for pinworms by sticking a piece of adhesive tape to the perineum and checking the tape under the microscope for the presence of eggs. When this problem exists, everyone living with the child should also be treated.

■ Examination After Acute Sexual Assault

If a child has been sexually abused within the past 48 to 72 hours, the medical provider will look for signs of both physical trauma to the child's body and sexual trauma to the child's oral, genital, and anal areas. The examiner will also assess the need for a forensic evidence kit (or rape kit—see Figure 10.8). It should be emphasized again that these kits are rarely needed unless there is a clear history that sexual trauma has occurred and deposition of evidence (saliva, sperm, hair) may have occurred (AAP 1999; Christian et al., 2000; Heger, Emans, & Muram, 2000). These kits involve invasive, uncomfortable, and often painful procedures that could be further traumatizing if not performed carefully and with sensitivity to the victim. Procedures include the following:

- In appropriate cases the examiner will use a cotton-tipped swab to obtain specimens from the skin, mouth, genital area, vagina, and anus of the victim (swabbing for saliva or semen deposited on or in the victim). Multiple swabs are obtained so that the lab has them in storage if a specimen is needed for repeat analysis or if a defense attorney who represents an identified perpetrator wants repeat, independent testing.

- The doctor may pass an ultraviolet light, called a Wood's lamp, over the child's clothing and body. Substances that fluoresce as a green color under this light may indicate seminal fluid and will be collected for analysis.

- The doctor may obtain specimens from the vagina, mouth, and rectum when indicated, for examination under a microscope, to detect the presence of motile (moving) or nonmotile (not moving) spermatozoa.

- If ejaculation is suspected or confirmed by history, the medical provider will collect specimens from the mouth, skin, vagina, or anus for a forensic lab to analyze for sperm or semen fluid chemicals such as acid phosphatase and P30 glycoprotein from the male prostate gland. Other laboratory tests, such as hair and fiber analysis and blood type (ABO typing) and DNA typing of body fluids, may also help determine the identity of the assailant. These will not be recovered if the assailant wore a condom. ABO blood typing that requires blood draws from the patient has been removed from these kits in many states.

- Hair may be pulled—not cut—from a victim's head and pubic area to identify hair from an assailant by comparing with the victim's hair. This is painful and is usually done as a last step in the process of the forensic kit. In many children who have not started puberty, there will of course be no pubic hair to collect.

- Blood is often drawn and saliva samples are obtained for the kit for ABO blood typing. Many adults secrete the protein of their blood type in saliva, and this may identify a perpetrator.

It should be cautioned that for most cases of sexual abuse of children, even when acute in a 48- to 72-hour period, a forensic evidence kit collection might not be warranted. Such collection may be requested inappropriately by uneducated police officers who conceive of "evidence" as being the same for both adults and children. Inappropriate collection by such kits may be traumatizing and painful to a child.

Finally, there may be evidence at a scene of an assault that could recover forensic evidence, such as semen on sheets or towels, blood evidence, or other material, objects, or surroundings described by the victim that could confirm the assault (Christian et al., 2000).

■ Physical Findings in Sexual Abuse

Attempts have been made to classify the physical examination findings in sexual abuse to indicate the degree of certainty of this diagnosis (Adams, Harper, & Knudson, 1992; Bays & Chadwick, 1993). The following is adapted from Bays and Chadwick (1993) and summarizes the different

Figure 10.8. Rape Kit. (From Giardino, Finkel, Giardino, Siedl, & Ludwig, 1992: 37. Copyright 1992 by Sage Publications. Adapted with permission.)

medical examination findings into classes. These classes list what findings are considered diagnostic for sexual abuse, consistent with sexual abuse but need corroborating history, or are inconclusive for sexual abuse.

Class 1. Specific and diagnostic findings even without a history consistent with abuse.

- Recovery of sperm, semen, or semen marker such as acid phosphatase from the body
- Pregnancy
- Fresh trauma to the genital or anal areas without a history consistent with accident
- Sexually transmitted diseases (specifically syphilis, gonorrhea, chlamydia, and HIV) without the history of transmission from birth or intravenous routes
- Hymenal abnormalities including a markedly enlarged opening to the vagina for child's age, transections or scars, and remnants of hymenal tissue without adequate surgical or accidental history

Class 2. Consistent findings with history and other supportive data are important in diagnosis.

- Hymenal abnormalities with "bumps," notches, clefts, irregular edges, asymmetry
- Marked enlargement of the hymenal opening

- Anal scars and skin tags outside the midline
- Anal dilatation without stool in rectum
- Irregularity of anal orifice with dilation
- Specific sexually transmitted disease not acquired at birth (e.g., *Trichomonas, Condyloma acuminata* [warts], or herpes)

Class 3. Findings often seen with sexual abuse but history and other data are very important in making the diagnosis of abuse.

- Major adhesions of the labia minora in girls out of diapers
- Area between vaginal area and anal area (posterior fourchette) cracks and bleeds easily
- Anal fissures
- Thickened perianal fissures
- A specific sexually transmitted disease that may commonly be transmitted nonsexually, such as bacterial vaginosis/ *Gardnerella vaginalis*

Class 4. Findings most often found in cases where sexual abuse has been ruled out by a careful history and/or in examinations of children where there is no concern for sexual abuse.

- Candida (yeast) infections
- Redness of the hymen and/or of vaginal, labial, and surrounding areas especially in prepubertal girls
- Hymenal variants (septate, imperforate, small bumps)
- Redness or darkening of skin around anus

■ Vaginal Irritation and Discharge in the Preadolescent Girl

The presence of vaginal discharge in the preadolescent girl usually suggests that a problem exists, possibly from infection, irritation, or a sexually transmitted disease. The medical provider may refer to irritation as vulvovaginitis or vaginitis, meaning inflammation of the vagina and surrounding area. The cause of the vaginitis can be by nonsexual infections or irritations, as well as by sexually transmitted infections (Arsenault & Gerbie, 1986). This section covers vulvovaginitis caused by nonsexually transmitted infection.

Normal Vaginal Discharge

Most newborn baby girls will experience a vaginal discharge, possibly with traces of blood, during the newborn period. This is normal and is the result of stimulation of the infant's vaginal mucosa by the mother's estrogen. It should disappear within seven to ten days. Thin white discharge caused by hormones also occurs in the months just prior to menarche (the beginning of menstruation) and is normal for preadolescents. Once a girl has reached adolescence, a small amount of gray-white non-foul-smelling discharge is normal and healthy.

Vaginal Discharge Due to Nonspecific Infections

☐ Hygiene

Approximately 70% of cases of nonspecific vulvovaginitis (inflammation of the area around the inner labia and the vaginal opening) are the result of poor hygiene. One of the most frequent causes of infection in children is back-to-front wiping, which causes fecal contamination of the vagina. In these instances, genital cultures may indicate particular bacteria, although the diagnosis is made by history and cultures are rarely indicated. It is important in these cases to educate both the parents and children about proper toilet training and hygiene. Repeated problems of improper hygiene may signal that the child is being improperly cared for and possibly neglected.

Another problem caused by poor hygiene is a vaginal adhesion, in which the labia minora adhere or stick together. This problem can cause pooling of urine as well as collection of feces and secretions and this contamination results in vaginal irritation. The medical provider will usually treat the problem by applying an estrogen cream to the skin to thin the adhesion so it opens. Surgical cutting of the adhesions is generally only done if urine flow is being obstructed.

☐ Local Irritation

Other common causes of irritation and discharge are chemicals, clothing, or cosmetics. Soap products used in both bathing and laundry may cause irritation, as can bubble bath, perfumes, and, in the older adolescent, douches and "feminine hygiene deodorants." Noncotton underwear, as well as tight-fitting jeans, pantyhose, tights, ballet leotards, rubber pants, plastic-covered paper diapers, or sanitary pads may all have a similar effect. In the case of nonspecific vulvovaginitis, it is important to consider the possibility of physical or sexual abuse with intentional application of some type of chemical irritant.

☐ Foreign Bodies

Foreign bodies may be the cause of vaginal irritation in a child, particularly when accompanied by a persistent, bloody, foul-smelling discharge. In these cases, the medical provider may inspect the vagina with a internal small speculum, otoscope, or vaginoscope. The most common foreign body is rolled up wads of toilet tissue (Herman-Giddens, 1994). Children may insert small objects such as toy parts and coins in the genital area. Pubic hairs retrieved from the vagina of a prepubertal girl are an almost definite sign of abuse.

Vaginal Discharge Due to Specific Nonsexually Transmitted Infections

Specific infections that are not sexually transmitted usually arise from a previously existing infection located elsewhere. Common culprits of these infections include the following:

- *Parasites.* One example would be pinworms, the small white worms that live in the large intestine and lay their eggs on the perianal skin. Sometimes worms may actually be recovered from the vagina. This is treated with antiparasite medication.

- *Bacteria from the gastrointestinal tract.* Examples would be salmonella, shigella, and E. coli from the child's own feces. Often oral antibiotics are needed but treatment of the gastrointestinal disease may simply involve oral fluids and time for the disease to resolve.

- *Bacteria from the respiratory tract.* An example of this would be streptococcal infections from the throat of the child, which can be transmitted by touching the genital-anal area. The most common is Group A streptococcus, which can cause a very red, itchy, swollen rash with or without a discharge. This is recovered with a strep culture just like a throat culture and treated with oral antibiotics (Mogielnicki, Schwartzman, & Elliott, 2000).

- *Bacteria from the skin.* These may cause rashes, the most common being *Staphylococcus aureus*, which causes impetigo, sometimes with blisters (bullous impetigo). This is treated with oral and topical antibiotics.

- *Fungal infections (candida).* These are common in infants and young children in diapers after prolonged antibiotic use and sometimes after skin breakdown from excessive diarrhea illness. Topical cream clears the infection.

■ Sexually Transmitted Diseases (STDs)

In cases of suspected sexual abuse, the medical provider may test the child for STDs. Whether or not the medical provider takes cultures for an STD depends on several factors: (1) the sexual abuse history, (2) symptoms and physical findings, and (3) the incubation period of the specific STD organisms relative to the alleged incident (Sirotnak, 1994; Sirotnak, 2004). The incubation time of a particular organism refers to the amount of time that elapses between the child's first contact with a disease and its initial appearance through cultures or physical symptoms. For example, a child who has been sexually abused the day before her exam may have a negative culture for a bacterial or viral STD that has an incubation period of three days or two weeks. The medical provider may want to re-culture a child who initially has a negative culture for any STD or give prophylaxis (preventive) antibiotic therapy for certain diseases, more commonly in adolescents who report vaginal rape. Cultures for STDs may be taken not only from the vagina but also from the rectum and pharynx, or throat.

It is important to realize that many diseases can be transmitted both sexually and nonsexually. Mothers may pass infections, such as syphilis or HIV infections, to their children by placental blood transfer in the womb or by the child's passage through the birth canal. As infants move through the birth canal they receive full contact with the mother's mucous membranes, thus making them susceptible to any STD that the mother may have. Remember that it is the actual passage through the birth canal that transmits such diseases. For example, infants delivered through a cesarean section should not contract diseases such as genital herpes or venereal warts from the mother. The presence of an STD in the preadolescent child is highly indicative of abuse, however, and the medical provider must consider other modes of transmission for some infections.

In rare cases, a disease may be transferred through fomites, that is, objects such as toilet seats, washcloths, or water. Some diseases may be innocently transferred from one person's hands to the vagina, anus, or mouth of another. Studies are clear on which specific infections can and cannot be transmitted in this way.

Testing

Listed below are the guiding principles to remember in determining the need for STD assessment in the sexually abused child (AAP, 2003; Sirotnak, 2004).

- The type of sexual abuse involving genital or anal contact that is alleged or disclosed

- The presence of acute trauma on examination

- The presence of any complaints or symptoms that may indicate an infection

- Contact with ejaculate, particularly with the mouth, vagina, anus, and any open area of trauma or wound

- The risk of an STD in the perpetrator from such factors as promiscuity, bisexual or homosexual activity, intravenous drug use, and the current presence or past diagnosis of an STD

- The risk of a preexisting infection or illness in an older child or adolescent that could predispose him or her to STD infection

- The epidemiology and presence of an STD in the child's living environment or community

Specific Sexually Transmitted Diseases

☐ *Chlamydia Trachomatis*

This bacterial STD can cause pelvic inflammatory disease and/or lifelong infertility if not treated. Children or adolescents with this disease should also be tested for gonorrhea and *Trichomonas vaginalis.*

Medical providers may test for this disease with immunologic tests or chlamydial cultures. The latter is preferred in sexual abuse cases, since some immunologic tests have been shown to have some false positive results, particularly with samples from the rectum. Newer DNA amplification tests, identifying specific bacterial DNA from a tissue swab, have been developed for both chlamydia and gonorrhea, with nearly equal ability to accurately detect the organism without these false positives. Cultures are still considered the "gold standard" until studies are completed comparing the performance of these new techniques with cultures (Hammerschlag, 1998).

Incubation is 1 to 2 weeks. Transmission can occur as a baby is born through the birth canal of an infected mother. Chlamydia can cause eye infections and pneumonia in newborns. Infants and very young children under 1 year of age can carry the organism (it can be "colonized") in the throat, vagina, and rectum with or without becoming symptomatic.

This STD in children and adolescents is always considered to be sexually transmitted. No cases have been reported of transmission via fomites. The treatment is oral antibiotics or intravenous antibiotics in a teenager or adult with pelvic inflammatory disease.

☐ Human Papilloma Virus (HPV), or *Condyloma Acuminata*

This virus causes venereal warts, which can appear as flat, fleshy, or cauliflowerlike lesions, either singly or in clusters, in the anorectal, perineal, or genital regions. The warts can also appear in the larynx, pharynx, or mouth. Certain types of HPV cause hand and foot warts, while other types cause genital and anal warts (Gutman, Herman-Giddens, & Phelps, 1993; Siegfried & Frasier, 1997). These types are identified by numbers and genetic typing in a lab. The genital types have been associated with abnormal PAP smears and cervical cancer in women, but there are no studies yet to determine if the presence of HPV in a child will lead to any predisposition to cancer later in life.

Incubation time is 6 weeks to 1 year or up to 2 years. Therefore, the current general recommendation is that any child under 3 years of age may have contracted HPV from the birth canal, and that any newly identified warts in a child over 3 years of age warrants a screen for sexual abuse risk factors and possibly for other STDs. Any child who is old enough to be interviewed should have this screen completed as well. Medical records of the child and mother should be reviewed by a medical provider in order to investigate whether a lesion was noted previously that could have been a wart or if the mother has a history of HPV or abnormal PAP smears (Siegfried & Frasier, 1997). Transmission can occur through vaginal births, sexual encounters, or close but nonsexual encounters from the hands to the mouth, genital, or anal region.

The treatment is removal with chemical topical medications, freezing, or surgical excision. Removal is indicated when a large number complicate hygiene, cause discomfort, or are internal in the vaginal or anal canal. Warts have a high recurrence rate after removal. Treatment is usually done by a pediatrician or dermatologist.

☐ *Gardnerella Vaginalis*

This STD is usually accompanied by a white, gray, or yellow malodorous discharge. It does not appear frequently in nonsexually abused prepubescent children. Its presence in the prepubertal child should raise suspicion of sexual abuse (Ingram et al., 1992). It is diagnosed by the positive "whiff test," where a positive fishy odor is given off when a swab of discharge is treated with a few drops of potassium hydroxide. The infection is treated with a short course of antibiotics.

☐ **Herpes Simplex Virus (HSV)**

Genital herpes is caused by herpes simplex virus and is one of the most frequently diagnosed STDs in adolescents and adults. Painful blister lesions (vesicles) develop on the genitalia, anus, or mucous membranes of the mouth.🔖 The disease may be confused with chicken pox or shingles. Incubation is 2 to 20 days, with an average of 6 days. Herpes simplex type 2 is the common genital infection, and type 1 is the cause of oral blisters and cold sores. Type 1 can be transmitted from the mouth to the genital area by hand contact or oral-genital contact (Christian, Singer, Crawford, & Durbin, 1997).

Transmission can occur through vaginal birth, oral-genital contact, genital-genital contact, or by the hands from the mouth to genitals. Fomite transmission has not been reported. A diagnosis is made by the appearance of the vesicles and by laboratory culture or rapid DNA tests. Symptomatic infections are often treated orally with the antiviral drug acyclovir to decrease the duration of outbreaks, which can be recurrent, as medication does not eradicate the virus from nerve cells, where it lies dormant.

☐ **Human Immunodeficiency Virus (HIV)**

Acquired immune deficiency syndrome (AIDS) is a disease that breaks down the body's immune system, or its ability to fight disease. The virus infects white blood cells (T-cells) and uses these cells to replicate in the infected human. Antiviral medications are used to suppress the virus replication. Other medications may be given to prevent opportunistic infections that occur when the immune system is severely compromised. These infections, along with malignancies, are the usual cause of death in AIDS patients. The overall diagnosis and treatment for AIDS has changed dramatically in the past decade, and the prognosis for the disease has shifted from being quickly terminal to controllable and chronic (Centers for Disease Control and Prevention, 2001; Gutman et al., 1991; Lindergren et al., 1998).

There are still misunderstandings about the transmission of HIV, even with better education about risk factors and the disease itself. The issues of confidentiality and stigma surrounding the diagnosis of HIV and AIDS are still important to remember when discussing the disease in patients and in human services clients.

The virus can be transmitted in the following ways:

- Sexual contact in which the body secretion (such as saliva, blood, feces, semen, or vaginal secretions) of an infected person comes into contact with the mucous membrane or open wound of another person.

- Shared needles of drug abusers, accidental needle sticks in health care or other settings, and contaminated blood or blood products used in blood transfusions or medical care. However, the incidence of transmission by blood products has decreased significantly since the implementation of universal blood screening in the United States.

- Transmission by mothers who are infected to their infants either during pregnancy or childbirth. Medication can be given to a mother during pregnancy and delivery to prevent transmission.

- Risk factors for HIV disease include promiscuity, intravenous drug abuse, homosexual or bisexual activity, and the presence of another bloodborne STD such as hepatitis or syphilis.

The virus has never been known to be spread through light or deep kissing (unless an open sore exists in the mouth), sneezing or coughing, hugging or touching an infected person, mosquitoes, or fomites.

Testing for AIDS can determine if a person has been exposed to the virus (is "HIV positive"). Because of the time it takes for the virus to manifest itself in the body, these antibody tests do not always indicate the presence of the virus. Newer tests can detect HIV DNA, can determine the viral load (how many particles of virus are in the blood), and can culture the virus from tissue, white blood cells, or blood. The routine HIV test that is ordered in cases of sexual assault is either an ELISA or a Western Blot and will be reported as reactive or nonreactive.

In cases of acute sexual assault in which there is transmission of blood or body fluid, especially with tissue damage during assault, preventive medicine can be given within hours of the rape to decrease the chance of acute HIV infection. This is very important in cases of both child/adolescent and adult rape. All of these medicines may have side effects and the administration must be monitored by a medical provider knowledgeable in their use. These medicines may be expensive, requiring rapid assessment of the family by a CPS worker for financial assistance.

If the worker encounters cases involving AIDS, it is crucial that the family be referred to the proper medical and supportive resources for medical treatment, education, and counseling.

Families may ask for HIV testing in cases of sexual abuse that might not need testing. Refer these cases to a medical provider for counseling. Request that the family sign a consent form to allow discussion with a medical provider if needed. A CPS worker should know his or her agency's internal policy on HIV testing and confidentiality.

Also, workers should be aware of the prevalence of HIV in their communities. More detailed information about AIDS can be obtained from the federal Centers for Disease Control (CDC) Web sites or at the local health department (CDC, 2001).

☐ *Molluscum Contagiosum*

This virus is relatively common among both adults and children. The signs of infection are the formation of flesh-colored, dome-shaped papules with central dimples on the skin. Incubation time ranges from 2 to 7 weeks and up to 6 months. Therefore, contact can occur long before the lesions appear.

Transmission occurs either sexually or nonsexually, via fomites or with contact with the skin of an infected person. When determining the mode of transmission, it is helpful to consider the site of the disease. Sores on the trunk and extremities may occur easily from play, while genital sores (genital *Molluscum contagiosum*) should raise the suspicion of sexual abuse (Bargman, 1986). Although the disease in children and infants is usually caused by nonsexual contact, the presence of *Molluscum contagiosum* does not rule out the possibility of sexual abuse. Treatment is by either mechanical or chemical removal of lesions.

☐ *Neisseria Gonorrhea*

The signs and symptoms of gonorrhea include purulent vaginal, penile, anal, or pharyngeal discharge, genital or anal swelling, painful urination, and redness, although patients may also be asymptomatic. Children who present with this disease should also be tested for syphilis and chlamydia.

Incubation time is 2 to 7 days. Transmission can occur through vaginal birth and it usually causes severe eye infection but can also cause blood, joint, and spinal fluid infections. Infants receive eye ointment as a routine precaution at birth. Diagnosis is made by culture of the discharge.

Beyond the immediate newborn period. *Neisseria gonorrhea* is *always* considered to be sexually transmitted. No cases have been reported of transmission via fomites (AAP Committee on Child Abuse and Neglect, 1998; Ingram, Everett, Flick, Russell, & White-Sims, 1997; Robinson, 1998; Sirotnak, 2004). Antibiotic treatment must be provided. Complications of untreated gonorrhea in adolescent females include pelvic inflammatory disease, which, like untreated or recurrent chlamydia, can affect fertility later in life.

☐ Syphilis (*Treponema Pallidum*)

This disease occurs in three stages. In the primary stage, the patient has small painless ulcers (chancres) of the skin and mucous membrane where contact has occurred, usually the genital, penile, or anal area, 10 to 90 days after the contact. Open, ulcerous lesions, or *chancroids*, can pass the disease when they are rubbed against another person. The secondary stage occurs 1 to 2 months later and causes a characteristic rash that includes hands and feet, headache, joint pain, or fever. A period of latency occurs between this stage and the tertiary stage, in which patients have blood antibodies but no external signs of disease. Relapses of the secondary stage are common. The tertiary stage occurs a variable number of years later and affects the heart muscle, bone, and brain.

The screening laboratory tests used in detecting these diseases are the VDRL and RPR. Other tests, called the treponemal tests (FTA-ABS and MHA-TP), are more specific and are used to confirm the diagnosis.

Incubation time is typically 3 weeks but it can range from 10 to 90 days. Syphilis is sexually transmitted when the diagnosis of birth transmission can be ruled out by medical history (Christian, Lavelle, & Bell, 1999; Sirotnak, 2004). Any child or adolescent diagnosed with syphilis should be tested for other STDs, including HIV and hepatitis B and C. Treatment will depend on the stage of disease and might include either intramuscular or intravenous penicillin.

☐ *Trichomonas Vaginalis*

This STD is relatively uncommon in prepubescent children. The presence of the organism should raise concern for sexual abuse. A frothy vaginal discharge with burning and itching is present, but both females and males can be asymptomatic. Tests for the presence of this disease is made by examination of the smear of the vaginal discharge or by culture.

Transmission can occur through vaginal birth and, in rare cases, through fomites (e.g., a wet washcloth). However, transmission occurs most commonly through sexual contact (Finkel & DeJong, 2001; Heger, Emans, & Muram, 2000). The incubation period is from 1 week to 1 month. Treatment is an oral antibiotic for the patient (and, if the patient is a sexually active adolescent, the partner).

☐ Pubic Lice

These organisms are spread by direct body contact. Body and hair lice in children are common pediatric conditions. Lice attach to specific body hair areas, and pubic lice are specific to the genital area. A lab technician can look at the lice under a microscope to determine the type. If pubic lice are diagnosed, evaluation of caregivers in the home should be done, and the possibility of sexual contact needs to be evaluated.

☐ Hepatitis B and C

These viruses, which are transmitted through birth, blood, or body fluids, including semen, cervical secretions, and saliva, and through intravenous drug use or accidental needle sticks in the health care environment, cause liver disease. Although children are immunized against hepatitis B during childhood, there may be some children who do not adequately respond to the immunization, or there may be decreasing levels of protection during adolescence.

The medical provider will do bloodwork for levels of antibody to the virus and to detect the presence of the virus in the patient as well. Acute hepatitis infection has an incubation period of 45 to 160 days. An acutely infected person then becomes a chronic carrier of the virus, and the virus predisposes that person to chronic liver disease and possible liver cancer later in life. Immunoglobulin can be given to acutely exposed individuals to prevent development of the disease. There is no effective treatment for the chronic stage of the disease, and chronic liver failure may lead to a liver transplant or death.

Sexual assault victims should be screened for their antibody level of protection and offered repeat immunization for hepatitis B. Child sexual abuse victims who have contact with blood or body fluid or have severe physical tissue trauma should also be screened. Because the type of screening often depends on the type and timing of the exposure, a medical provider will need to determine which testing is needed.

Finally, another hepatitis virus warrants mention. Hepatitis A is a virus that is transmitted through the fecal-oral route, often via contaminated food from handlers who do not wash hands. It can be spread in day-care or health care centers the same way from materials in contact with a contaminated stool. The virus causes a febrile diarrhea and abdominal pain illness with liver inflammation (hepatitis) and in children it is usually self-limited and minor but in adults it can cause liver damage. This hepatitis virus is not usually considered an STD but adults can contract this by consensual oral-anal contact. Treatment is supportive for the acute disease, hepatitis A.

Immunoglobulin may help fight the virus, and preventive vaccination is often recommended in day-care or health care workers.

Table 10.2 summarizes these infections and their modes of transmission and significance in child sexual abuse (AAP, 1999; AAP, 2003; McCann, Voris, & Simon, 1992).

■ Female Genital Mutilation

Medical practitioners in areas with a high rate of African immigration are encountering a form of circumcision, defined by the World Health Organization as female genital mutilation (FGM). FGM is practiced primarily in North Africa, Asia, and various Middle Eastern countries, with an incidence as high as 90% of female infants, children, and adolescents in some countries. The procedure occurs most often in children between 4 and 8 years of age. It is a cultural, rather than religious, practice shared by Chris-

Table 10.2. Summary of Sexually Transmitted Diseases

Disease	Evidence of Sexual Abuse	Maternal or Neonatal Transmission	Nonsexual Human Transmission	Transmission via Fomites
Chlamydia trachomatis	Strong	Yes	No	No
Condylma acuminata	Strong	Yes	Possible	No
Gardnerella vaginalis	Possible	Unclear	No	No
Genital herpes	Probable	Yes	Yes	No
Molluscum contagiosum	Possible	Yes	Yes*	Yes
HIV	Strong	Yes	No**	No
Neisseria gonorrhea	Strong	Yes	No	No
Syphilis	Strong	Yes	Yes***	No
Trichomonas vaginalis	Strong	Yes	No	Yes

* Transmitted through open lesions. Look at site of transmittance to determine sexual abuse.

** Transmitted through contaminated needles of intravenous drug users and blood products only. Not documented for other fomites.

*** Transmitted through rubbing open lesions (chancroids). Look at site of transmittance to determine sexual abuse.

tians, Muslims, and Jews. The practice is maintained for various reasons: to preserve group identity; to ensure cleanliness and health (because of a belief that the clitoris is "dirty"); to preserve virginity and family honor; and to further the desirability of the female as a marriage partner.

The extent of the procedure varies, from excision and removal of the clitoral hood and/or the clitoris to the most extreme form called infibulation, in which the clitoris and the labia minora are removed and the tissues surrounding the urethral and vaginal openings are stitched together, leaving only a small opening for urine and menstrual flow. The procedure is usually performed by a local lay practitioner, using a knife, razor, or broken glass without anesthesia or sterile technique. Immediate risks to the child include blood loss, shock, and severe infection. When infibulation takes place, the female is at future risk for labor and delivery complications.

The American Medical Association, the World Health Association, the American College of Obstetricians and Gynecologists, and the AAP have all opposed FGM as a medically unnecessary practice with serious, potentially life-threatening complications (AAP Committee on Bioethics, 1998). In 1996, the U.S. Congress enacted legislation that criminalized the performance of FGM on all children below the age of 18. Many African countries are now promoting educational programs to discourage the practice, although immigrant families still frequently return to their native countries to obtain the procedure for their daughters. The AAP further "recommends that its members actively seek to dissuade families from carrying out FGM and provide patients and their parents with compassionate education about the physical harms and psychological risks" (AAP Committee on Bioethics, 1998). It is strongly suggested that community educational efforts be instituted utilizing the services of native counselors sensitive to the family cultural beliefs. Health and human service providers need to develop a compassionate approach to children and families who have had the procedure performed.

Case Example

An 8-year-old girl was seen by a community pediatrician for persistent foul-smelling vaginal discharge. Cultures were negative for any causative organisms and frequent baths and genital cleaning did not improve the situation. The family returned to their African country for an extended visit with family. Upon return, at the child's next pediatric visit, the pediatrician noted that the child's clitoral area had been removed. The father acknowledged that the procedure had been carried out by a medical practitioner in their native country. Of note, the vaginal discharge had not improved and was finally diagnosed as a dermatological problem.

Had this procedure been performed in the United States it would have been considered child abuse. Because the example occurred outside the country, it is not prosecutable within the United States. However, efforts should be made to educate the family about this practice in case there are other children or there are emotional consequences for the child.

■ Overall Likelihood of Medical Diagnosis of Sexual Abuse

In summary, the decision about the likelihood of abuse is made on the basis of the history (presenting physical and behavioral symptoms, disclosures during interview), physical exam, and laboratory evidence. The standard of care is to take a careful history, review symptoms and signs of disease or condition, conduct a physical examination, and consider any other differential diagnoses and interpretations of any labs or other studies. Remember that a case in which there is a clear statement of sexual abuse ("someone touched on my privates") along with a normal exam and negative testing would usually be founded as probable sexual abuse.

■ Sexual Abuse Treatment

Medical Treatment

The medical treatment will vary according to the extent and nature of the injury and whether the child is either at risk for or has contracted an STD (CDC, 2002; Finkel & DeJong, 2001). For example, sexual partners of adolescents may need to be evaluated and treated for STDs. Injuries from minor physical trauma (bruises, scratches, fissures, superficial lacerations or cuts) may only need monitoring as these will heal on their own. Watching for signs of infection, increased bleeding, pain, or discomfort with urination or defecation are standard care. Sitz baths will help minor discomfort.

A child who has undergone severe acute genital or anal abuse from penetration may need to be evaluated by a surgeon or gynecologist for repair of injury. These severe cases will be evident to both the medical provider and the worker. The complications of such severe trauma should be discussed with the medical provider.

Children may be prescribed oral antibiotics for STD treatment, as noted in the section above. Some topical creams or ointments for minor irritation might be needed.

Mental Health Treatment

The psychological effects of sexual abuse can range from minor and brief trauma-related symptoms to severe psychological trauma that is life altering (Koverola & Friedrich, 2000; Olafson & Boat, 2000; Paradise, Rose, Sleeper, & Nathanson, 1994; Swanston, Tebbutt, O'Toole, & Oates, 1997). All children who experience any type of sexual abuse should receive some form of counseling. ◨

The following examples of child sexual abuse definitely warrant therapy.

- Children who have been repeatedly abused over a long period of time by one or more offenders

- Children who have suffered a particularly traumatic form of abuse, especially those cases in which there was significant physical trauma and those in which there was a significant amount of aggression, humiliation, exploitation, or embarrassment

- Children and adolescents who have been previously abused and have subsequently become sexual offenders

- All cases of incest within the family. This should include support therapy for the nonoffending parent or guardian

- All cases in which there are significant short-term effects and intense trauma symptoms such as nightmares, bed-wetting, flashbacks, phobias, or anxiety attacks

- All cases in which the child wants to talk with a professional

- Cases in which family members need advice and support in dealing with the situation

- Cases in which there will be possible legal action of a contested nature in which the child might be called on to testify (parent not believing or supporting child, requiring court petition or contentious divorce-custody situation)

Some cultural groups may use specific healing ceremonies for children who have been sexually abused. Psychotherapy is not always considered by every culture as an appropriate approach to healing. It is important to explore the cultural context of the event of sexual abuse and learn about the approaches to healing that may be specific to the family and child's cultural or spiritual beliefs. For example, some cultures may view the victim differently, as changed or not virginal, and this can affect the child's future emotional development.

The CPS worker should familiarize herself with local professionals who are trained, skilled, and competent in the medical and psychological assessment and treatment of sexually abused children. The AAP has a section on child abuse and neglect and maintains a membership list by state of such medical experts. The local mental health agency may also have referral guidance and resources for CPS workers and families.

A healthy outcome depends on protective, supportive caregivers and a safe and stable environment, as well as access to age- or developmentally appropriate mental health services. Unless cultural taboos are discovered, or there are culturally appropriate alternative treatment methods in place, a caregiver who does not follow through with either recommended medical or mental health services for a sexually abused child should be considered neglectful. Strong consideration of a court-ordered treatment plan for the family is warranted.

References

Adams, J., Harper, K., & Knudson, S. (1992). A proposed system for the classification of anogenital findings in children with suspected sexual abuse. *Adolescent and Pediatric Gynecology, 5,* 73–75.

Adams, J. A., Harper, K. H., Knudson, S., & Revilla, J. (1994). Examination findings in legally confirmed child sexual abuse: It's normal to be normal. *Pediatrics, 94*(3), 310–318.

American Academy of Pediatrics. (2003). Sexually transmitted diseases. In L. K. Pickering (Ed.), *2003 red book: Report of the committee on infectious diseases* (26th ed.). Elk Grove Village, IL: Author.

American Academy of Pediatrics Committee on Bioethics. (1998). Female genital mutilation. *Pediatrics, 102,* 153–156.

American Academy of Pediatrics Committee on Child Abuse and Neglect. (1998). Gonorrhea in prepubertal children. *Pediatrics, 101*(1), 134–135.

American Academy of Pediatrics Committee on Child Abuse and Neglect. (1999). Guidelines for the evaluation of sexual abuse of children: Subject review. *Pediatrics, 103*(1), 186–191.

American Academy of Pediatrics Committee on Psychosocial Aspects of Child and Family Health, & Committee on Adolescence. (2001). Sexuality education for children and adolescents. *Pediatrics, 108*(2), 498–502.

Arsenault, P., & Gerbie, A. (1986). Vulvovaginitis in the preadolescent girl. *Pediatric Annals, 15*(8), 577–585.

Atabaki, S., & Paradise, J. E. (1999). The medical evaluations of the sexually abused child: Lessons from a decade of research. *Pediatrics, 104*(1), 178–186.

Bargman, H. (1986). Genital molluscum contagiosum in children: Evidence of sexual abuse? *Canadian Medical Association Journal, 135*(5), 432–433.

Bays, J., & Chadwick, D. (1993). Medical diagnosis of the sexually abused child. *Child Abuse and Neglect, 17*(1), 91–110.

Berenson, A. B. (1995). A longitudinal study of hymenal morphology in the first 3 years of life. *Pediatrics, 95*(4), 490–496.

Berenson, A. B., Chacko, M. R., Wiemann, C. M., Mishaw, C. O., Friedich, W. N., & Grady, J. J. (1999). A case-control study of anatomic changes resulting from sexual abuse. *American Journal of Obstetrics and Gynecology, 182*(4), 820–834.

Berenson, A. B., Chacko, M. R., Wiemann, C. M., Mishaw, C. O., Friedich, W. N., & Grady, J. J. (2002). Use of hymenal measurements in the diagnosis of previous penetration. *Pediatrics, 109*(2), 228–235.

Bond, G. R., Dowd, M. D., Landsman, I., & Rimsza, M. (1995). Unintentional perineal injury in prepubescent girls: A multicenter prospective report of 56 girls. *Pediatrics, 95*(5), 628–631.

Centers for Disease Control and Prevention. (1999). *HIV/AIDS surveillance report, 11*(2), 1–44. Retrieved from http://www.cdc.gov/hiv/stats/hasr1102.htm

Centers for Disease Control and Prevention. (2002a). 2002 sexually transmitted disease treatment guidelines [Electronic version]. *Morbidity & Mortality Weekly Report, 51*(RR-6), 1–81. Retrieved from http://www.cdc.gov/std/treatment/rr5106.pdf

Centers for Disease Control and Prevention (2002b). Sexual assault or abuse of children [Electronic version]. *Morbidity & Mortality Weekly Report, 51*(RR-6), 1–80. Retrieved from http://www.cdc.gov/std/treatment/8-2002TG.htm#Assault ofChildren

Christian, C. W., Lavelle, J., & Bell, L. M. (1999). Preschoolers with syphilis. [Electronic version]. *Pediatrics, 103*(1), e4. Retrieved from http://www.pediatrics. org/cgi/content/full/103/1/e4

Christian, C., Lavelle, J., DeJong, A., Loiselle, J., Brenner, L., & Joffe, M. (2000). Forensic evidence findings in prepubertal victims of sexual assault. *Pediatrics, 106*(1), 100–104.

Christian, C. W., Singer, M. L., Crawford, J. E., & Durbin, D. (1997). Perianal herpes zoster presenting as suspected child abuse. *Pediatrics, 99*(4), 608–610.

DeJong, A., & Finkel, M. (1990). Sexual abuse of children. *Current Problems in Pediatrics, 20,* 489–567.

Emans, S., Woods, E. R., Flagg, N. T., & Freeman, A. (1987). Genital findings in sexually abused, symptomatic and asymptomatic girls. *Pediatrics, 79*(5), 778–785.

Finkel, M. A., & DeJong, A. (2001). Medical findings in child sexual abuse. In R. M. Reece (Ed.), *Child abuse: Medical diagnosis and management* (2nd ed.). Philadelphia: Lippincott Williams & Wilkins.

Friedrich, W. N., Fisher, J., Broughton, D., Houston, M., & Shafran, C. R. (1998). Normative sexual behavior in children: A contemporary sample. [Electronic version]. *Pediatrics, 101*(4),1–8. Available at http://www.pediatrics.org/cgi/content/full/101/4/e9

Friedrich, W. N., Grambsch, P., Broughton, D., Kuiper, J., & Beilke, R. (1991). Normative sexual behavior in children. *Pediatrics, 88*(3), 456–464.

Gardner, J. (1992). Descriptive study of genital variation in healthy, nonabused premenarchal girls. *Journal of Pediatrics, 120*(2), 251–257.

Giardino, A. P., Finkel, M. A., Giardino, E. R., Seidl, T., & Ludwig, S. (1992). *A practical guide to the evaluation of sexual abuse in the prepubertal child.* Thousand Oaks, CA: Sage.

Gutman, L., Herman-Giddens, M., & Phelps, W. (1993). Transmission of human genital papillomavirus disease: Comparison of data from adults and children. *Pediatrics, 91*(1), 31–38.

Gutman, L. T., St. Claire, K. K., Weedy, C., Herman-Giddens, M. E., Lane, B. A., Niemyer, J. G., & McKinney, R. E., Jr. (1991). Human immunodeficiency virus transmission by child sexual abuse. *American Journal of Diseases of Children, 145*(2), 137–141.

Haka-Ikse, K., & Mian, M. (1993). Sexuality in children. *Pediatrics in Review, 14*(10), 401–407.

Hammerschlag, M. R. (1998). Sexually transmitted diseases in sexually abused children: Medical and legal implications. *Sexually Transmitted Infections, 74*(3), 167–174.

Heger, A., Emans, S. J., & Muram, D. (2000). *Evaluation of the sexually abused child* (2nd ed.). New York: Oxford University Press.

Heger, A., Ticson, L., Velasquez, O., & Bernier, R. (2002). Children referred for possible sexual abuse: Medical findings in 2,384 children. *Child Abuse & Neglect, 26*(6–7), 645–659.

Herman-Giddens, M. E. (1994). Vaginal foreign bodies and child sexual abuse. *Archives of Pediatrics & Adolescent Medicine, 148*(2), 195–200.

Hillman, D., & Solek-Tefft, J. (1988). *Spiders and flies: Help for parents and teachers of sexually abused children.* Lexington, MA: Lexington Books.

Ingram, D. L., Everett, V. D., Flick, L. A., Russell, T. A., & White-Sims, S. T. (1997). Vaginal gonococcal cultures in sexual abuse evaluations: Evaluation of selective criteria for preteenaged girls. *Pediatrics, 99*(6), 9–16.

Ingram, D., White, S. T., Lyna, P. R., Crews, K. F., Schmid, J. E., Everett, V. D., & Koch, G. G. (1992). *Gardnerella vaginalis* infection and sexual contact in female children. *Child Abuse & Neglect, 16*(6), 847–853.

Jenny, C., Kuhns, M. L., & Arakawa, F. (1987). Hymens in newborn female infants. *Pediatrics, 80*(3), 399–400.

Kadish, H. A., Schunk, J. E., & Britton, H. (1998). Pediatric male rectal and genital trauma: Accidental and nonaccidental injuries. *Pediatric Emergency Care, 14*(2), 95–98.

Koverola, C., & Friedrich, W. (2000). Psychological effects of child sexual abuse. In A. Heger, S. Emans, & D. Muram (Eds.), *Evaluation of the sexually abused child* (2nd ed.). New York: Oxford University Press.

Lindergren, M. L., Hansin, I. C., Hammett, T. A., Beil, J., Fleming, P. L., & Ward, J. W. (1998). Sexual abuse of children: Intersection with the HIV epidemic [Electronic version]. *Pediatrics, 102*(4), e46. Retrieved from http://pediatrics .aappublications.org/cgi/content/full/102/4/e46

McCann, J., & Voris, J. (1993). Perianal injuries resulting from sexual abuse: A longitudinal study. *Pediatrics, 91*(2), 390–397.

McCann, J., Voris, J., & Simon, M. (1992). Genital injuries resulting from sexual abuse: A longitudinal study. *Pediatrics, 89*(2), 307–317.

McCann, J., Wells, R., Simon, M., & Voris, J. (1990). Genital findings in prepubertal girls selected for nonabuse: A descriptive study. *Pediatrics, 86*(3), 428–439.

McCauley, J., Gorman, R., & Guzinski, G. (1986). Toluidine blue in the detection of perineal lacerations in pediatric and adolescent sexual abuse victims. *Pediatrics, 78*(6), 1039–1043.

Mogielnicki, N. P., Schwartzman, J. D., & Elliott, J. A. (2000). Perineal group A streptococcal disease in a pediatric practice. *Pediatrics, 106*(2), 276–281.

Muram, D. (1999). Treatment of prepubertal girls with labial adhesions. *Journal of Pediatric and Adolescent Gynecology, 12*(2), 67–70.

Muram, D., Arheart, K. L., & Jennings, S. G. (1999). Diagnostic accuracy of colposcopic photographs in child sexual abuse evaluations. *Journal of Pediatric and Adolescent Gynecology, 12*(2), 58–61.

Olafson, E., & Boat, B. W. (2000). Long-term management of the sexually abused child: Considerations and challenges. In R. M. Reece (Ed.), *Treatment of child abuse: Common ground for mental health, medical and legal practitioners.* Baltimore, MD: Johns Hopkins University Press.

Paradise, J. E., Rose, L., Sleeper, L. A., & Nathanson, M. (1994). Behavior, family function, school performance, and predictors of persistent disturbance in sexually abused children. *Pediatrics, 93*(3), 452–460.

Robinson, A. J. (1998). Sexually transmitted organisms in children and child sexual abuse. *International Journal of STD & AIDS, 9*(9), 501–511.

Ryan, G., & Blum, J. (1994). *Childhood sexuality: A guide for parents.* Denver, CO: Kempe Children's Center.

Schoentjes, E., Deboutte, D., & Friedrich, W. (1999). Child sexual behavior inventory: A dutch-speaking normative sample. *Pediatrics, 104*(4), 885–894.

Siegfried, E. C., & Frasier, L. D. (1997). Anogenital warts in children. *Advances in Dermatology, 12,* 141–167.

Sirotnak, A. P. (1994). Testing sexually abused children for sexually transmitted diseases: Who to test, when to test and why. *Pediatric Annals, 23*(7), 370–374.

Sirotnak, A. P. (2004). Sexually transmitted diseases in child sexual abuse. In A. P. Giardino & R. Alexander (Eds.), *Child maltreatment: A clinical guide and photographic reference* (3rd ed.). Philadelphia: Elsevier.

Summit, R. (1983). The child sexual abuse accommodation syndrome. *Child Abuse & Neglect, 7*(2), 177–193.

Swanston, H. Y., Tebbutt, J. S., O'Toole, B., & Oates, K. (1997). Sexually abused children 5 years after presentation: A case controlled study. *Pediatrics, 100*(4), 600–608.

11

Andrew P. Sirotnak
Joyce K. Moore
Jean C. Smith

Neglect

A school official calls the local CPS office with concerns of a student who might be neglected. He seems hungry and thin. He is poorly kept and looks and smells dirty. A medical provider voices concern about an infant who is not growing properly. Her mother seems distant and unconcerned. These and similar situations may be problems of neglect, the most prevalent form of child maltreatment in the United States today. These cases are difficult not only in their frequency but also in the obscurity of their diagnosis and variety of treatments. In our society, neglect is easily confused with poverty, ignorance, or parents or caregivers who are overwhelmed with other problems. The treatment of neglect is often protracted, combining the efforts of many different agencies and professionals. The medical provider will work with a CPS worker not only in treating the child's immediate problem but also in monitoring his growth and development through the course of his treatment. In this form of maltreatment, the combined efforts of many professionals are crucial.

In a national study of the incidence and prevalence of child abuse, the U.S. Department of Health and Human Services (2004) reports that in 2002 there were over twice as many neglect cases as physical and sexual abuse cases. In fact, of all cases of abuse and neglect that year, 60.5% involved neglect, while 28.5% involved physical or sexual abuse. The treatment of child neglect involves several different actions; many will require a worker's exclusive interaction with a medical provider. In this chapter, neglect is divided into the categories of failure to thrive, physical neglect, medical neglect, substance abuse and neglect, and safety neglect.

■ Failure to Thrive

Failure to thrive (FTT) is a nonspecific term applied to infants and young children who are failing to grow in a normal fashion. 💻 The diagnosis is most often made in children under the age of 3, in large part because these children both grow quickly and depend on parental assistance to meet even their most basic needs. Failure to thrive may be organic, meaning that the growth failure is caused by an underlying disease; nonorganic, meaning that the cause is psychosocial in origin and not due to underlying disease; or mixed, with organic and nonorganic factors interacting. To further complicate the matter, many children present with failure to thrive with an underlying medical condition complicated by a dysfunctional or maladaptive interaction with the parent or caregiver. It should be stated clearly that, ultimately, caloric intake is the issue. The calories are not being offered to the child, the child is not taking the offered calories, the child is using calories at an increased rate, or the calories are not being absorbed into the body from the gastrointestinal system. Medical and psychological evaluations are needed to clarify the pattern for each child.

Maternal deprivation has been one of the traditional explanations for nonorganic failure to thrive (NOFT). It has been long known that infants deprived of touch and interaction fail to grow and die at a very high rate. Similar patterns of growth failure have been observed in homes where the mother or caregiver may be present physically but, because of depression, substance abuse, or other problems, is unable or unwilling to provide for the infant's most basic needs.

The role of the whole family must also be considered in the assessment and, in particular, the management of children with NOFT (Drotar, 1991). The family's economic and social circumstances can affect the availability of food within the household. Even if the family has an external resource, such as the Women, Infants, and Children (WIC) Supplemental Food Program available to them, dysfunction or crisis may interfere with their actually obtaining the food or formula. Some families may alter the infant's diet because of well intentioned but erroneous beliefs about nutrition. For example, switching a 2-month-old infant from breast-feeding or formula to whole milk because of concerns of "colic" or "allergies" will result in insufficient calories for growth. Additionally, in disorganized or violent families, a consistent pattern of feeding or mealtimes is either nonexistent or frequently disrupted. Thus the infant does not receive consistent and regular caloric intake over time.

Disorders of attachment (bonding) between the parent, usually the mother, and the child typically manifest themselves after the first 3 months. ❑ At this time, the child needs responses and stimulation beyond simple clothing and food. While the FTT may be uncovered much later, growth failure secondary to lack of bonding can often be traced back to the second 3 months of life. It is important to understand that the child, by his nature or temperament, may be a major contributor to the parent-child interaction. Babies with colic or babies who sleep excessively and never cry, even when hungry, play a significant role in the way the parent or caregiver responds to them. Other contributing factors to attachment disorders include marital stress, financial distress, and prolonged separation between the mother and child at birth because of hospitalization, among others.

Later in the first year of life (after 6 months), the infant will begin to organize her own behaviors and develop more independence. A child who is thwarted in her endeavors may begin to battle her parents and assert control in those few areas open to her. Appetite is one of the few areas in which a parent cannot take control from the child. Sometimes children refuse to eat when not allowed to feed themselves. Parents who insist on maximum cleanliness during eating with constant interruptions to wipe the hands, face, plate, tray, and so on, may find that the child has little interest in food.

The consequences of FTT can be severe. The child, deprived of an adequate intake of calories, will break down fat and muscle to maintain growth of the brain. A child who is failing to thrive usually becomes abnormal with respect to low weight first. Subsequently, the child will slow in height growth. Small head size and delayed growth of the brain are seen as manifestations of severe and prolonged FTT. Long-term consequences in addition to small stature include mental retardation, behavior problems, learning difficulties, and a delay in language skills.

When to Suspect FTT

The warning signals of potential FTT may be apparent before the baby is ever born. If the medical provider is forewarned that a mother may have problems nurturing her child, precautions can be taken before, during, and after the birth to help reduce these chances. Therefore, it is essential that the CPS worker, as well as any medical providers involved with pregnant women, look for signals that may predict this form of neglect. A mother may need special attention if any of the following signals occur:

- She denies the pregnancy or fails to seek prenatal care until she is near term.
- She attempts a self-induced abortion.
- She fails to exhibit normal "nesting" behavior in the home in preparation for the child.
- She considers putting the child up for adoption, then changes her mind at the last moment.
- She has or has had an alcohol or drug problem.
- She has or has had a psychiatric disorder, including postpartum depression.
- She has no emotional support from the baby's father or from her family or friends.
- She has no financial support.
- She has a history of being abused or neglected herself.
- She is not able to hold, feed, or care for the child for an extended time following the birth.

Once the mother has given birth to her child, watch her behavior, or that of the caregiver, around the baby. Does she handle him roughly, like a package, or hold him close to her body? Does she talk and smile at him, or does she ignore him? A baby with NOFT may present with the following systems:

- A weak, pale, and listless appearance. Instead of smiling, cooing, and maintaining eye contact, the baby stares vacantly with the typical "radar gaze."

- The habit of sleeping in a bizarre, curled-up, fetal position, with fists tightly closed.

- Self-stimulatory behavior, such as rocking back and forth in bed as the baby lays on her back (creating bald patches on the back of the head) or banging her head repeatedly against her crib.

- Dirt and feces under long, ragged fingernails, severe diaper rash, a dirty face, hands, feet, and body.

- Obvious delays in developmental and motor function (see Appendix B).

Although some of these cases are due to lack of money or education and can be solved with financial aid and counseling, it is still imperative that all malnourished children be examined by a medical provider. Not only will he or she initiate treatment for the existing malnourishment, but the medical provider will also be able to monitor the child's growth and development in the future.

The Importance of the History in FTT

One of the most important tools in determining the course of treatment for FTT is a detailed, accurate history. The medical provider may ask specific questions about the feeding of the infant.

- Is the infant breast-fed? If so, were there any problems? If he or she is not breast-fed, what formula is used? How is it prepared? How often is the child fed?

- How is the infant fed? (Propping the bottle on a pillow in the crib not only suggests a lack of maternal contact but also the possibility that the child is not getting enough food.)

- How is the infant's appetite? How does the caregiver know when he or she is full? (Infants who drift to sleep during feeding may be listless and apathetic from lack of stimulation or malnourishment, or they may simply sleep a lot naturally.)

- Has the infant experienced any diarrhea or vomiting? How do his or her stools look? In addition, the history should seek to reveal any factors other than FTT that might be the cause of the child's malnutrition.

- How large are the infant's biological parents? (Genetics are often a contributing factor to a child's short stature.)

- Were there any problems in the pregnancy? Was the child born prematurely? Did the mother receive adequate prenatal care?

- Is the child on any medications?

- Has the child had any serious illnesses?

- How often does the infant sleep? Is he or she active during waking hours?

If the medical provider does not have access to the infant's mother or caregiver, the case history and report to the medical provider should include information such as that listed above. This may require contacting previous medical providers.

The medical provider will want to know of any factors in the psychosocial history that may indicate maternal difficulties. In addition to the high-risk factors listed above in the section "When to Suspect FTT," the CPS worker should attempt, with the medical provider, to determine the nature of the relationship between the mother or caregiver and the child. It is usually hard, in one conversation, to gain a true assessment of a caregiver's parenting skills or an infant's temperament. It may be helpful to ask the caregiver to describe a typical day with her infant. How often does she hold him? Do they play together? Is he a difficult child? What does she do when he cries? Many parents may purposely avoid holding or cuddling their baby for fear of spoiling him. Others may feel that their child is rejecting them, when in reality, they simply have a less responsive child.

Once NOFT is diagnosed, communication with the parents or caregivers is essential to uncover the fundamental cause of the problem and the steps to be taken to cure it. Obviously, the best time for the detection of these problems is before the infant is born. Unfortunately, many cases are not recognized until the infant is born and begins to suffer. From this pool of information, the CPS worker, the medical provider, other counselors, and educators can create a course of treatment and rehabilitation tailored for that family's needs. In some situations, placement outside the home may be the only solution.

The Medical Provider's Assessment

☐ Monitoring Height, Weight, and Head Circumference

In the initial assessment, the medical provider will obtain all previous measurements of height, weight, and head circumference and chart these on a standard growth curve (see Figures 11.1, 11.2, 11.3, and 11.4). ✒ These curves can compare the infant's weight and length to those of healthy infants nationwide. This will help the medical provider determine if a child

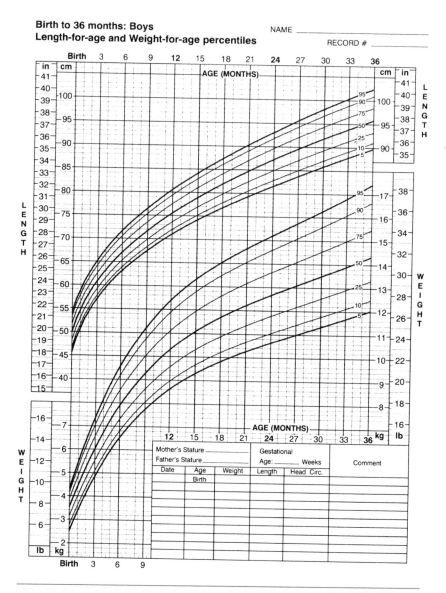

Figure 11.1. Growth Chart for Boys—Length and Weight. (Developed by the National Center for Health Statistics in collaboration with the National Center for Chronic Disease Prevention and Health Promotion)

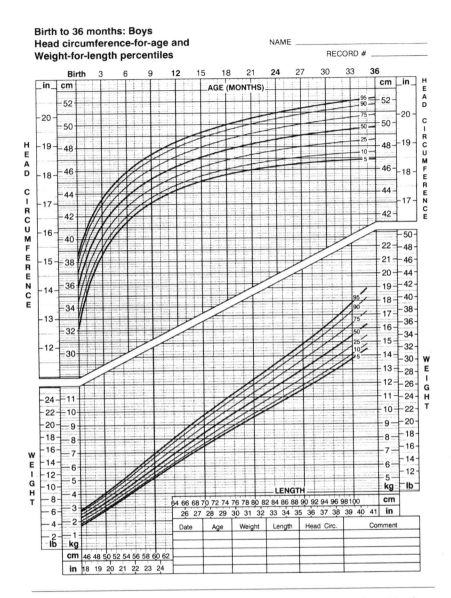

Figure 11.2. Growth Chart for Boys—Head Circumference. (Developed by the National Center for Health Statistics in collaboration with the National Center for Chronic Disease Prevention and Health Promotion)

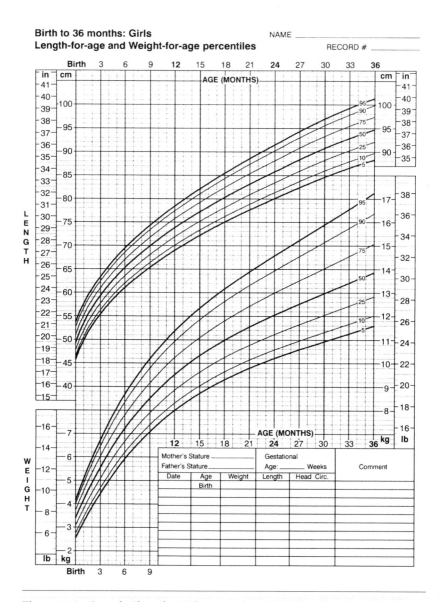

Figure 11.3. Growth Chart for Girls—Length and Weight. (Developed by the National Center for Health Statistics in collaboration with the National Center for Chronic Disease Prevention and Health Promotion)

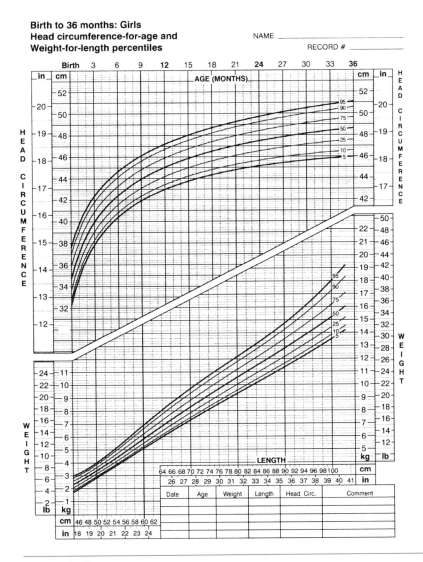

Figure 11.4. Growth Chart for Girls—Head Circumference. (Developed by the National Center for Health Statistics in collaboration with the National Center for Chronic Disease Prevention and Health Promotion)

is small because he or she is malnourished or small because that is his or her natural, inherited size. Obviously children's heights and weights will vary drastically according to their genetic makeup. Those whose parents are of short stature may be short themselves, with a weight in a lower percentile. If the concept of percentiles is difficult for the parent or caregiver to understand, the child's age-weight can be used. The idea that her 2-year-old is the size of a 1-year-old may be more understandable to a mother than the fact that the child's weight is in the 3rd percentile. In the assessment and treatment, the medical provider will want to monitor these measurements frequently (see the section entitled "Treatment of FTT"). The existence of the following conditions may arouse a medical provider's suspicion of FTT:

- A child whose percentile drops dramatically. For example, an infant who normally exists in the 90th percentile but drops to the 50th percentile.

- All children whose height and weight are below the 3rd percentile.

Growth charts frequently show "leveling" periods (or declines) at age periods that correspond with family stress periods. A common phenomenon in FTT children is "stair step" growth, which appears when the child is fed by some source other than the primary caregiver, perhaps by a visiting public health nurse or during a stay in the hospital. Infants who undergo drastic weight gain only during these periods, with no weight gain otherwise, are classic examples of NOFT. The following case history gives an example of this phenomenon.

Case Example

Daniel was identified at birth as being high risk for FTT because his mother was schizophrenic. The mother was taking her medications, seeing her psychiatrist regularly, and staying with her mother and sister at home.

Daniel's aunt accompanied him and his mother to the first two well-child visits. At about 6 months of age, Daniel's mother left her mother's and stayed sometimes with Daniel's father. She also stopped her medication and stopped seeing her psychiatrist.

Daniel's weight went from between the 25th and 50th percentiles to the 10th at 9 months of age. During this time, he did not lose weight, but it was apparent from the growth chart that he was not gaining appropriately.

When 10 months old, Daniel had actually lost weight and was less than the 5th percentile—he "fell off the growth chart" for his weight. At this time, the mother was "roaming" the streets with Daniel, sometimes staying with her mother or with Daniel's father. She would forget to feed herself as well as Daniel.

The medical provider contacted CPS, who helped the mother maintain residence with Daniel's father for supervision. Two more episodes of falling off the weight chart occurred when Daniel's mother left the father's home with Daniel on her own accord. Of importance, Daniel's height and head circumference at this time (about 12 months) also began to level off.

Placement in a local residential development center showed dramatic increase in weight gain back to the 25th percentile. The father was participating in care with the goal for Daniel to be discharged to his father's home and continue to have supervised care. Daniel's mother again assumed care in the father's home and again

Daniel fell off the growth curve for weight, height, and head circumference. Foster care placement was initiated and Daniel again regained to the 25th percentile.

☐ Laboratory Examination

The history and physical are the most important tools in assessing FTT. Laboratory studies can be kept to a minimum and a feeding trial in the hospital begun. The minimum studies include a complete blood count; serum electrolytes (an analysis of sodium, potassium, bicarbonate, blood urea nitrogen, and creatinine in the blood); a urinalysis; a stool examination for blood and fat; a thyroid test; a test for cystic fibrosis; and an X-ray of the chest. If any of these preliminary studies suggest an abnormality, they should be followed up with other tests to clarify the reason for the abnormality.

☐ Psychosocial Evaluation

Initiating social work and dietitian interviews about feeding as soon as the medical workup has begun, instead of waiting for the medical tests to return, is very helpful. This usually involves observing a feeding with the primary caregiver, which can help identify problems with the interactions early in the assessment.

▨ Differential Diagnoses

As in all abuse and neglect allegations, one of the medical provider's primary concerns will be to rule out any differential conditions, organic or nonorganic, that may be causing the failure to gain weight. Once these are diagnosed, the child may require special treatment, such as a limited diet, medications, or possibly surgery. It is important to assess the mother's or caregiver's ability to care for the child's special needs. At first, she may need help in feeding him, or taking him to and from the medical provider's office. If there are concerns about the mother's capabilities in caring for a sick child, it is important that these concerns are expressed to the medical provider, who can help assess the situation. Problems in the following organ systems can all lead to organic failure to thrive:

- Lungs (chronic infection)
- Kidneys (loss of protein or other chemicals in urine, failure of the kidney or infection)
- Intestines and stomach (chronic vomiting or poor absorption of nutrients)
- Liver (hepatitis, defect in using or processing nutrition)
- Hormone system (thyroid or adrenal gland dysfunction)
- Cardiac system (heart disease with chronic failure)

It is not uncommon for new mothers or caregivers to inadvertently feed babies incorrectly, perhaps giving the wrong dilutions of formula or not feeding them enough. Other mothers may have problems breast-feeding their infants. Some babies are simply poor feeders, with poor sucking reflexes. Although these cases are types of NOFT, they are not necessarily volitional neglect. It is crucial that these mothers work closely with a nurse or other medical provider to learn correct feeding and care of their babies.

Treatment of FTT

The first step in treating the FTT infant is determining her need for immediate hospitalization. In cases involving severe malnutrition, dehydration, or suspected physical abuse, the medical provider will probably hospitalize the child. Sometimes, hospitalization is a routine part of assessment. Unfortunately, many NOFT children do not gain weight until the second or third week of hospitalization or longer. In fact, some actually *lose* weight during hospitalization, perhaps due to the various testing procedures requiring fasting, along with the actual trauma of hospitalization and separation from the home. If infants are fed a high-calorie, high-protein diet and given lots of nurturing and stimulation yet still fail to gain weight, they most likely have a medical problem other than NOFT. Once NOFT is diagnosed, the goals of treatment include proper feeding, nurturing, and care, as described below.

Correct the Malnutrition

This is usually achieved by feeding the child a high-calorie, high-protein diet, with frequent feedings and close monitoring of his or her weight, height, and head circumference. Infants may be hospitalized to achieve maximal care, or feeding can be administered out of the home through visits by public health nurses or trips to the clinic for mother and child. Remember, it is *very* important that these infants have *constant* monitoring from day to day. Consider these points:

- Does the mother have adequate transportation to the clinic? If not, has this been arranged?

- Can the mother be relied on to keep her appointments? If not, hospitalizing the child should be considered.

- Can the mother understand, remember, and carry through with the proper feedings and nurturing of the child? If not, hospitalizing the child should be considered.

- Can the mother afford to buy appropriate food, vitamins, and medication for the child? If not, has this been taken care of?

- Does the mother have any help from family, partner, or friends? Those without support may need extra attention.

The CPS worker should give the medical providers and hospital social workers contact information with the explicit request that they call when the infant is released. CPS should begin services and monitoring immediately once the mother and child have returned home.

☐ **Provide Nurturing and Care**

Again, this must be provided either by the parents or substitutes. Parents will need support and assistance in adapting to the new styles of parenting required for their babies.

■ Physical Neglect

Children who suffer from lack of proper food, hygiene, clothing, or shelter may, in extreme circumstances, be classified as victims of physical neglect. These cases are often reported by teachers, caregivers, or neighbors, who interact with children on a day-to-day basis.

▦ Malnutrition

The effects of malnutrition are similar to those seen in FTT babies. The difference between these two conditions is mainly the age of the child. Malnutrition is part of failure to thrive, but a child may have grown so well as an infant, that, even when malnourished, he or she does not meet the growth failure criteria for FTT. In both situations, it is important to remember that the neglect may not be volitional and could be caused by poverty and/or lack of education. However, it is harder for a parent to make mistakes feeding older children, who, unlike infants, will tell them when they are hungry.

Children who are malnourished may be drowsy and/or pale due to anemia, which is a lack of red blood cells caused by iron deficiency. They may have extended abdomens and a generally skinny, undernourished appearance. They may have "pinched faces"; prominent ribs; wasted, "wrinkled" buttocks; and thin extremities. Some children may refuse to eat or experience vomiting and diarrhea.

The first step in diagnosing this problem will include a thorough assessment of the home environment and the reasons for the child's lack of food. It is a good idea to contact the child's school or day care to inquire about his or her eating habits. How much food and what does he or she bring to school? How long has the problem persisted? Are siblings in the same condition? (One child who suffers while his or her siblings do not is most likely the victim of intentional neglect.) Does he or she have bizarre eating habits, for example, eating from garbage cans or drinking from the toilet? The information from these questions will also be helpful to the medical provider in the diagnosis and treatment.

In these particular cases, the role of the medical provider is similar to his or her role in the diagnosis and treatment of FTT. First, he or she must confirm the existence of malnutrition and investigate for any differential medical problems. In the exam, the medical provider will chart the child's height, weight, and head circumference on a growth curve. It will be important to keep track of these measurements from day to day. It may be helpful to have the school nurse keep these records. The medical provider may put the child on a special high-calorie and/or high-protein diet. If, following treatment, the child still does not gain weight, he or she may require more testing and/ or removal from the home.

Hygiene

Sometimes schools or day cares will express concern that a child is always dirty or that he smells like urine, feces, or dirty feet. Some children may be covered in insect bites or have continual infestation with lice. Infants may have severe diaper rash or "cradle cap," a condition in which flaky, crusty skin appears on the scalp, face, and head. Unfortunately, one of the most harmful aspects of bad hygiene is the ostracization children experience as peers inevitably tease them.

There are no set standards for when a child is "too" dirty. Obviously, cases in which the child's health is at risk should be given strict attention, but usually the course of action is that of education, both for the parents and the child. It is best to instruct parents and caregivers to bathe the child at least twice a week. CPS should attempt to remain uninvolved in the cases of dirty children unless all other resources, such as voluntary agencies' services through the department of social services, health clinics, and public health nurses, have been depleted. Severe conditions that do not improve after repeated attempts to offer help to the family might, in some circumstances, be a red flag for chronic neglect. Any conditions such as severe diaper rash, lice, impetigo, scabies, or severe insect bites should be examined by a medical provider who can not only treat the child but also help educate the parent or caregiver.

Psychosocial Short Stature/Psychosocial Dwarfism

A severe form of FTT has also been called abuse dwarfism, emotional deprivation dwarfism, and psychosocial growth failure, in addition to psychosocial short stature or psychosocial dwarfism.

Psychosocial short stature (PSS) is a rare disorder of short stature and growth failure of infancy, childhood, and adolescence that is seen in association with emotional deprivation and/or a pathological psychosocial environment. Often a disturbed relationship exists between child and caregiver. Psychological factors of emotional deprivation have been shown to cause the transient growth hormone deficiency seen in these children. Nutritional or caloric deprivation alone is not always a major causal factor. This type of severe deprivation of nutrition, nurturing, and care may be sensationalized by the media and unfortunately those stories are often accurate in the description of the physical and emotional neglect that leads to this rare condition.

Several pediatric endocrinologists, specialists in the hormone systems that regulate puberty and growth, have researched and categorized several now generally accepted subtypes. Specific diagnostic and therapeutic interventions are recommended for these children.

The pathophysiology is complex in that it involves nutritional, psychological, and environmental factors. Endocrine disturbances of growth hormone, secondary thyroid dysfunction, and growth hormone levels are abnormal. Linear growth—that is, height—is obviously delayed. Growth arrest lines (lines seen on x-rays that indicate bones have stopped growing) are seen in long bones and temporary widening of cranial sutures has been reported. Sleep disturbance and abnormal pain tolerance are seen. Cognitive functioning may be preserved but psychological outcomes associated with emotional maltreatment can be severe.

There are three subtypes based on age and other factors.

Type I. Age of onset is during infancy with usually gradually severe failure to thrive (FTT), with no bizarre behaviors, but often depressed affect exhibited by children. They have normal growth hormone secretion. There is usually no overt parental rejection and this may be considered a severe form of infant FTT. There is an unknown responsiveness to growth hormone treatment. Hospitalization for improved nutrition is needed.

Type II. Age of onset is greater or equal to three years; some of these children have FTT. They usually exhibit bizarre behaviors and are very often depressed. There is decreased or absent growth hormone secretion. Significant parental rejection or pathology is evident. There is minimal responsiveness to growth hormone therapy. Hospitalization for improved nutrition may be needed and removal from the disturbed caregiver is typically a mandatory part of treatment.

Type III. Age of onset is either in infancy or during older childhood but children are not usually FTT and do not usually exhibit bizarre behaviors. They have normal growth hormone secretion and have no overt parental rejection. There is, however, significant response to the administration of growth hormone so this is a part of treatment (Blizzard & Bulatovic, 1996; Green, Campbell, & David, 1984).

The following historical factors are important for a pediatrician and endocrinologist in making the diagnosis of classic PSS.

- A presence of history suggesting a severe psychological disturbance in a child with bizarre behaviors around food and water acquisition, despite seemingly adequate food calorie and fluid intake and its usual availability (e.g., excessive eating and drinking, hoarding food, gorging and vomiting, eating from garbage bins, drinking from toilets, and stealing food).

- Sleep disturbances (insomnia or night wandering); overtly abnormal behaviors (withdrawal, apathy, anxiety, irritability, temper tantrums, extreme shyness, "accident prone," self-injurious).

- Developmental delays (speech, cognitive, psychomotor retardation).

- A caregiver who appears to have psychopathology and the relationship with the child seems abnormal. Mothers can be depressed, anxious, have personality disorders, be victims of domestic violence, have substance abuse or an addiction, or marital instability (usually the spouse or father of child is absent).

- Abnormal endocrine function (thyroid, growth hormone, puberty hormones) that normalizes when the child is removed from the unsafe and non-nurturing environment.

- Malnutrition or inadequate caloric intake are not demonstrated to be the primary cause of growth failure.

- Diagnosis is confirmed by the removal of the child from the environment and demonstration of catch-up growth, improvements in behaviors, and normalization of the hormonal disturbances.

The physical examination of an infant or child with PSS will show a short child and may be mistaken for that of growth hormone deficiency from other causes. Many, but not all, children will be underweight for height and a few may be overweight for height as well as short for chronological age. A distended abdomen and enlarged liver and spleen may be seen.

A skin exam may show signs of abuse (scars, burns, pattern injuries). The medical providers will order a number of tests to assess malnutrition, to rule out other organic causes of severe growth failure, and will possibly request some x-rays to look for growth arrest in the bones and rule out tumors in the brain that can affect the pituitary that is important in growth. Some hormone levels take a significant time to analyze and get results from a lab. These children must be seen by pediatric specialists and always warrant a psychological evaluation.

Treatment typically begins with removing the child from the dangerous or non-nurturing environment. This intervention, with appropriate mental health treatment, improves many of the child's abnormal behaviors. Other medical and hormone therapies, depending on the results of testing, may be needed. Therapy with a child psychiatrist or psychologist may include medication. Return to the previous environment has been demonstrated to result in rapid deceleration of the improved growth rate.

Addressing the psychosocial pathology in the child's environment *must* occur if returning the child to the previous caregiver is considered. Many such caregivers have their own histories of abuse or neglect and may require intensive mental health therapy to be able to parent effectively. Court-ordered treatment plans should be mandatory. The outcome of this condition depends on early identification, the severity of the malnutrition, the treatability of the parental pathology and improvement of the behavioral disturbances, and the provision of a continued safe and nurturing environment for the child. For example, a parent with a severe history of abuse as a child with no mental health treatment and who has limited cognitive functioning and chronic substance abuse is certainly at high risk for treatment failure. Returning a child to this environment without demonstrated involvement in and improvement with intensive therapy is a risk. Careful monitoring of growth and development and emotional health, whether reunited with the parent in treatment or in foster care, is crucial.

■ Medical Neglect

A young asthmatic boy is repeatedly brought to the emergency room only when his condition is so severe that he immediately goes into intensive care. The parents of a girl with congenital cataracts refuse to consent to eye surgery, which would prevent her eventual blindness. When a child with a treatable serious chronic disease or handicap has frequent hospitalizations or significant deterioration because the parents ignore medical recommendations, court-enforced supervision or even foster placement may be required. Some parents may refuse treatment based on religious grounds. Others are simply anxious and afraid about a disease and treatment that they do not understand.

In such circumstances, the primary goal is identifying and nullifying the parents' specific concerns about treatments or hospitalization. Although the medical provider will be the most knowledgeable source of information, the parents may relate more comfortably with the CPS worker; as a liaison between the parents and the medical provider, the worker may play the most important role in this process. For good results, both the worker and the medical provider should attempt to include both parents in the decision process. When a medical provider feels that a child's need for treatment is severe enough to justify a court order, the worker will need to work with him or her in this endeavor.

Barton Schmitt (1981) breaks this form of neglect into clear categories that include serious acute illnesses, life-threatening chronic diseases, disabling diseases, and handicapping chronic diseases. The CPS worker may experience all of these in working with children, and although each case invariably differs from another, the worker should be familiar with these problems.

Serious Acute Illnesses

These are the cases usually considered emergencies. Examples are parents who refuse to allow a blood transfusion to save a child in shock or parents who refuse to admit a severely dehydrated child to the hospital. When parents consistently refuse to sign a consent form in these circumstances, the court must intervene and do so quickly. Also, diseases that endanger the public safety can evoke a court order if the parents refuse treatment.

Life-Threatening Chronic Diseases

Chronic diseases are long-lasting ones, such as asthma or diabetes mellitus. Sometimes children with diseases such as these experience frequent medical problems because their parents or caregivers ignore medical recommendations for home treatment.

Chronic illnesses are added stresses for families, but about two-thirds of these families will cope with such stress either very well or adequately. The remaining one-third who cannot adapt adequate coping strategies to care for their chronically ill child will need identification and support to ensure their child receives appropriate care.

Disabling or Handicapping Chronic Diseases

These cases involve children who will develop permanent disfigurements or disabilities if they do not receive treatment. Examples are children with congenital glaucoma or cataracts, which will eventually cause blindness if surgery is not performed. Although parents eventually can be persuaded of the need for surgery in these conditions, those who persist in their refusal will eventually need to be taken to court, which can usually be swayed to intervene once the risks and benefits of treatment are reviewed.

Substance Abuse and Neglect

Parental addiction to alcohol, cocaine, heroin, and other drugs has led to one of the more complex and devastating problems in child neglect and abuse. Recent studies have identified parental substance abuse as occurring in 40% to 60% of the cases of child maltreatment. The alarming rate of substance abuse occurring during pregnancy has been well documented during the last decade, with estimated illegal drug use identified in 10% to 24% of all pregnancies. The problem of parental addiction thus encompasses all aspects of child maltreatment: physical abuse; sexual abuse; physical, emotional, and medical neglect; and, additionally, the potential for harm to the infant during the prenatal period. For more information on this issue, see chapter 13.

Pregnancy and Substance Abuse

Pregnant women who are addicted to drugs or alcohol are at far greater risk for a range of medical problems that adversely affect the health of the mother and the developing fetus. Drug-dependent mothers have an increase in obstetrical problems such as poor nutrition, anemia, and infections, including tuberculosis. Often prostitution is used to provide money to support this habit, thus creating an even greater risk to contract sexually transmitted diseases and HIV infection in particular, leading to serious problems for both the mother and unborn child. Cocaine use, which constricts blood vessels, has been documented to lead to a variety of major obstetrical complications such as infections of the amniotic fluid and sac, premature rupture of the membranes (which protect the fetus from infections), abruptio placenta (an early separation of the placenta leading to loss of blood and oxygen supply to the fetus), intrauterine growth retardation, and premature birth.

The pregnant addicted woman is less likely to seek or adequately follow through on routine prenatal care although their pregnancies are usually high-risk and could benefit most from even closer care than other pregnancies. In addition to the direct risks to their own health such as infections, high blood pressure, malnutrition, and bleeding, pregnant addicted women are more likely to be physically abused themselves. All of these complications can lead to a high rate of spontaneous abortions and, for those infants who reach delivery, serious problems. Mothers who do not receive prenatal care are more likely to give birth to low birth-weight infants and these babies are more likely than a normal birth-weight infant to die during the first four weeks of life.

Because these infants are born prematurely, have low birth weights, and acquire infections at birth and prenatally from the mother, they are at increased risk for all the problems related to these conditions, such as requiring mechanical ventilation and oxygen to breathe; bleeding into the brain from the rupture of small, fragile blood vessels; overwhelming infections needing antibiotics; and an inability to suck mothers' breasts effectively, leading to artificial feeding. Infants exposed prenatally to cocaine, heroin, and methadone can experience life-threatening withdrawal symptoms shortly after birth so that medical providers now are constantly on the lookout for problems in the delivery room unique to the resuscitation of such a baby. In the immediate newborn period, infants exposed to cocaine exhibit problems with irritability, making these babies difficult to console.

When pregnant mothers drink, the alcohol can cause problems described as fetal alcohol syndrome. The unique infant traits associated with fetal alcohol syndrome are as follows:

- An unusual face, including droopy eyelids and smaller-than-usual eye slits
- Active alcohol withdrawal symptoms after birth
- Congenital heart defects
- Low birth weight and sustained smallness in size for age
- Moderate mental retardation

The negative impact of drugs and alcohol on the development of infants is well documented when problems such as those discussed above exist. Sudden infant death syndrome is reported to be higher in cocaine-exposed babies, but other studies contradict this. Some infants can become "boarder babies" and are essentially abandoned, or their mothers die from an AIDS-related infection or obstetrical complications associated with substance abuse.

There is still much controversy in the studies of long-term impact of prenatal exposure to substances such as cocaine, if the infant is lucky enough not to have immediate problems. Most current research points to the powerful impact of the environment of substance-abusing caregivers on the development of the child, making it difficult, if not impossible, to separate prenatal effects from those caused postnatally.

Prenatal screening for substance abuse can be useful to identify high-risk pregnancies and offer close care and support to the pregnant mother. Unfortunately, a major obstacle to obtaining prenatal care is the lack of programs designed specifically for addicted pregnant mothers. Most drug treatment programs have focused on males and not on the unique issues of women and their special needs during pregnancy. Another obstacle to obtaining prenatal care is the fear of retribution and the all too frequent desire to punish the pregnant woman.

Comprehensive programs that can identify the addicted mother, offer drug addiction treatment, and provide necessary support services are most likely to meet the unique needs of substance-abusing mothers. These services would include adequate housing, counseling for sexual and domestic violence, child care, health care (including family planning and well-child care, in addition to prenatal care), education, training, and employment.

The Family and Substance Abuse

The combined stresses of substance dependency and demands of infants and children for routine care can create a volatile environment in which physical neglect or abuse is very likely to occur. One study of parental substance abuse and child maltreatment showed alcohol abuse to be significantly related to physical abuse but not to sexual abuse, while cocaine abuse was the opposite, with a significant association to sexual abuse but not to physical abuse. Severe neglect can occur by the actual physical absence of the parent because of drug-seeking behaviors, prostitution, or incarceration. The drug addiction and participation in trafficking create in both the child and family's social environment a volatile climate with frequent exposures to actual violence. Even if the parents themselves are not drug abusers, child development can be impacted by the direct observation of shootings, knifings, and other violent acts and by changes in caregiving practices such as restricting the child's outdoor activities.

Parents who are high on drugs or alcohol cannot provide the very basic needs of infants and children for food, hygiene, and sleep, let alone respond to the more subtle cues for physical and social interactive nurturing. Some addicted parents may also have concurrent personality disorders magnifying the distortions of parent-child interactions.

Addicted parents have impaired judgment and can consciously or unconsciously "use" their children to help deal with their addiction problems. This can be as obvious as prostituting a child for money to buy drugs to the more subtle plan of a mother to breast-feed her baby with the mistaken assumption it will help her "stay clean."

Most substance-abusing families have a multitude of other problems that create an environment of high risk for child maltreatment. Current research would indicate that continued parental addiction easily can prevent or undo other interventions. Thus there is a real need to provide effective treatment programs for addicted parents and provide protection for children whose parents refuse or fail at these treatment efforts. See chapter 13 for more information on this topic.

■ Safety Neglect

Barton Schmitt defines safety neglect as any situation where an injury occurs because of a gross lack of supervision. This might involve leaving poisons, open heaters, knives, or guns within the child's reach. Repeated dog bites by the family dog also represent a dangerous home environment. Obviously, every child will sustain minor injuries or traumas during the childhood years. No parent can watch his or her infant or young child every minute of the day. It is when these accidents are repeated and severe that medical providers and CPS workers should become concerned about neglect. It is estimated that before the age of 3, children have not developed an adequate sense of safety awareness; normally, children below this age should not be allowed the freedom and independence that may lead to serious injuries.

Parents will need education on child safety; they may need financial help in making their home "accident proof"; for example, placing screens around open heaters, putting plugs in electrical outlets, using smoke detectors, or placing safety catches on cabinets. One indicator of safety neglect is the parents' or caregivers' concern for the child. Watch how they handle the child and react to his injury. If a baby who has fallen off the sofa is brought to the medical provider and then left unattended on the examining table, one should be concerned about the parents' ability or desire to protect that child.

Ideally, if a medical provider reports an injury that he or she considers a product of gross safety neglect, the CPS worker would contact any medical providers that might have records of previous accidents. If the child is new to the agency, it may be necessary to look out of the county or even to another state for this information. This time-consuming and often frustrating process may seem meaningless at times, but it may uncover critical problems that need to be treated. In the history, ask the parents or caregivers questions about *specific* injuries that might have occurred:

• Has the child had any previous fractures or broken bones? If so, what were the circumstances surrounding each event?

• Has the child ever accidentally ingested a poisonous substance? If so, what was the substance and where was it located in the home? What precautions have been taken to avoid this problem in the future?

• Has the child had any previous burns? How severe were they? How exactly did they happen?

• What other accidents has the child had and how serious were they?

In summary, child neglect is the most prevalent form of child maltreatment. Its presentations are varied both in form and severity and can be present with any other form of maltreatment. CPS workers must be as aggressive in the identification and treatment of child neglect as with all other forms of child abuse.

References

Blizzard, R. M., & Bulatovic, A. (1996). Syndromes of psychosocial short stature. In F. Lifshitz (Ed.), *Pediatric endocrinology* (3rd ed., pp. 83–93). New York: M. Dekker.

Drotar, D. (1991). The family context of nonorganic failure to thrive. *American Journal of Orthopsychiatry, 16,* 23–24.

Green, W. H., Campbell, M., & David, R. (1984). Psychosocial dwarfism: A critical review of the evidence. *Journal of the American Academy of Child Psychiatry, 23*(1), 39–48.

Schmitt, B. (1981). Child neglect. In N. Ellerstein (Ed.), *Medical aspects of child abuse and neglect* (pp. 297–306). New York: John Wiley.

U.S. Department of Health and Human Services, Administration for Children, Youth, and Families. (2004). *Child maltreatment 2002.* Washington, DC: U.S. Government Printing Office.

12 Andrew P. Sirotnak

Emotional Maltreatment

Emotional maltreatment can be considered either neglectful or abusive, and like other forms of maltreatment it can occur within a pattern or range of severity and duration and be associated with other forms of abuse and neglect. Thus, this form of maltreatment has often been hard to define, to recognize, and to address with CPS involvement. This section will suggest a framework of assessment and treatment for the CPS worker based on child development and literature from experts in this area.

■ Definition and Incidence

The definition of emotional maltreatment under the Federal Child Abuse Prevention and Treatment Act (CAPTA) is a repeated pattern of caregiver behavior or an extreme incident of behavior that conveys to children that they are worthless, flawed, unloved, unwanted, endangered, or only of value in meeting another's need. Psychological maltreatment includes acts of commission as well as acts of omission (CAPTA, 1974). In state statutes, emotional maltreatment is defined in many different ways; therefore, it is advisable to review the exact wording of the state's definition. 🖳

The true incidence of emotional maltreatment is impossible to determine. The U.S. Department of Health and Human Services (USDHHS) report on child maltreatment (2005) indicates a rate of 0.6/1,000 for emotional abuse, compared to a rate of 15/1,000 for all other forms of child maltreatment. Emotional maltreatment by itself consistently accounts for less than 10% of all reports of confirmed child abuse in the United States annually according to USDHHS data. Data on the age and sex of victims follow the national child abuse data in that younger children, particularly under age 5 are at increased risk due to the many developmental stages that encompass these years. Beyond these first several years, however, emotional maltreatment also occurs, often along with other forms of abuse and neglect. For example, the infant or young child whose basic needs are ignored and fails to thrive physically is likely also neglected emotionally as basic maternal interactions that promote attachment, bonding, and social development of the infant are disturbed. The young child who is repeatedly subjected to sexual abuse by a nonprotective parent is at risk for psychological damage and this, by definition in many states, is considered emotional maltreatment.

Emotional abuse and neglect of children or emotional maltreatment has *at its core* parental behavior that has the impact of an injury to the child's psychological and emotional health. Emotional maltreatment, therefore, can be considered to underlie *all* types of abuse and neglect.

Many theorists have divided emotional maltreatment into two areas: emotional abuse (including verbal or emotional assaults and threatened harm) and emotional neglect (including inadequate affection, refusal to provide adequate care, or knowingly allowing maladaptive behavior such as delinquency) (O'Hagan, 1993). The more commonly suggested definition concludes that emotional abuse is not an isolated event but rather a pattern of psychically destructive behavior that may include rejecting, isolating, terrorizing, ignoring, and corrupting (Garbarino, Guttman, & Wilson Seeley, 1986). Each form is listed below with examples.

Rejecting

Rejection involves those behaviors that constitute abandonment. "Mild" rejection is confined to isolated incidents, while "moderate" and "severe" rejections are more frequent and generalized. During infancy this may involve abandonment or refusing to return smiles and vocalization. For older children, it might involve leaving the child home from family outings, belittling or scapegoating the child, or subjecting him or her to verbal humiliation, degrading comments, and inappropriate criticism.

Isolating

Isolating involves those behaviors that rob the child of his or her opportunity to develop normal social relations. These parents or caregivers teach their children to avoid social contact beyond the parent-child relationship, sometimes punishing the child for making social overtures to other children or adults. A mother may isolate her child because of mental illness, violence in the home, or the occurrence of an abnormal attachment or enmeshment. The child who is viewed as "vulnerable" because of special needs or chronic illness may be at risk of being isolated by a parent.

Terrorizing

Parents or caregivers who terrorize their children may intentionally stimulate intense fear by threatening them with extreme or sinister punishment, thus creating an environment of unpredictable threat. During infancy this may involve teasing and scaring the child or reacting with extreme responses to infantile behavior. For older children, it may involve intense direct threats to the child's everyday sense of security, safety, and well-being. This may be especially pertinent in situations of a mother and a boyfriend in the home where he is in care of the children, exposes the family to violence or threat of harm, or uses harsh or physical discipline. A battered mother may allow this to happen or ignore the events intentionally, or such events may be out of her control. Regardless, the behavior is emotionally abusive and physical or sexual abuse by a person in the home should be a consideration.

Ignoring

Ignoring refers to parents or caregivers who are so psychologically preoccupied with themselves and their surroundings that they are unable to respond to the child's psychological needs. These parents or caregivers may erect a "barrier of silence" in the child's presence and refuse to engage in conversation or show interest in the child's daily activities, concentrating on other relationships, which displaces the child as an object of affection. Again, a parent may be aware of such behavior or have related problems such as drug abuse, mental illness, or indiscriminate poor judgment in choosing relationships. A common example of how neglect and emotional maltreatment intersect would be a parent who chooses to engage in drug use, engages in promiscuous sexual activity to support drug use, and ignores the child as part of his or her personal life and responsibility.

Corrupting

Corrupting refers to parental behaviors that "mis-socialize" children and reinforce them in antisocial or deviant patterns, especially in the areas of aggression, sexuality, or substance abuse. These behaviors tend to make the child unfit for normal social experience (Garbarino, Guttman, & Wilson Seeley, 1986). The sexually inappropriate environment, the parent who does not protect a child from or ignore the outcry of sexual abuse, the acceptance of a culture of violence in the home, or substance abuse in the home—all are examples of this form of emotional maltreatment. For example, the child of a methamphetamine-abusing parent who can describe how the drug is cooked or how the parents or caregivers engage in sexual activity while doing drugs lives in a "corrupting environment."

Yet another way of looking at emotional maltreatment is to define it broadly as psychological maltreatment and then subcategorize emotional abuse. Psychological maltreatment is a term preferred by others as it attempts to distinguish between emotional abuse and psychological abuse. *Emotional* abuse is seen as the sustained, repetitive, inappropriate emotional response to the child's own expression of emotion and its accompanying expressive behavior. *Psychological* abuse is the sustained, repetitive, inappropriate behavior that damages or substantially reduces the creative and developmental potential of crucially important mental faculties of a child; these include intelligence, memory, recognition, perception, attention, language, and moral development (O'Hagan, 1993).

In consideration of cultural practices that may be misconstrued as emotional abuse, another definition qualifies that emotional abuse involves acts or omission by parents that jeopardize "the development of self esteem, of social competence, of the capacity for intimacy, of positive and healthy interpersonal relationships" and recognizes some child-rearing practices that may seem harmful to other cultures (Garbarino & Gilliam, 1980). For example, a culture may have historically considered having an adolescent male attempt survival on his own in a remote setting to encourage independence and strength. A child who is forced to kneel for hours at a time praying and fasting might be considered abusive by some but a cultural norm for the child's family by others. Finally, CPS workers should also be aware of a set of definitions from the American Professional Society on the Abuse of Children (APSAC) that are practical and helpful summary guidelines. Psychological maltreatment is outlined in six forms: spurning, exploiting/corrupting, terrorizing, denying emotional responsiveness, isolating, and denying mental health care, medical care, or education (APSAC, 1995).

■ High-Risk Factors in Emotional Maltreatment

As in all forms of abuse and neglect, there are certain conditions that indicate that families are at high risk for emotional maltreatment. Specific areas of family functioning as they relate to a child's emotional, physical, and cognitive development may be used as a guide to identify those risk factors. In general, remember that provision of a child's physical needs, social relationships, and developmental and emotional needs are vital to overall health. Families may harm children by either oversupplying or undersupplying these important tasks (Hamerman & Ludwig, 2000).

Situations specific to the family dysfunction or societal pressures impacting the family are both important. Risk factors may include an unwanted pregnancy, having a child for unrealistic reasons, adolescent first-time parents, adults whose needs were not met in their own childhood, alcoholism, substance abuse, domestic violence, mental illness, separation, and divorce.

Factors in the child's environment that are a risk for emotional maltreatment include social isolation, poverty, unemployment, poor housing conditions, crime, and limited or no access to community services and resources. Parental characteristics that can be risk factors are similar to those noted as risk for any form of abuse, and include mental illness, depression, alcohol or substance abuse problems, lack of knowledge about child development, disagreement over parenting styles between parents, strict physical discipline, marital problems, low self-esteem, and the parent's own history of abuse or neglect as a child. Finally, the child who has special needs, is developmentally disabled, or has behavioral or emotional problems already is at increased risk for emotional maltreatment.

■ Parental Assessments

A number of professional psychological assessment tools are available that can be of diagnostic help when requesting an evaluation of parents or caregivers in the context of emotional maltreatment. Several assessment tools of parental functioning (listed below) have been developed that can be administered by psychologists or social workers trained to use them. Each is focused at operationalizing psychological abuse in ways that can be measured reliably (Hamerman & Ludwig, 2000).

- The Parenting Risk Scale (PRS) is an interviewing tool that assesses parents in five key areas: emotional availability, control, psychological disturbances, knowledge base, and commitment (Mrazek, Mrazek, & Kinnert, 1995).

- The Psychological Maltreatment Rating Scale (PMRS) evaluates mother-child dyads and is helpful in discerning between maltreating parents and comparison parents (Brassard, Hart, & Hardy, 1993).

- The Child Abuse and Trauma Scale (CAT) is another quantitative index of the frequency and extent of various negative experiences (Sanders & Becker-Lausen, 1995).

■ Diagnosis of Emotional Maltreatment

Although the signs and symptoms listed below often present to a primary care provider, unless other forms of child abuse are evident or glaring family risk factors are uncovered, the general practice medical provider may not recognize the emotionally maltreated or abused child. As children grow older, unless they are chronically ill they do not visit the medical provider very often, except to obtain a school physical. Schoolteachers, not medical providers, will report neglect more frequently and this is an opportunity for CPS workers to evaluate for the possibility of emotional maltreatment. It is critical, therefore, that CPS workers have a framework for definition and have an identification or "diagnosis" of the signs and symptoms of emotional maltreatment. ▣

▦ Core Principles for the Evaluation of Emotional Maltreatment

- Evaluation of the child-family relationship in terms of the above areas of the physical and social environment and family functioning that relate to the child's development

- Knowledge of the child's developmental age and the expected milestones

- Description of the form of emotional maltreatment and the suspected severity and chronicity

- Assessment for other forms of child abuse including physical harm and sexual abuse

- Critical and careful assessment of parental functioning and the ability to quantify the parents' or caregivers' ability to meet the child's needs

- An evaluation of relatives or kinship providers

Signs and Symptoms of Emotional Maltreatment in the Child

The signs and symptoms of the emotionally abused or neglected child are quite variable and are similar to those seen in other forms of abuse and neglect. They may vary according to the age, sex, and developmental stage of the child. They may depend on or be influenced by the type, severity, and chronicity of the family dysfunction and abuse.

Most important, CPS workers should take the time to listen to the child and to the peers, teachers, and caregivers that know the child. A child may have and express feelings of inadequacy, isolation, of being unwanted, or simply feel unloved. Expressions of low self-esteem and unworthiness are common and certainly are warning signs.

The response of a male or female child may be one of outward hostility, aggression, delinquency, or other behavioral disturbances. These may set the child up for physical abuse and neglect as well. Inward responses may include depression, self-destructive behaviors, withdrawal, and then self-harm and suicide ideation or attempts. Physical complaints are common such as vague somatic complaints (headaches, stomachaches, and nervous habits), sleep disturbances, or eating and feeding disorders. For example, a 6-year-old boy living in a home with a drug-addicted or alcoholic parent who is ignored by the parent, never praised for his school work, and isolated from peers may show signs of either depression or aggression. Likewise, a 10-year-old girl who is overweight, teased by her stepfather, and degraded by her mother may become depressed, self-destructive, and express low self-esteem to a teacher or become a target for sexual abuse by a grooming predator.

Finally, a child removed from parents or caregivers for other forms of abuse and neglect may exhibit these behaviors or make such statements. Consideration of emotional maltreatment as a "co-morbid finding" is possible only if the CPS worker remembers a framework of definition and presentation of this form of child abuse.

■ Treatment for and the Outcome of Emotional Maltreatment

It is impossible to construct a complete list of sequelae or outcomes of emotional maltreatment. Individual children are all unique in their sensitivity and vulnerability to this form of maltreatment. While some children will manifest clear psychological and/or physical delays, others may not react at all. The range of necessary assessment and treatment is beyond the scope of this text. The following are helpful core principles in treatment planning for the family and child where emotional maltreatment is a major concern.

- A thoughtful, stepwise approach of treatment should always begin with an attempt to stop all forms of child maltreatment; to make efforts at normalizing the child's environment, growth, and development; and to address the damage that has been done by the emotional maltreatment and/or other abuse. Identification and treatment of other forms of child maltreatment (physical abuse, sexual abuse, physical or nutritional neglect) is crucial.

- Difficulty in definition and identification of emotional maltreatment makes it difficult to recommend a specific mode or strategy for treatment and to identify which is most effective. Few treatments have been systematically or carefully evaluated.

- Family therapy, individual parent and child therapy, therapeutic preschools and other day treatment–type schools for older children, and group therapy are all models that can be applied in either the short term or long term. Understanding the cultural background of a family is important in designing any treatment or intervention.

- Underlying parental pathology absolutely must be identified, diagnosed, and adequately treated. Mental illness, substance abuse or addiction, personality disorders, and behaviors that effect interpersonal and family conflict resolution are key components. Any lack of cooperation over time with diagnosis and treatment should be considered carefully, and issues of treatability, permanency, and continued protection of the child might lead to relinquishment counseling or termination of parental rights.

- The ultimate goal is to help children who are growing older understand the effects of emotional maltreatment on their childhood development and, eventually, to protect their own functioning as adults and as potential parents.

Emotional maltreatment is particularly difficult to define and treat but should be considered in any situation of child maltreatment. The impact of emotional maltreatment on children can be just as potent as a severe physical injury and thus warrants immediate and sustained intervention. Safety from mental injury is as important as safety and protection from physical harm. Understanding this multidimensional form of maltreatment will result in better outcomes for children and families.

References

American Professional Society on the Abuse of Children. (1995). *Practice guidelines: Psychosocial evaluation of suspected psychological maltreatment in children and adolescents.* Chicago: Author.

Brassard, M. R., Hart, S. N., & Hardy, D. B. (1993). The psychological maltreatment rating scales. *Child Abuse and Neglect, 17,* 715–729.

Child Abuse Prevention and Treatment Act, 42 U.S.C. 5106g(4) (1974).

Garbarino, J., & Gilliam, G. (1980). *Understanding abusive families.* Lexington, MA: Lexington Books.

Garbarino, J., Guttmann, E., & Wilson Seeley, J. (1986). *The psychologically battered child.* San Francisco: Jossey-Bass.

Hamerman, S., & Ludwig, S. (2000). Emotional abuse and neglect. In R. M. Reece (Ed.), *Treatment of child abuse: Common ground for mental health, medical and legal practitioners.* Baltimore: Johns Hopkins University Press.

Mrazek, D. A., Mrazek, D. M., & Kinnert, M. (1995). Clinical assessment of parenting. *Journal of the American Academy of Child and Adolescent Psychiatry, 34*(3), 272–282.

O'Hagan, K. (1993). *Emotional and psychological abuse of children.* Toronto: University of Toronto Press.

Sanders, B., & Becker-Lausen, E. (1995). The measurement of psychological maltreatment: Early data on the child abuse trauma scale. *Child Abuse and Neglect, 19*(3), 315–323.

U.S. Department of Health and Human Services, Administration on Children, Youth, and Families. (2005). *Child maltreatment 2003.* Washington, DC: U.S. Government Printing Office.

13
Kathryn M. Wells

Substance Abuse and Child Maltreatment

Substance abuse and child maltreatment are intricately related, putting children from families where substance abuse is present at risk for abuse and neglect. Parental addiction to alcohol, marijuana, heroin, cocaine, methamphetamine, and other drugs has led to one of the more complex and devastating problems in the field of child welfare. Data from the 1996 National Household Survey on Drug Abuse (NHSDA) reveal that an estimated 8.3 million children, 11% of all children in the United States, live with at least one parent who is in need of substance abuse treatment (Huang, Cerbone, & Gfroerer, 1998). Substance abuse includes the abuse of legal drugs (alcohol, prescription drugs, over-the-counter drugs) as well as illegal drugs (cocaine, heroin, marijuana, and methamphetamines). Many substance abusers are also polysubstance users and the abuse of legal substances may be as detrimental to parental functioning as abuse of illicit substances.

■ The Problems of Substance Abuse Faced by the CPS System

Research has confirmed a strong connection between substance abuse and child maltreatment (Child Welfare League of America [CWLA], 1992; White et al., 1995). In one study that controlled for many variables, children whose parents were abusing substances were found to be 2.7 times more likely to be abused and 4.2 times more likely to be neglected than other children whose parents were not substance abusers (Kelleher, Chaffin, Hollenberg, & Fischer, 1994; U.S. Department of Health and Human Services [USDHHS], 1998; White et al., 1995). In fact, in a 1998 survey of the 50 state child protection service agencies, the National Committee to Prevent Child Abuse (now Prevent Child Abuse America) reported that 85% of the states indicated that substance abuse was one of the two leading problems exhibited by families reported for child maltreatment (Wang & Harding, 1999), with poverty being the other most frequently reported issue.

The combined stresses of substance abuse and the demands for the routine care of infants and children can create a volatile or otherwise vulnerable environment in which neglect or physical abuse can occur. Parents or caregivers who are high on drugs or alcohol will not respond appropriately to the cues an infant or child gives for both physical and social interactive nurturing. A parent or caregiver who abuses substances has impaired judgment and priorities and is unable to provide the consistent care, supervision, and guidance that children need. Additionally, these homes are often plagued with other problems including diversion of resources (money, time, energy, and emotional support) from the children to drug habits, criminal activity, other physical and mental illness of the caregivers, poor parenting skills, and domestic violence. Finally, many drugs make adult caregivers violent, paranoid, and angry, creating a situation where the caregiver is more prone to injure or neglect their children (Bays, 1990). For all these reasons, substance abuse is clearly a critical factor in child welfare (USDHHS, 1999).

Children who grow up in these homes have poorer outcomes (behaviorally, psychologically, socially, and physically) than children whose parents or caregivers do not abuse substances. These children also have an eightfold increased risk of substance abuse themselves. Additionally, children who were abused during their childhood have a greater risk of substance abuse later in life, highlighting the importance of breaking this cycle of addiction (Bennett & Kemper, 1994).

CPS workers should carefully assess abusive families for drug and alcohol problems as parental substance abuse is associated with a higher risk of recurrent child abuse and neglect. When compared to nonsubstance-abusing parents, substance abusers had a 50% higher rate of previous reports of child abuse and neglect, presented greater risk to their children, more frequently rejected court-ordered services, and were more likely to have their children permanently removed from their homes (Murphy et al., 1991).

Parental substance abuse has been linked to the most serious outcomes of all cases of child maltreatment including fatalities. In fact, data by Reid, Macchetto, and Foster (1999) indicate that substance abuse by caregivers is associated with as many as two-thirds of all cases of child maltreatment fatalities. In this study, 51% of these deaths involved physical abuse while 44% involved neglect and 5% involved multiple forms of child maltreatment.

Prenatal Drug Exposure

Prenatal drug exposure, although only one aspect of the link between substance abuse and child maltreatment, may be accompanied by additional effects on the infant's health before birth and in the immediate neonatal period. These children are often not identified because their mothers do not disclose their substance abuse for fear of prosecution as well as of losing their children. However, this may be the most effective time for intervention, as motherhood is often the only legitimate social role that is valued by drug-dependent women, and most women in treatment are quite concerned about how their substance abuse has affected their children. Therefore, pregnancy and motherhood are times of increased motivation for treatment. Therefore, even if her rights to previous children have been terminated, a new birth may be motivation for a mother to comply with a treatment program for the sake of the new child.

Studies that have tried to assess the direct risks to children exposed to drugs in utero have found it difficult to disassociate the negative effects of the actual drug exposure from the negative effects of other variables including poor prenatal care, poor prenatal nutrition, prematurity, and an adverse postnatal environment. However, the identification of maternal substance abuse in the prenatal period should serve as a red flag for potential risks in the postnatal environment. In fact, recent studies have shown that drug-exposed infants may be at greater risk of harm in the postnatal environment than in the prenatal environment. Therefore, it is important for CPS workers to use identification of prenatal exposure to drugs or alcohol as an opportunity to address the multiple other issues that the family may be confronting.

Pregnant women who are substance abusers are at far greater risk for a range of medical problems. They are at risk for many different kinds of infections, including HIV, sexually transmitted diseases, tuberculosis, hepatitis, syphilis, endocarditis, and pulmonary infections. In addition, they may display nutritional deficiencies and anemia, as well as toxin-induced organ damage to the heart, lungs, liver, or kidneys. Additional obstetrical complications include infections of the amniotic fluid and sac, premature rupture of the membranes (which protect the fetus from infections), abruptio placenta (an early separation of the placenta that can lead to loss of blood and oxygen supply to the fetus), intrauterine growth retardation, and premature birth. Frequently women who are using substances do not seek out adequate prenatal care, which places the infant and the mother at increased risk. Mothers who do not receive prenatal care are more likely to give birth to low birth-weight infants, which places the infants at increased risk of death and other complications during the first 4 weeks of life.

Neonatal complications of maternal substance abuse include immune system abnormalities, jaundice, blood sugar difficulties, brain bleeds, growth abnormalities, neonatal withdrawal syndrome (neonatal abstinence syndrome), pneumonia, infections, and increased risk for death from SIDS (sudden infant death syndrome). Because these infants are often born prematurely, they frequently have low birth weights and are at increased risk for a host of problems related to prematurity. These complications may include needing mechanical ventilation and oxygen, bleeding into the brain from rupture of small fragile blood vessels, overwhelming infections requiring antibiotics, and poor feeding, often requiring artificial feeding assistance.

Prenatal substance abuse can lead to specific medical and developmental problems for the child in addition to the overall obstetrical and neonatal complications. For example, depending on the gestational age of the fetus when the drug was used, there may be congenital abnormalities of any major organs system such as the neurologic, pulmonary, renal, or digestive systems. Additionally, there has been a great deal of research that has shown long-term developmental and behavioral issues in children exposed to drugs and alcohol in utero. The potential effects of maternal substance abuse on the infant depend greatly on the substance being used and its frequency, duration of use, and quantity. Often, women use multiple chemicals in combination, placing the infant at even further risk.

Alcohol ingested by the pregnant woman does cross the placenta to the fetus. Therefore, any amount of alcohol ingested during pregnancy may harm the infant. Alcohol-related birth defects (ARBD) occur in 1 out of 200 births worldwide and account for 5% of all congenital anomalies, as well as 10% to 20% of all cases of mental retardation. Fetal alcohol syndrome (FAS) is a constellation of physical characteristics, as well as behavioral and developmental problems, that children exposed to alcohol in utero may display. The unique infant traits associated with this syndrome may include the following:

- Facial characteristics, including an abnormally small head, a low nasal bridge, small eyes, flatness in the middle part of the face, a short nose, and a thin upper lip

- Irritability

- Low birth weight and/or sustained smallness in size for age

- Moderate intellectual impairment

- Motor problems, including hypotonia

- Seizure disorder

- Frequent hyperactivity and attentional impairment in childhood

Fetal alcohol effect (FAE) is the disorder displayed by children who are alcohol exposed and display behavioral and developmental difficulties without the physical or facial characteristics of FAS.

Heroin and methadone addiction are also associated with all the prematurity and low birth-weight problems just described for prenatal exposure to alcohol and drugs. In addition, these infants can experience life-threatening withdrawal symptoms shortly after birth. This is called the neonatal abstinence syndrome and these children may even require medication intervention for treatment of the syndrome while in the hospital.

The effects of prenatal exposure to cocaine and methamphetamine are the subject of numerous studies. ◻ The problems of methamphetamine-exposed babies, which are similar to the problems found in cocaine-exposed babies, may include the following:

- They may have prenatal problems such as early separation of the placenta in labor, irregular heartbeat, prematurity, and growth retardation while in utero.

- Some problems that may be identified at birth are brain abnormalities with areas of decreased blood or oxygen supply, and a variety of birth defects (particularly gastrointestinal).

- These infants may have poor sucking and feeding difficulties after birth.

- Cocaine-exposed infants are noted to be quite irritable, to have a shrill cry, and to be very difficult to console. Methamphetamine-exposed infants are sleepy and lethargic for the first few weeks, to the point of not waking to feed. After the first few weeks, they resemble cocaine-exposed infants, becoming quite jittery, having a shrill cry, and often startling at the slightest stimulation.

- Cases of sudden infant death syndrome have been reported to be higher in cocaine- and meth-exposed babies, but this has recently been debated due to many other factors.

- These children may display long-term delays in development. Although research is being done in this area, it is difficult to separate the effects of cocaine or methamphetamine prenatally from the poor family functioning and environmental conditions that are likely to occur in these families. It is important to understand that this is true for all children whose parents abuse substances.

Therefore, more important than the individual medical and developmental complications of the prenatal drug or alcohol exposure is the correlation of prenatal substance abuse with poor outcomes in relation to postnatal outcomes. Alcohol- and drug-related cases are more likely to result in foster care than other child welfare cases. Of children prenatally exposed to drugs, at least 10% to 20% enter foster care at birth and another one-third enter foster care within 1 year. Once in foster care, children with parents or caregivers who have substance abuse problems tend to remain in care for longer periods of time. This raises particular challenges given the many conflicting timelines that are imposed for families dealing with these issues. The child has a developmental timeline in which he or she will grow and develop a tremendous amount over the first 3 years of his or her life, making this a critical time for consistency. The timeline for substance addiction recovery for the parent is a lifetime, with much intervention and support needed especially in the beginning of the recovery. Additionally, there are new guidelines imposed on families involved in the child welfare system, requiring a permanency plan to be established by one year after placement of the child. Finally, there are other financial timelines such as TANF (Temporary Assistance for Needy Families) funding that play a role in meeting the families' needs.

Case Example

Five-year-old Dora went into foster care 9 months ago after her mother was arrested for methamphetamine use. The criminal charges were dropped but the CPS case remains open. Mom has been quite inconsistent with attending treatment. For the first 2 months, she had clean UAs, attended all counseling sessions, and visited Dora frequently. She relapsed after 2 months and stopped visiting for a while but she is now back in treatment and fairly consistent with her visitations with Dora. When visitation does occur, Dora and her mother clearly enjoy and love each other. Mom had a positive UA last week but did attend visitation later in the week. The next court hearing is 2 weeks away and the CPS worker struggles to make a recommendation about permanency.

Many infants born to substance-abusing mothers become boarder babies (left with caregivers such as friends or relatives for extended periods of time) and are often essentially abandoned. In some cases, their mothers die early from problems related to their substance use such as organ failure, infections like HIV or hepatitis, or violence.

Those infants who do go home with a parent who is abusing substances are at an increased risk for medical and environmental neglect because of their special medical needs. These children are often fussier and more difficult to console and may easily frustrate any caregiver. If this situation is coupled with the caregiver's use of a substance to deal with the stress, the risk to the child is further increased. For example, the fact that small infants usually communicate their needs by crying can cause additional frustrations for a caregiver that uses drugs or alcohol to cope. Therefore, the parent may use more drugs to try to temper her anxiety. Unfortunately, the use of drugs may lead to further difficulty with anger and the caregiver may finally become so frustrated and upset that she may abuse the infant. The use of drugs and alcohol has been linked to a lower frustration threshold.

Direct exposure of children to drugs after birth is an important consequence that is often overlooked. These children may accidentally ingest substances that are left accessible to them in the home or become victim to passive exposure to marijuana, methamphetamines, phencyclidine (PCP), and crack cocaine when these drugs are smoked by caregivers in their presence (Bateman & Heargarty, 1989; Heidemann & Goetting, 1990; Mirchandani et al., 1991), although it is unclear how much of the drug the child can get passively through smoke alone. There have also been reports of caregivers forcing ingestion of an illicit substance or alcohol for amusement of the caregiver or to produce a desired effect such as trying to quiet the child. One study showed 11% of adolescent females surveyed in one treatment program admitted to deliberately intoxicating children they were babysitting by blowing marijuana smoke in their faces (Schwartz, Peary, & Mistretta, 1986). Further studies have shown dangerously high levels of alcohol and illegal drugs through breast-feeding infants of mothers who are active substance abusers (Chaney, Franke, & Waadlington, 1988; Chasnoff, Lewis, & Squires, 1987; Little, Anderson, Ervin, Worthington-Robert, & Clarren, 1989). Other studies have provided disturbing evidence of cocaine exposure in children including a children's hospital study in which 5% of children screened had urine specimens containing cocaine or its metabolite (Shannon, Lacouture, Roa, & Woolf, 1989). Possible routes of exposure considered were breast-feeding, intentional administration, accidental ingestion, and possibly, though not proven, passive inhalation. Exposure to cocaine, methamphetamine, and PCP may produce signs and symptoms of intoxication that may include lethargy, vomiting, seizures, apnea, coma, and death (Bays, 1994).

Environmental Concerns

Another risk to children in substance-abusing homes is when they are present in homes where methamphetamine is being manufactured. Clandestine labs, most commonly used to manufacture methamphetamine, are rapidly increasing. Once most commonly found in rural areas and on the West Coast as well as in the Midwest, these toxic sites are rapidly moving into urban and suburban areas as well as to the eastern United States. The labs utilize multiple hazardous chemicals including strong acids (e.g., hydrochloric acid, sulfuric acid, muriatic acid), bases (e.g., sodium hydroxide or lye), anhydrous ammonia, lithium, red phosphorus, and solvents (e.g., Coleman fuel, Toluene, Heet, acetone, drain cleaner, starting fluid, denatured alcohol) to convert pseudoephedrine or ephedrine to methamphetamine. Children are found in about 30% to 35% of these environments and these "homes" are extremely dangerous for multiple reasons. The hazardous chemicals used in the manufacturing process are often improperly stored such as within the refrigerator and within reach of curious children. Numerous reports tell of children ingesting these dangerous chemicals with resultant severe illness and even death. Many of these chemicals produce noxious vapors and recent studies from National Jewish Hospital and Research Center indicate that these vapors (including hydrochloric acid, phospine gas, anhydrous ammonia, and iodine) permeate every porous surface in the home (Martyny, Arbuckle, McCammon, & Erb, n.d.). These vapors also contain methamphetamine itself, which is also found on every vertical and horizontal surface in the home. The manufacturing process requires combining these chemicals often with the use of heat, creating an environment that is extremely flammable and explosive. Because these chemicals are not meant to be used in this manner, the long-term implications of these combinations are not known. These homes need to be considered contaminated until they have undergone extensive cleanup and have been released for safe occupation by building inspectors.

Case Example

Lilah (4 years old) and Omar (2 years old) were found wandering in a home identified as a methamphetamine lab. They are now in foster care and are doing well but are suffering from a host of medical conditions including respiratory problems, severe dental issues, and developmental delays. Thus far, the medical providers have not been able to diagnose the root cause of their conditions but speculate that it is a combination of the toxic environment and chronic neglect they experienced.

Methamphetamine labs pose multiple dangers not directly related to the chemicals used in the manufacturing process. A large number of these children test positive for methamphetamine at the time of removal from the home containing the lab. Additionally, because of the paranoid features of methamphetamine use, the caregivers almost always have weapons readily accessible in the home. They also frequently engage in violent behavior such as domestic violence and child physical abuse. Needles are often found lying out in the open and accessible to children. Methamphetamine considerably increases the sex drive of users, making them extremely hypersexual and increasingly interested in pornography, including that of a very graphic nature. Therefore, a large amount of graphic X-rated material may be found in these homes and children may not only be exposed to this material but are often victimized themselves. Finally, because the use and manufacturing of the drug becomes paramount to the caregiver, these children rarely have appropriate medical and dental care, support, guidance, encouragement, and the discipline that they need. It is for all of the above reasons that these children should always be considered endangered and out-of-home placement must be immediately explored.

■ Safety Plans

Safety and support plans using foster homes, extended family, and community members are essential to the continuing safety and well-being of the children and the continuing recovery of substance-abusing parents. ⌨ However, studies of the families of substance-abusing mothers point out the vicious cycle of parents being neglected or abused as children and then perpetuating the neglect and abuse with their own children. As with other aspects of child neglect and abuse, the prime concern is protection of the child. Comprehensive programs that can identify the addicted parent, offer substance abuse addiction education and treatment, and provide necessary support services are most likely to meet the unique needs of substance-abusing mothers.

Substance abuse treatment programs that are culturally responsive, immediately available, and include full wraparound services are the key to offering the parent the best chance at recovery and the child the best possible outcome. These services might include family group planning meetings with the extended family and community support providers, adequate housing, counseling for sexual and domestic violence, child care, health care (including family planning and well-child care, in addition to prenatal care), mental health care assistance if needed, education, training, and employment.

Sometimes a bias against the child's grandparents may exist, because a child's grandparents may automatically be "blamed" for producing a substance-abuser-turned-parent. Thus, grandparents or other relatives of a substance-abusing parent may be unnecessarily overlooked as caregivers. However, the reality that must be considered is that substance abuse and addiction are often generational. Since time limits for reunification are more difficult to accomplish when substance abuse is involved, consideration of placement with relatives becomes an even more critical issue if the child is to remain connected with family and not be unnecessarily adopted outside of the extended family. It is still important, however, to carefully evaluate all placement options.

Most drug treatment programs have focused on males and not on the unique issues for women and their special needs during pregnancy and beyond during the parenting years. Some of these issues include the need for child-care assistance, transportation, and job skills training. Many of these women also need assistance with issues related to domestic violence, infectious diseases (such as HIV, hepatitis, tuberculosis), and mental health. It is clear that more treatment programs where mothers reside with their children are needed. In addition, front-loading services and expanded family and community support can be an effective means of keeping children in the home while parents recover from substance abuse and co-occurring mental health concerns, or receive other needed remedial or rehabilitative services (Metsch et al., 1995). Substance abuse treatment must be a major component of the treatment plan for these families and needs to be made available in a timely manner. However, when caregivers fail to comply with drug and alcohol treatment programs within court-ordered guidelines, early termination of parental rights should be considered so that the child can be placed in a permanent living situation where they can grow physically, emotionally, developmentally, and intellectually.

It is clear that substance abuse and addiction to both legal and illegal drugs play a major role in the child welfare field. Therefore, it is extremely important for CPS workers to carefully and compassionately assess for and identify families dealing with issues of substance use and abuse in an effort to avoid escalation to potentially severe and even deadly situations for the children living in these homes.

References

Bateman, D. A., & Heargarty, M. C. (1989). Passive freebase cocaine ("crack") inhalation in infants and toddlers. *American Journal of Diseases in Children, 143,* 25–27.

Bays J. (1990). Substance abuse and child abuse—Impact of addiction on the child. *Pediatric Clinics of North America, 37,* 881–904.

Bays, J. (1994). Child abuse by poisoning. In R. M. Reese (Ed.), *Child abuse: Medical diagnosis and management* (pp. 69–106). Philadelphia: Lea & Febiger.

Bennett E. M., & Kemper, K. J. (1994). Is abuse during childhood a risk factor for developing substance abuse problems as an adult? *Journal of Developmental and Behavioral Pediatrics, 15,* 426–429.

Chaney, N. E., Franke, J., & Waadlington, W. B. (1988). Cocaine convulsions in a breast-feeding baby. *Journal of Pediatrics, 112,* 134–135.

Chasnoff, I. F., Lewis, D. E., & Squires, L. (1987). Cocaine intoxication in a breast-fed infant. *Pediatrics, 80,* 836–838.

Child Welfare League of America & North American Commission on Chemical Dependency and Child Welfare. (1992). *Children at the front: A different view of the war on alcohol and drugs.* Washington, DC: Child Welfare League of America.

Heidemann, S. M., & Goetting, M. G. (1990). Passive inhalation of cocaine by infants. *Henry Ford Hospital Medical Journal, 38,* 252–254.

Huang, L., Cerbone, F., & Gfroerer, J. (1998). Children at risk because of parental substance abuse. In Substance Abuse and Mental Health Administration & Office of Applied Studies, *Analyses of substance abuse and treatment need issues* (Analytic Series A-7). Rockville, MD: Substance Abuse and Mental Health Services Administration.

Kelleher, K., Chaffin, M., Hollenberg, J., & Fischer, E. (1994). Alcohol and drug disorders among physically abusive and neglectful parents in a community-based sample. *American Journal of Public Health, 84,* 1586–1590.

Little, R. E., Anderson, K. W., Ervin, C. H., Worthington-Robert, B., & Clarren, S. K. (1989). Maternal alcohol use during breast-feeding and infant mental and motor development at one year. *New England Journal of Medicine, 321,* 425–430.

Martyny, J. W., Arbuckle, S. L., McCammon Jr., C. S., & Erb, N. (n.d.). *Methamphetamine contamination on environmental surfaces caused by simulated smoking of methamphetamine.* Retrieved from http://www.colodec.org/medical/documents/Meth%20smoking%20experiment.pdf

Metsch, L. R., Rivers, J. E., Miller, M., Bohs, R., McCoy, C. B., Morrow, C. J., Bandstra, E. S., Jackson, V., & Gissen, M. (1995). Implementation of a family-centered treatment program for substance-abusing women and their children: Barriers and resolutions. *Journal of Psychoactive Drugs, 27,* 73–83.

Mirchandani, H. G., Mirchandani, I. H., Hellman, F., English-Rider, R., Rosen, S., & Laposata, E. A. (1991). Passive inhalation of free-base cocaine ("crack") smoke by infants. *Archives of Pathological Laboratory Medicine, 115,* 494–498.

Murphy, J. M., Jellinek, M., Quinn, D., Smith, G., Poitrast, F. G., & Goshko, M. (1991). Substance abuse and serious child maltreatment: Prevalence, risk, and outcome in a court sample. *Child Abuse and Neglect, 15,* 197–211.

Reid, J., Macchetto, P., & Foster, S. (1999). *No safe haven: Children of substance-abusing parents.* New York: National Center on Addiction and Substance Abuse at Columbia University.

Schwartz, R. H., Peary, P., & Mistretta, D. (1986). Intoxication of young children with marijuana: A form of amusement for pot-smoking teenage girls. *American Journal of Diseases in Children, 140,* 326.

Shannon, M., Lacouture, P. G., Roa, J., & Woolf, A. (1989). Cocaine exposure among children seen at a pediatric hospital. *Pediatrics, 83,* 337–341.

U.S. Department of Health and Human Services, Administration for Children and Families, Substance Abuse and Mental Health Administration, Office of the Assistant Secretary for Planning and Evaluation. (1999). *Blending perspectives and building common ground. A report to Congress on substance abuse and child protection.* Washington, DC: Substance Abuse and Mental Health Administration.

U.S. Department of Health and Human Services, Public Health Service, Substance Abuse and Mental Health Services Administration, & Office of Applied Studies. (1998). *National household survey on drug abuse: Main findings, 1996.* Rockville, MD: Substance Abuse and Mental Health Services Administration.

Wang, C. T., & Harding, K. (1999). *Current trends in child abuse reporting and fatalities: The results of the 1998 annual fifty state survey.* Chicago: National Committee to Prevent Child Abuse.

White, W. L., Illinois Department of Children and Family Services, & Illinois Department of Alcoholism and Substance Abuse. (1995). *SAFE 95: A status report on Project Safe, an innovative project designed to break the cycle of maternal substance abuse and child neglect/abuse.* Springfield, IL: Illinois Department of Children and Family Services.

14

Kathryn M. Wells
Charmaine R. Brittain

Violence in the Home

Understanding and responding to child maltreatment requires an appreciation of the impact of family dynamics. Along with other factors, the presence of family violence in the home must be assessed for and addressed carefully and thoroughly to increase the children's safety.

Family violence—which may also be called domestic violence, intimate partner violence, spouse abuse, battering, or partner violence—is generally defined as the intentional infliction of harm or injury by one intimate partner to another (National Research Council, Institute of Medicine, 1998). Multiple studies have shown that severe physical violence against intimate partners is often accompanied by other forms of maltreatment (Graham-Bermann, 1998; Straus, Hamby, Boney-McCoy, & Sugarman, 1995; Tolman, 1989), so the definition of domestic violence should be expanded to include forms of emotional maltreatment and verbal and sexual abuse (Koss et al., 1994). Domestic violence usually continues over a long period of time and may become more frequent and severe over time. Anyone—regardless of age, gender, race, ethnicity, economic status, education, or religion—can be a victim of domestic violence. Most victims are females, but males can be abused by females, and a person can be abused by someone of the same gender. Women are more likely to be seriously injured by their partners than men. Intimate partner violence is associated with both short- and long-term problems, including physical injury and illness, psychological symptoms, economic costs, and death (National Research Council, 1996).

It is well documented that child abuse frequently occurs in homes where domestic violence exists (Zink et al., 2004). However, a great deal of research is needed in this area. In fact, research in the field of domestic violence is about 15 years behind that of child abuse (Graham-Bermann, 2002). Although reporting of child abuse is mandatory, there is no such requirement for domestic violence. Cases of domestic violence are also not well documented and tracked (Graham-Bermann, 2002). One estimate, thought to be conservative, reports the overall rate of domestic violence in the United States is 28% of all married couples per year (Straus & Gelles, 1990). A recent survey by the Center for the Advancement of Women (2003) indicated that 92% of American women rank domestic and sexual violence as one of their top priorities. The 1995–1996 National Violence against Women Survey reported that 1.5 million women and 834,700 men were raped or physically assaulted by their intimate partner within the previous 12 months (Tjaden & Thoennes, 2000). The survey further showed that among women who are physically assaulted or raped by an intimate partner one in three is injured each year, with more than 500,000 women requiring medical treatment. It is estimated that 10 million children witness domestic violence each year (based on data from 1975 and 1985 national surveys) (Straus, 1992). Battered women who are pregnant frequently report that the target of the violent assault is the abdomen and subsequently the fetus (McFarlane, Parker, & Soeken, 1995; Seng et al., 2001). Physical violence against pregnant women has been calculated to be as high as 154 per 1,000 up to the fourth month of gestation and 170 per 1,000 from the fifth through the ninth month of gestation (Seng et al., 2001). In fact, as many as 324,000 women each year experience intimate partner violence during their pregnancy (Gazmararian et al., 2000). However, none of these figures takes into account the frequency, intensity, duration, and nature of the abuse. Most disturbingly, in the United States, people are more likely to be assaulted, beaten, or killed by their own family members than by outsiders (Straus, Gelles, & Steinmetz, 1980).

In families where adult domestic violence is occurring, a high incidence of child abuse coexists. A growing body of research points to pervasive connections between child abuse and domestic violence. According to 45% to 70% of women in shelters, their batterers have also committed some form of child abuse (figures from different shelters vary). A review of 200 substantiated cases of child maltreatment in Massachusetts found that 30% of the case records also mentioned adult domestic violence (Herskowitz & Seck, 1990). A survey of 6,000 American families found that 50% of men who frequently assaulted their wives also frequently abused their children (Straus & Gelles, 1990).

More severe and fatal cases of child abuse are often linked to domestic violence. A 1993 Oregon study reported the presence of domestic violence in 41% of families where child abuse or neglect resulted in critical injuries or death (Oregon Children's Services Division, 1993). Forty-three percent of child fatalities in Massachusetts in 1992 occurred in families where the mother reported herself to be a victim of domestic violence (as cited in Schechter & Edelson, 1994).

Witnessing domestic violence may put children at risk for increased emotional problems. It is estimated that between 3.3 million and 10 million children witness domestic violence each year (Carlson, 1984; Straus, 1992). Child witnesses of domestic violence have been found to show increased aggressive and antisocial behavior, as well as more anxiety, depression, and temperamental problems and lower self-esteem than children who have not witnessed domestic violence (Schechter & Edelson, 1994).

These multiple connections make clear that child abuse and domestic violence advocates often serve the same population of families. In order to serve these families more effectively and to prevent further violence, a coordinated response is needed when families come to the attention of service providers for either child abuse or domestic violence issues.

Because of the strong correlation between domestic violence and child physical abuse, workers should always consider that children of victims present when domestic violence occurs are also at risk for child abuse. Also, in all reported cases of child abuse, there should be additional consideration given to the possibility of coexistent intimate partner abuse. In addition, children of women abused during pregnancy should be considered to be at greater risk for later child abuse. It has been shown that battered women are six times more likely to be reported for child abuse than nonbattered women (Campbell, 1994). One study showed that each additional act of violence toward the woman increased the odds of the batterer abusing the child by an average of 12% and violence by the woman toward the male partner increased the odds of the female partner physically abusing the child by an average of 4% (Ross, 1996).

Children who live in homes where family violence exists are often subjected to different forms of maltreatment ranging from emotional and psychological abuse to severe physical or sexual abuse. It is important to recognize that the less severe forms of maltreatment may be equally or more harmful to the exposed children if the incidents and exposures are repeated frequently enough. Therefore, workers need to assess for and document several factors when recording children's exposure to domestic violence including the range and frequency of the violent experiences and whether the children experience the violence directly or indirectly—for example, whether they see it, hear it, or just know about it (Barnett, Manly, & Cicchetti, 1993).

Domestic violence can lead to child physical abuse in several ways. First, the child may attempt to intervene in a violent situation, causing the angry parent to redirect his or her anger toward the child. Second, the child may accidentally be struck by a blow or item that was originally directed at the other parent. For example, a piece of furniture is thrown and hits the child instead of the intended target. Finally, it has been shown that battered parents tend to overdiscipline their children in an effort to control children's behavior because of fears that the violent partner may discipline the children more aggressively. Additionally, children may be used by the batterers to coerce the other parent in conjunction with a violent incident (Jaffe & Geffner, 1998; Jaffe, Poisson, & Cunningham, 2001). Abused women are twice as likely as nonabused women to abuse their children (Gayford, 1975; Walker, 1984) and male batterers are believed to abuse their children twice as often as battered women (Giles-Sims, 1985; Jouriles & Norwood, 1995). Additionally, the severity of abuse to the woman is felt to be directly linked to the severity of abuse to the child (Bowker, Arbitell, & McFerron, 1988; Straus & Gelles, 1990). Another form of child maltreatment that can be considered in the context of family or domestic violence is that of parental kidnapping. Studies show that over 350,000 children are abducted each year (Finkelhor, Hotaling, & Sedlak, 1990). These situations frequently occur because of child custody and visitation disputes.

Whether the child's exposure to the violence is intentional or not, it is clear that domestic violence has deleterious effects on the child. In fact, a Carnegie report, *Saving Youth from Violence* (Carnegie Corporation of New York, 1994), identified violence in the home, including child abuse and exposure to domestic violence, as one of the major stressors and traumas that contribute to the development of aggressive and anxious behavior in young children. Children who witness their mothers being abused can experience a variety of behavior problems, including anxiety, withdrawal, depression, and aggression (McFarlane, Groff, O'Brien, & Watson, 2003). Some of these children may actually go on to display symptoms of posttraumatic stress (Richters & Martinez, 1993). Further, these children may develop developmental delays (Graham-Bermann, 1998; Margolin, 1998) and problems with interpersonal relationships (Graham-Bermann, 1996; McFarlane, Groff, O'Brien, & Watson, 2003).

Several factors contribute to family violence and should be considered when assessing families for the risk of child abuse. ◤ By understanding these important red flags, the worker can potentially identify high-risk environments before the abuse occurs in order to provide the appropriate support for the family. Understanding these factors also assists the worker in developing a comprehensive and effective treatment plan. Obtaining a complete social history is the first critical feature and should include the following factors:

- Safety of the index child and other children in the home
- Prior social service or criminal involvement; physical and/or emotional "isolation" of the family
- Family crisis/stressors; single and/or young parents
- Method of discipline and parental roles
- Parents' past victimization
- Mental illness
- Domestic violence
- Drugs and/or alcohol
- Firearms
- Exposure to household hazards
- Composition of the household

Intimate partner violence in the home often predates child abuse, thus increasing the importance of accurate identification (Stark & Flitcraft, 1996).

Additionally, child abuse and abuse of the child's mother by her partner strongly correlates with a history of poor social support, increased life stressors, psychiatric illness in the mother, and unwanted pregnancy (Wilson et al., 1986). Perpetrators of intimate partner violence may lack some social skills, such as communication skills, particularly in the context of problematic situations with their intimate partners. A high number of perpetrators of intimate partner violence report more depression, lower self-esteem, and more aggression than nonviolent intimate partners. Evidence indicates that violent intimate partners may be more likely to have personality disorders such as schizoidal/borderline personality, antisocial or narcissistic behaviors, and dependency and attachment problems (Holtzworth-Monroe, Bates, Smutzler, & Sandin, 1997). Child abuse itself is also strongly associated with a history of childhood violence in the mother and her partner, previous abuse of children by the mother's partner, a poor relationship between the mother and her parents, low self-esteem in the mother, and lack of attendance at prenatal classes (Wilson et al., 1986). Several conditions have been identified to be associated with a batterer's later maltreatment of a child: dissolution of the marriage, separation, and a husband committed to dominance and control over the family members (Bowker, Arbitell, & McFerron, 1988). Finally, substance abuse has been strongly linked to domestic violence (Gondolf, 1993). It is estimated that in 45% of cases of intimate partner violence, men had been drinking, and in about 20% of cases, women had been drinking (Roizen, 1993).

The link between intimate partner violence and child abuse in families is so strong that CPS workers should carefully assess for and recognize signs that violence is occurring in the home and consider whether the children may have witnessed violence. Workers need to consider the dynamics of domestic violence when assessing whether the children or the batterer need to be removed from the home. Victims of this violence also need to be familiar with available community resources (e.g., shelters, advocacy groups) in order to provide better protection for their children (McKernan McKay, 1994). Finally, placement decisions need to take into consideration potential risks, with the best custody decisions being coupled with counseling and support services for the custodial parent (Ross, 1996).

■ Family Violence and Animal Abuse

A strong correlation exists between animal abuse, family violence, and other forms of community violence. Child and animal protection professionals have recognized this link, noting that abuse of both children and animals is connected in a self-perpetuating cycle of violence. Several studies have documented the link between violence to animals and to people with co-occurring rates ranging from 24% to 85% (Balkin & Schoen, 2004). While there is a wide range in the co-occurrence, it is indicative that the link between animal violence and domestic violence exists and is sufficiently concerning. When animals in a home are abused or neglected, it is a warning sign that others in the household may not be safe. In addition, children who witness animal abuse are at a greater risk of becoming abusers themselves.

A survey of pet-owning families with substantiated child abuse and neglect found that animals were abused in 88% of homes where child physical abuse was present (DeViney, Dickert, & Lockwood, 1983). A study of women seeking shelter at a safe house showed that 71% of those having pets affirmed that their partner had threatened, hurt, or killed their companion animals, and 32% of mothers reported that their children had hurt or killed their pets (Ascione, 1998). Still another study showed that violent offenders incarcerated in a maximum-security prison were significantly more likely than nonviolent offenders to have committed childhood acts of cruelty toward pets (Merz-Perez, Heide, & Silverman, 2001).

Clearly, family violence is detrimental to the physical and emotional well-being of children, and CPS workers must identify these situations and work to ensure a safer environment for children. Timely identification of children at risk in homes with family violence is critical to beginning the healing process. Counseling is recommended and encouraged for both adult and child victims of family violence. For child witnesses of domestic violence, counseling assists in helping them understand that they should not feel responsible for the violence, identifying and expressing their feelings in a healthy manner, and developing the use of safe coping mechanisms to deal with feelings of anger (Thormachlen & Bass-Felf, 1994). Prevention of family violence should focus on addressing associated and contributing factors, facilitating improved communication skills within the family, and empowering individuals to seek available resources and support to develop and improve appropriate coping mechanisms (Kornblit, 1994).

■ Safety Assessment/Lethality Assessment

In confirmed domestic violence cases, the first consideration should be to assess the safety of the victim and the children in the home and respond swiftly to the situation to develop a plan to provide for and respond to safety considerations. ⬛⬉

To assess safety and develop a safety plan, the CPS worker should engage in the following activities:

- Meet with the domestic violence victim alone. Arranging a private meeting can be difficult, but being unable to meet alone with the victim can signal danger related to the level of control that the alleged offender has over the family. It may be necessary to meet in a neutral place such as a park or coffee shop or at the victim's office. When private meetings are difficult, consult with a supervisor on how to proceed. Arrange to view and interview the children outside of the presence of the alleged offender as well. Provide assurances of concern about the safety of the victim as well as her children at each meeting. Provide assurance that the offender will not be confronted with information provided by the victim but do explain the limits of confidentiality.

- Explain the advantages of court intervention or criminal prosecution as the best means to deter future violence in most cases. Explain that statistically it has been shown that the cycle of domestic violence as well as child abuse often continues and escalates where there is no intervention by the court system. If a court intervention has occurred and a restraining order or a no-contact order is in place, explain that safety and treatment options *must* be guided by this order (e.g., no family or couples counseling is permitted).

Ask the victim questions to assess the nature of the relationship and the level of dangerousness of the offender. See the questions listed below for areas to assess.

Questions to Assess Patterns of Verbal, Emotional, Physical, or Sexual Abuse

- Has your partner called you degrading names, emotionally insulted you, or humiliated you at home or in public?
- Has your partner destroyed your possessions, broken furniture, pulled the telephone cord out, or punched holes in walls or doors?
- Has your partner threatened to injure you, himself, your children, or other family members?
- Has your partner hit, slapped, pushed, kicked, choked, or burned you?
- Has your partner threatened to use or used a weapon against you or threatened to kill you or to commit suicide? Does he have a gun or rifle at home?
- Has your partner hurt your pets? (Explain that it is also against the law to abuse animals and that this can be reported to animal protection officials.)
- Has your partner recklessly endangered you or your children (e.g., driving too fast with you and the children in the car or driving when drunk)?
- Has your partner behaved violently or been arrested for violent crimes?

- Has your partner forced you to perform sex acts, prevented you from using birth control, or hurt you during pregnancy? Have you been forced into prostitution or pornography?

- Has your partner forced you to abuse drugs or other substances?

Questions to Assess Risk to Children in Domestic Violence Situations

- Has your partner threatened to hurt or kill your children?

- Has your partner threatened to "snatch" your children?

- Has your partner hurt you in front of your children or while you were holding your children?

- Has your partner accused you of being an unfit parent or threatened to take the children away from you or call social services?

- Has your partner physically hurt your children by hitting, slapping, punching, kicking, beating, burning, or shaking them? (Observe whether there are marks on the children indicative of abuse.)

- Has your partner touched your child in ways that made you feel uncomfortable? Do you suspect sexual abuse?

- Has your partner asked your children to tell him where you go during the day?

- Does your partner force your children to participate in or watch abuse of you? Has your partner forced your children to watch him rape you?

- Do your children behave in violent ways similar to your partner?

- Have your children tried to stop violence by your partner or protect you in violent situations?

- Have your children been fearful of leaving you alone?

- Have your children hurt themselves or pets?

- Have your children overheard violence against you?

- Have your children exhibited physical, emotional, or behavioral problems at home, school, or day care?

- Are your children displaying symptoms that may be indicative of the effect of the violence against you on them:
    - difficulty sleeping and/or nightmares
    - poor appetite or eating problems
    - difficulty with concentration

- persistent sadness or depression
- low energy
- withdrawal
- violence toward you or siblings
- running away
- alcohol or drug abuse
- destroying toys or other objects
- fear of leaving you
- fear of being alone with the batterer

Questions to Assess the Victim's History and Willingness to Seek Help

If the victim has disclosed, this information will help in the planning for her safety and that of her children:

- Have you ever told anyone about the abuse and what happened when you did?

- Have you ever left home as a result of the abuse? Where did you go? Did you take your children with you?

- Have you called the police, filed for a restraining order, or pressed criminal charges because of abuse? What was the result? Do you have a restraining order now? Is it temporary or permanent?

- Have you or your partner participated in counseling for the abuse? Was your partner court-ordered to attend counseling? What was the result?

- Have you ever gone to a battered women's support group or shelter? Have you called a domestic violence crisis line to talk? Was it helpful?

- Do you blame yourself for the abuse or believe that the maltreatment is your responsibility?

- Have you fought back against your abuser? What happened?

- When was the last domestic violence incident?

- Has your partner ever threatened to kill you, your children, or anyone else in the family?

- Has your partner ever threatened or attempted to commit suicide?

■ Safety Planning for Battered Victims and Their Children

Safety planning should begin with a general assessment of the danger to the victim and the children. A general understanding of the power structure within the family and the victim's assessment of the danger to him or herself and the children should be developed, as battering is typically a power and control issue. A CPS worker should respect the victim's right to self-determination but should explain that help is available and that intervention may be the only way to deter future violence. Safety for the victim and her children should always remain the first consideration.

Listed below are general questions that can be asked to begin safety planning:

- How dangerous do you think your partner is?

- What dangerous actions do you think your partner is capable of?

- Do you have any current injuries or health problems?

- What do you think is the best way to keep you and your children safe?

- How do you understand the violence and how is it affecting your view of yourself, your children, and the future?

- How do you believe your children understand the violence?

If the answers to these initial questions suggest extreme danger to the victim and the children are identifying with the offender, the worker should postpone any further interviews with the victim and other family members until safety is more evident. If the children are in danger or have been abused, however, the worker should act immediately to protect them. A formal written personalized safety planning form is suggested to help prevent violence to the victim and any children in the home.

Safety plans for those preparing to leave a relationship may include the following:

- Keeping emergency and important phone numbers near the phone and teaching children how and when to use them.

- Telling neighbors about the violence and telling them to call police if necessary.

- Making a list of safe places to go in an emergency (e.g., family members' homes, friends' homes, police station, shelter).

- Putting cash aside in a safe place for emergencies and in a separate bank account if possible.

- Creating a code word to use with children or friends so they can call for help.

- Keeping copies of important documents and keys outside of the house. For example, having a suitcase packed and available at a neighbor or relative's home or hidden in the garage.

• Remembering important items when leaving the house, such as identification, birth certificates for self and children, medications, driver's license, passport, green card, car registration, insurance papers, school records, keys, social security card, and social security numbers for all family members. These items should be kept together in a safe, easily accessible place, or duplicates should be available to avoid creating suspicion.

Children should be made aware of how to be safe if violence erupts in the home. Children should do the following:

• Leave or hide if parents/partners are fighting.

• Telephone a friend, police, or 911 for emergency situations.

• Run to get someone to help or to summon assistance from other adults or police, such as a friend or neighbor.

• Go to an older sibling for help.

When children do not know who to turn to for help, CPS workers should help them to identify specific individuals or agencies who can assist, how to call for help, and what to say.

Personalized Safety Plan

The following steps represent a plan for increasing safety and preparing in advance for the possibility for further violence. Each plan should be customized for the individual and follow these general steps.

Step 1: Safety during a violent incident. Sometimes violent incidents cannot be avoided. During a violent incident, know how to leave the residence immediately or contact a friend or relative who can call law enforcement. Teach children when and how to call 911 and how to avoid physical violence by moving to a safe place or using strategies to de-escalate the situation.

Step 2: Safety when preparing to leave. Battered people frequently leave the residence they share with the battering partner. Leaving must be done strategically in order to increase safety. Batterers often strike back when they believe that their partners are leaving a relationship.

Step 3: Safety in own residence. There are many things that a person can do to increase her safety in her own residence (e.g., locking doors, removing weapons). It may be impossible to do everything at once, but safety measures can be added step by step.

Step 4: Safety with a restraining or protection order. Many batterers obey restraining or protection orders, but one can never be sure which violent partner will obey and which will violate restraining or protection orders. The victim may need to ask the police and the courts to enforce these orders.

Step 5: Safety on the job and in public. Each battered person must decide if and when she will tell others that her partner has battered her and that she may be at continued risk. Friends, family, and coworkers can help to protect women. Each woman should consider carefully which people to invite to help secure her safety.

Step 6: Safety and drug or alcohol consumption. Most people living in a domestic violence situation consume alcohol. Many consume mood-altering drugs. Much of this consumption is legal and some is not. The legal outcomes of using illegal drugs can be very hard on a battered woman, may hurt her relationship with her children, and put her at a disadvantage in other legal actions with her battering partner. Therefore, women should carefully consider the potential cost of the use of illegal drugs or alcohol. But beyond this, the use of any alcohol or other drugs can reduce a woman's awareness and ability to act quickly to protect herself from her battering partner. Furthermore, the use of alcohol or other drugs by the batterer may give him or her an excuse to use violence. Therefore, in the context of drug or alcohol consumption, a person who is being battered needs to make specific safety plans.

Step 7: Safety and emotional health. The experience of being battered and verbally degraded by partners is usually exhausting and emotionally draining. The process of building a new life for the person who has been battered takes much courage and incredible energy.

Step 8: Items to take when leaving. When women leave partners, it is important to take certain items with them. Beyond this, women sometimes give an extra copy of papers and an extra set of clothing to a friend just in case they have to leave quickly.

CPS workers can facilitate breaking the cycle of violence in the home with proper assessment, intervention, and support services. The CPS mandate of ensuring children's safety depends on the entire family's freedom from violence.

References

Ascione, F. R. (1998). Battered women's reports of their partners' and their children's cruelty to animals. *Journal of Emotional Abuse, 1,* 119–133.

Balkin, D., & Schoen, K. (2004). Lawyers: A critical segment addressing the link. *Protecting Children, 19*(1), 13–23.

Barnett, D., Manly, J. T., & Cicchetti, D. (1993). Defining child maltreatment: The interface between policy and research. In D. Cicchetti & S. L. Toth (Eds.), *Child abuse, child development, and social policy* (pp. 7–73). Norwood, NJ: Ablex.

Bowker, L. H., Arbitell, M., & McFerron, J. R. (1988). On the relationship between wife beating and child abuse. In K. Yllö and M. Bograd (Eds.), *Perspectives on wife abuse* (pp. 158–174). Newbury Park, CA: Sage.

Campbell, J. C. (1994). Child abuse and wife abuse: The connection. *Maryland Medical Journal, 43,* 349–350.

Carlson, B. E. (1984). Children's observations of interpersonal violence. In A. R. Edwards (Ed.), *Battered women and their families* (pp. 147–167). New York: Springer.

Carnegie Corporation of New York. (1994). Saving youth from violence. *Carnegie Quarterly, 39,* 1–15.

Center for the Advancement of Women. (2003). Is your mother's feminism dead? New agenda for women revealed in landmark two-year study [Press release]. Retrieved July 20, 2004, from http://www.advancewomen.org/for_reporters/press_releases.php

DeViney, E., Dickert, J., & Lockwood, R. (1983). The care of pets within child abusing families. *International Journal for the Study of Animal Problems, 4,* 321–329.

Finkelhor, D., Hotaling, G. T., & Sedlak, A. (1990). *Missing, abducted, runaway, and thrown-away children in America: First report.* Washington, DC: Juvenile Justice Clearinghouse.

Gayford, J. (1975). Wife battering: A preliminary survey of 100 cases. *British Medical Journal, 1,* 194–197.

Gazmararian, J. A., Petersen, R., Spitz, A. M., Goodwin, M. M., Saltzman, L. E., & Marks, J. S. (2000). Violence and reproductive health: Current knowledge and future research directions. *Maternal and Child Health Journal, 4*(2), 79–84.

Giles-Sims, J. (1985). A longitudinal study of battered women. *Family Relations, 34,* 205–207.

Gondolf, E. (1993). Treating the batterer. In M. Hansen & M. Harway (Eds.), *Battering and family therapy: A feminist perspective* (pp. 105–118). Newbury Park, CA: Sage.

Graham-Bermann, S. A. (1996). Family worries: The assessment of interpersonal anxiety in children from violent and nonviolent families. *Journal of Clinical Child Psychology, 25*(3), 280–287.

Graham-Bermann, S. A. (1998). The impact of woman abuse on children's social development. In G. W. Holden, R. Geffner, & E. N. Jouriles (Eds.), *Children and marital violence: Theory, research, and intervention* (pp. 21–54). Washington, DC: American Psychological Association.

Graham-Bermann, S. A. (2002). Child abuse in the context of domestic violence. In J. E. Myers, L. Berliner, J. Briere, C. T. Hendrix, C. Jenny, & T. A. Reid (Eds.), *The APSAC handbook on child maltreatment* (pp. 119–129). Thousand Oaks, CA: Sage.

Herskowitz, J., & Seck, M. (1990, January). *Substance abuse and family violence, part 2: Identification of drug and alcohol usage in child abuse cases in Massachusetts.* Boston: Massachusetts Department of Social Services.

Holtzworth-Monroe, A., Bates, L., Smutzler, N., & Sandin, E. (1997). A brief review of the research on husband violence: Part I: Maritally violent versus nonviolent men. *Aggression and Violent Behavior, 2*(1), 65–99.

Jaffe, P., & Geffner, R. (1998). Child custody disputed and domestic violence: Critical issues for mental health, social services and legal professionals. In G. W. Holden, R. Geffner, & E. N. Jouriles (Eds.), *Children exposed to marital violence: Theory, research, and applied issues* (pp. 371–408). Washington, DC: American Psychological Association.

Jaffe, P., Poisson, S., & Cunningham, A. (2001). Domestic violence and high conflict divorce: Developing a new generation of research for children. In S. A. Graham-Bermann & J. L. Edelson (Eds.), *Domestic violence in the lives of children: The future of research, intervention and policy* (pp. 189–202). Washington, DC: American Psychological Association.

Jouriles, E. N., & Norwood, W. D. (1995). Physical aggression toward boys and girls in families characterized by the battering of women. *Journal of Family Psychology, 9,* 69–78.

Kornblit, A. L. (1994). Domestic violence—An emerging health issue. *Social Science & Medicine, 39,* 1181–1188.

Koss, M. P., Goodman, L. A., Browne, A., Fitzgerald, L. F., Keita, G. P., & Russo, N. F. (1994). *No safe haven: Male violence against women at home, at work, and in the community.* Washington, DC: American Psychological Association.

Margolin, G. (1998). Effects of domestic violence on children. In P. K. Trickett & C. J. Schellenbach (Eds.), *Violence against children in the family and in the community* (pp. 57–102). Washington, DC: American Psychological Association.

McFarlane, J. M., Groff, J. Y., O'Brien, J. A., & Watson, K. (2003). Behaviors of children who are exposed and not exposed to intimate partner violence: An analysis of 330 black, white, and Hispanic children. *Pediatrics, 112*(3), 202–207.

McFarlane, J., Parker, B., & Soeken, K. (1995). Abuse during pregnancy: Frequency, severity, perpetrator, and risk factors of homicide. *Public Health Nursing, 12,* 284–289.

McKernan McKay, M. (1994). The link between domestic violence and child abuse: Assessment and treatment considerations. *Child Welfare, 73*(1), 29–39.

Merz-Perez, L., Heide, K. M., and Silverman, I. J. (2001). Childhood cruelty to animals and subsequent violence against humans. *Journal of Offender Therapy and Comparative Criminology, 45,* 556–573.

National Research Council. (1996). *Understanding violence against women.* Washington, DC: National Academy Press.

National Research Council, Institute of Medicine. (1998). *Violence in families: Assessing prevention and treatment programs.* Washington, DC: National Academy of Sciences.

Oregon Children's Services Division. (1993). Task force report on child fatalities and critical injuries due to abuse and neglect. Salem, OR: Oregon Department of Human Resources.

Richters, J., & Martinez, P. (1993). The NIMH community violence project: I. Children as victims of and witnesses to violence. *Psychiatry, 56,* 7–21.

Roizen, J. (1993). Issues in the epidemiology of alcohol and violence. In S. E. Martin (Ed.), *Alcohol and interpersonal violence: Fostering multidisciplinary perspectives* (NIAAA Research Monograph No. 24) (pp. 3–36). Bethesda, MD: National Institute on Alcohol Abuse and Alcoholism.

Ross, S. (1996). Risk of physical abuse to children of spouse abusing parents. *Child Abuse and Neglect, 20,* 589–598.

Schechter, S., & Edelson, J. (1994). *In the best interest of women and children: A call for collaboration between child welfare and domestic violence constituencies.* St. Paul, MN: Minnesota Center against Violence and Abuse, School of Social Work, University of Minnesota.

Seng, J. S., Oakley, D. J., Sampselle, C. M., Killion, C., Graham-Bermann, S., & Liberzon, I. (2001). Posttraumatic stress disorder and pregnancy complications. *Journal of Obstetrics and Gynecology, 97,* 17–22.

Stark, E., & Flitcraft, A. (1996). *Women at risk: Domestic violence and women's health.* Thousand Oaks, CA: Sage.

Straus, M. A. (1992). Children as witnesses to marital violence: A risk factor for life-long problems among a naturally representative sample of American men and women. In D. F. Schwartz (Ed.), *Children and violence: Report of the twenty-third Ross roundtable on critical approaches to common pediatric problems* (pp. 98–109). Columbus, OH: Ross Laboratories.

Straus, M. A., & Gelles, R. J. (1990). *Physical violence in American families.* New Brunswick, NJ: Transaction.

Straus, M. A., Gelles, R. J., & Steinmetz, S. (1980). *Behind closed doors: Violence in the American family.* Garden City, NJ: Anchor.

Straus, M. A., Hamby, S. L., Boney-McCoy, S., & Sugarman, D. (1995). *The revised Conflict Tactics Scales (CTS2).* Durham, NH: Family Research Laboratory.

Thormachlen, D. J., & Bass-Felf, E. R. (1994). Children: The secondary victims of domestic violence. *Maryland Medical Journal, 43,* 355–359.

Tjaden, P., & Thoennes, N. (2000). *Full report of the prevalence, incidence, and consequences of intimate partner violence against women: Findings from the National Violence against Women Survey* (Report for grant 93-IJ-CX-0012, funded by the National Institute of Justice and the Centers for Disease Control and Prevention). Washington, DC: National Institute of Justice.

Tolman, R. (1989). The development of a measure of the psychological maltreatment of women by their male partners. *Violence and Victims, 4,* 159–177.

Walker, L. (1984). *The battered woman syndrome.* New York: Springer.

Wilson, L. M., Reid, A. J., Midmer, D. K., Biringer, A., Carroll, J. C., & Stewart, D. E. (1986). Antenatal psychosocial risk factors associated with adverse postpartum family outcomes. *Canadian Medical Association Journal, 154,* 785–799.

Zink, T., Kamine, D., Musk, L., Morgan, S., Field, V., & Putnam, F. (2004). What are providers' reporting requirements for children who witness domestic violence? *Clinical Pediatrics, 43*(5), 449–460.

15

Andrew P. Sirotnak

Child Abuse Fatalities

The death of a child as a result of abuse or neglect often represents the tragic failure of our society to identify at-risk families and to protect vulnerable children. Yet even in the most well-designed and well-delivered community systems of child protection and public health, children will die from physical abuse or neglect.

Data from the U.S. Department of Health and Human Services (2005) for 2003 showed that an estimated 1,500 children died from abuse or neglect for an incidence rate of 2.00 per 100,000 children. Children under 4 years of age accounted for 78.7% of child fatalities and children less than or equal to 1 year accounted for almost 60% of all fatalities. Inconsistent state reporting, uninvestigated suspicious child deaths, and deaths misidentified as accidental or SIDS are factors in these numbers being an estimate only.

Most children are killed by a parent or caregiver; often both parents or caregivers are responsible and both genders are equally victimized. Despite many high-profile cases in recent years, the national data reports that only 10.7% of these families had received services in the five years prior to the deaths.

The CPS worker's role, and the involvement of the CPS agency in a child abuse fatality investigation, will vary depending on state statutes, agency policy, and whether there has been prior contact with the child or family. Reports involving a child fatality may also come to the agency's attention, because the safety of other children who will either remain in a home or be placed out of home until an investigation is completed must be assessed. CPS workers also play a crucial role in both local and state child fatality review teams.

All child abuse deaths should be considered preventable. Through a multidisciplinary child fatality review process, system problems can be addressed, coordinated protocols for death investigations can be developed, and agencies can work together to both identify children at risk and prevent severe injury and death. 🖙

■ Investigation of Child Abuse Deaths

The investigation of sudden or unexpected deaths in infants and children begins with a detailed history. ⬛ This will eventually include a review of past medical care records and hospital records. Often the initial information comes from the emergency responders or paramedics who arrive at the scene of the death. Coroners may also respond to the death scene. The most important part of the investigation is often the scene of death. CPS workers may respond to the scene with police or the coroner and might play a role in this part of the investigation. During the investigation, CPS workers will be interested in responses to the following questions:

- Is there evidence of neglect, disarray, or impoverishment in the home environment?

- Is there enough or any food in the home?

- Are there obvious safety concerns in the home, such as access to dangerous chemicals, weapons, drugs or medications, or electrical wires? The majority of home drownings, for example, are related to bath or pool safety and neglect should be carefully considered.

- Is there anything that suggests impairment of a parent or caregiver such as alcohol, drugs, or drug paraphernalia?

■ Medical Examiners, Coroners, and Pathologists

In each state, an individual or agency is usually responsible for the completion of a postmortem investigation of all suspicious deaths. The professional role of the coroner or medical examiner and his or her education will vary by county and/or state. For example, this individual may be a physician who has board certification in pathology and who may have additional forensic pathology training and certification, or a mortician, a law enforcement official, or even an elected or appointed citizen with no medical training whatsoever. CPS workers should know what system is in place in their counties, surrounding counties, and states. Each state department and county department of human services should have some contact or liaison within the coroner or medical examiner system.

The Role of the Pathologist

It is not the CPS worker's role to determine the *medical* cause of death; however, it is important to understand the *mechanics* of a pathologist or medical examiner's investigation of a child's death. A pathologist's investigation of the circumstances leading to the child's death may also provide the worker with clues in assessing the living conditions and environment of the child that died, the parent or caregiver, and, most important, those children who are still living in the home. An autopsy, or postmortem examination, should be performed by an appropriate medical examiner or forensic pathologist on children in every case of an unexpected, unexplained, or suspicious death. Again, this will vary by county and state protocol.

Questions that the pathologist should attempt to answer about the sudden death of an infant or child include the following:

- Was death related to abuse or neglect injury or of complications of injury or neglect? Is there a mechanism of injury known and, if so, is that consistent with the injury seen?

- When did the injury occur in relation to the time of death? Can the time of death be determined with any reasonable accuracy?

- Did any delay in seeking medical care contribute to the death?

- Is there any evidence of recurrent or chronic injury to the child? Or is this injury a single event?

- Were illegal drugs, toxins, poisons, or medications involved in the death?

- Is there evidence of failure to thrive and is this related to nutrition or some underlying disease or condition?

The pathologist, through the actual autopsy, will attempt to determine the following:

- If there was any natural disease process that could have caused the death,

- If the child has any anatomic and/or pathological finding that is not consistent with the history given by the parent or caregiver, and

- If the injuries are consistent with any other possible explanations.

A thorough postmortem exam would include the following:

- A meticulous examination of the external appearance, noting and photographing any bruises, abrasions, burns, or signs of blunt trauma, strangulation, malnutrition, or neglect. The body will be measured and weighed and compared to standard growth curves, much like a live child will be treated during routine health care. Photos are taken during an autopsy of both external and internal findings.

- A complete postmortem skeletal survey X-ray, noting any old or healing fractures and their location, age, and number. For example, fractures often seen in physical abuse, such as the metaphyseal chip fracture and rib fractures, might be seen on a postmortem x-ray.

- Cultures for various infections that might have caused the death.

- Investigation for head injuries, the most frequent cause of child abuse death in infants and young children. In the investigation the pathologist will look for fractures of the skull, any external or scalp hemorrhages, subdural hematomas, or other injuries from blunt force trauma or shaken baby syndrome.

- Investigation for chest trauma: for example, broken ribs, punctured lungs, or traumatic bleeding in the internal chest cavity.

- Investigation of gastric contents to help estimate the time of death.

- Investigation of the internal organs such as the liver, spleen, pancreas, bladder, kidney, or gastrointestinal tract for any lacerations or bruises caused by blows to the abdomen.

- Investigation of sexual abuse, including examination for signs of trauma and possibly forensic evidence kit collection.

- Analysis for signs of starvation or malnutrition, including testing of blood components such as electrolytes, urea nitrogen, creatinine, and glucose. When a finding of starvation is expected, the doctor will need to investigate the child's previous medical records to look at growth patterns prior to illness or death.

- Analysis of body fluids or tissues for the presence of illegal drugs, medications, or toxic substances.

The coroner will often perform microscopic tissue studies to look for things like infections, tissue or cell damage, or specific tissue and cell changes or abnormalities that might indicate a medical condition related to the death. For example, an enlarged liver might show abnormal cells and structures that could indicate a metabolic disease that mimics SIDS. This would be important for the family to know as well so future genetic counseling could be arranged.

Many of these tests might take weeks to months to be completed, especially if they are sent to a referral source outside the local county or state, such as to a university medical center or national disease laboratory.

■ Cause and Manner of Death

The coroner or medical examiner will then dictate a report of an autopsy and its findings. *It is important to understand what the final autopsy report means to the investigation.* The cause and manner of death will be listed in the report and on the death certificate.

National standards for the death certificate exist and are reported to the county and state health departments in order to track these vital statistics. Each state has a registrar of vital statistics that tracks all births and deaths. The official death certificate is usually kept in such an office.

The *cause* of death is defined as the chain of events or the disease process that led to the death. For example, cause of death in a child could be sudden unexplained cardiac failure, pneumonia, blood infection, complications of leukemia, extreme prematurity, severe brain swelling due to blunt force trauma, or SIDS. The cause may list some specific events that led to the final determination of the manner of death. The manner of death is defined as the circumstances of the death. These are *natural, suicide, homicide, accidental, undetermined,* and *SIDS.* For example, for a 4-month-old baby who dies from abusive head injury, the cause could be listed as "acute subdural hematoma, brain edema and herniation from brain trauma" and the manner as "homicide." For a murdered, battered child, cause might be listed as "multiple contusions, fractures, and liver laceration from blunt force trauma" and the manner as "homicide."

A child who has leukemia and died from infection complication would be listed as a "natural" death. Accidental, suicide, and homicide manner of death determination depends greatly on the investigation by agencies who report to the coroner. For example, although a gunshot wound to the head might appear to be suicide, the death scene investigation might indicate homicide.

Often child deaths that may be related to neglect are not recognized as such, and the CPS worker investigating may still need to address significant family issues. This is one area of child death investigations where misidentification and misclassification of manner of deaths still occurs (Crume, DiGuiseppi, Byers, Sirotnak, & Garret, 2002). This relates again to the level of education, training, and child abuse experience—as well as the basic consideration of abuse or neglect—that a coroner might have. For example, the case of a toddler who is left home alone by the parent or caregiver and starts a fire and dies of smoke inhalation should be considered a case of neglect. It might very well be listed as *cause of death: smoke inhalation,* and *manner of death: homicide,* or *manner of death: accidental.* It cannot be emphasized too greatly that the CPS workers must know the degree of experience or child abuse death expertise of the coroner and bring other possibilities to his or her attention if overlooked.

■ Sudden Infant Death Syndrome (SIDS)

The cause of SIDS is still unknown, and research is being performed to understand this cause of death in infancy. Most infants who die of SIDS are under 1 year old, and close to 90% are under 6 months old. The incidence of SIDS has been decreasing in the United States in the past decade. The "Back to Sleep Campaign" of the American Academy of Pediatrics (2001) has directed education efforts during primary care about placing infants to sleep on their back. There has been a demonstrated decrease in SIDS incidence rates with this campaign. Current research is still looking at why SIDS may occur more frequently in infants who are placed on their stomachs and if other environmental factors are involved. This is important to remember, as some families may have limited access to primary care and may not receive this SIDS education and other families may for cultural reasons put infants to sleep on their stomach.

The usual presentation is that a previously healthy infant is fed or bathed, put to bed, and later found dead. There may be foamy discharge in the infant's mouth or nose, and if the infant has been dead overnight, lividity and rigor (dependent pooling of blood and stiffness) may be present. An autopsy may be completely normal or show petechiae in the lungs or heart tissue. There is usually no other autopsy finding. The autopsy findings in suffocation deaths can be identical. A physical exam or autopsy exam that shows physical trauma, signs of neglect or malnutrition, or other disease immediately excludes the diagnosis of SIDS.

The evaluation of SIDS must include a scene investigation and a complete medical and social history. The family investigation must not indicate or identify risk factors for abuse. The coroner or medical examiner may call the CPS agency to inquire if any such information exists regarding the family and children in the home. A coroner protocol for SIDS may exist in the county or state, and CPS workers need to be familiar with that protocol. The AAP has a policy statement that was written to guide pediatricians in the evaluation of SIDS and child abuse death.

The family and siblings of a SIDS infant need immediate support services and grief counseling. Families should not be confronted with the fact that "child abuse needs to be ruled out" but a balanced approach of concern and sympathy with objectivity for the possibility of an abuse or neglect situation until the investigation is complete.

■ Emotional Effects of Child Death

The emotional and psychological effects of a child death are readily apparent when working with a family. It is important to recognize the range of grief response in parents and care providers. ⌘ Likewise, a family member who has no seemingly appropriate or a very abnormal response might be a warning sign for an investigator or CPS worker. The worker, in collaboration with victim support services from law enforcement or a local SIDS program, may be the only access for family support. Mental health services in many communities may be limited. Child advocacy centers, local children's hospitals or community hospitals with pediatric or nursery services, and local or state child fatality review teams might have a list of resources for family grief support. The worker may be the best qualified individual to provide support to a grieving family who is involved in a case of child death from abuse, neglect, or SIDS.

Additionally, cumulative or vicarious trauma response in families and professionals is a risk. The worker who has any personal struggle in the case of child death should access help from colleagues, supervisors, an internal employee support program, and/or mental health professionals. The death of a child—regardless if related to abuse or neglect—can add additional stress and risk for vicarious trauma for a professional.

The CPS worker plays a vital role in the investigation of sudden unexpected deaths in children and of child abuse or neglect deaths. Immediate response with law enforcement to scene investigations or hospitals to assess the safety of the family, making placement decisions, participation in child protection team meetings, assisting with interviews of family and siblings, and coordinating follow-up voluntary or court-ordered treatment services are all important. Multidisciplinary child fatality review committees, both within human services and within public health settings, require open participation and sharing of information by all agencies, including human services. It is only through coordinated, protocol-driven investigation of child deaths that agencies can review and develop coordinated policies and procedures for investigations and effective prevention strategies.

References

American Academy of Pediatrics, Committee on Child Abuse and Neglect. (2001). Distinguishing sudden infant death syndrome from child abuse fatalities. *Pediatrics, 107*, 437–441.

Crume T., DiGuiseppi, C., Byers, T., Sirotnak, A. P., & Garret, C. (2002). Underascertainment of child maltreatment fatalities by Colorado death certificates 1990–1998. [Online version]. *Pediatrics, 110*(2), e18. Retrieved from http://www.pediatrics.org/cgi/content/full/110/2/e18

U.S. Department of Health and Human Services, Administration on Children, Youth and Families. (2005). *Child maltreatment 2003*. Washington, DC: U.S. Government Printing Office.

Appendix A

Well-Child Care and Immunizations

Andrew P. Sirotnak

All infants and children need immunizations against the common preventable child-hood diseases. This is the cornerstone of pediatric health care. Immunizations prevent death and disability from these serious diseases. Many of these immunizations are required before children can enter school. All immunizations, both required and recommended, should be given at the appropriate ages according to a schedule recommended by the American Academy of Pediatrics (AAP). 🖳

These recommendations for immunizations coincide with the minimum standards for well-child checkups during which growth and development are assessed and anticipatory guidance and education are provided to parents and caregivers. 🖳 Five visits before 24 months of age are recommended.

■ Minimal Standards for Well-Child Checkups

- Newborn nursery examination and reexamination in two to four days if discharged in less than 48 hours after delivery.

- Visits at 1, 2, 4, 6, 12, 15, 18, and 24 months, which coincide with current recommended immunization schedules (see Figure A.1). Assessment of developmental milestones occurs at these visits.

- After 24 months, children are seen annually for routine preventive care and immunization boosters between 4 and 6 years, 11 and 12 years, and then between 13 and 18 years.

- Different assessments may be required at certain ages, depending on the level of risk (e.g., lead screening, developmental screening, cholesterol screening, and tuberculin skin testing). All visits include a health history, examination, and anticipatory guidance on behavior, development, educational progress, injury prevention and safety, and sexuality during adolescence.

Time should be taken at visits to discuss sexual abuse prevention and domestic violence screening; however, many practices may not always take time to follow such guidelines. It is important for a CPS worker to recognize that families may not always

215

Recommended Childhood and Adolescent Immunization Schedule
United States • 2005

	Range of Recommended Ages			Catch-up Immunization			Preadolescent Assessment					
Vaccine▾ Age▶	Birth	1 mo.	2 mo.	4 mo.	6 mo.	12 mo.	15 mo.	18 mo.	24 mo.	4–6 y	11–12 y	13–18 y
Hepatitis B	HepB #1 (only if mother HBsAg (–))	HepB #2				HepB #3					HepB series	
Diphtheria, Tetanus, Pertussis			DTaP	DTaP	DTaP		DTaP			DTaP	Td	Td
Haemophilus influenzae Type b			Hib	Hib	Hib	Hib						
Inactivated Poliovirus			IPV	IPV	IPV					IPV		
Measles, Mumps, Rubella						MMR #1				MMR #2	MMR #2	
Varicella						Varicella					Varicella	
Pneumococcal			PCV	PCV	PCV	PCV			PCV	PPV		
Influenza					Influenza (Yearly)					Influenza (Yearly)		
— · — · — Vaccines below line are for selected populations — · — · —												
Hepatitis A										Hepatitis A Series		

Figure A.1. Immunization Schedule. (Centers for Disease Control, the Advisory Committee on Immunization Practices, the American Academy of Pediatrics, and the American Academy of Family Physicians)

get the same level of education about child abuse or violence prevention, depending on the practice or clinic a family attends.

■ **Immunization**

Although children are not allowed to enter school unless they have been immunized (or an exemption formally claimed), this important part of well-child care should be started long before the child enters school. Unfortunately, some parents or caregivers are uninformed about the immunization process and may delay or avoid taking the child to a health care provider, thinking they can "catch up" later and get the immunizations all at one time, or think the immunizations are not really necessary. If parents or caregivers do not understand this process and the importance of immunizations both personally and from a public health perspective, a thorough explanation should be provided by a medical provider. A CPS worker can help the family understand the process and the rationale for obtaining immunizations. The medical provider should keep up-to-date records of the child's shots and provide a copy to the parent or caregiver. Some offices and public health clinics have computerized databases for this purpose, and others may use a standard "shot record" card. Because the required vaccines may be free at any public health clinic or federally funded immunization program, financial problems should not interfere with this process. Be aware, however, that funding in every state may be affected for many budget reasons and regularly check with the local public health department or local clinic about vaccine availability.

If a child has not received any shots by the first 1 and a half years after birth, the county health department may intervene and help the family, but again, the bur-

Table A.1. Catch-Up Schedule for Children, Age 4 Months through 6 Years

Minimum Interval between Doses

Dose One (Minimum Age)	Dose One to Dose Two	Dose Two to Dose Three	Dose Three to Dose Four	Dose Four to Dose Five
Diphtheria and tetanus toxoids and acellular pertussis vaccine (DTaP) (6 weeks)	4 weeks	4 weeks	6 months	6 months
Inactivated polio vaccine (IPV) (6 weeks)	4 weeks	4 weeks	4 weeks	
Hepatitis B vaccine (HepB) (birth)	4 weeks	8 weeks (and 16 weeks after first dose)		
Measles, mumps, and rubella vaccine (MMR) (12 months)	4 weeks			
Varicella vaccine (VAR) (12 months)				
Haemophilus influenzae type b conjugate vaccine (Hib) (6 weeks)	4 weeks: if 1st dose given before 12 months 8 weeks (as final dose): if 1st dose given at age 12–14 months No further doses needed: if first dose given at or after age 15 months	4 weeks: if current age is less than 12 months 8 weeks (as final dose): if current age is 12 months or older and 2nd dose given before age 15 months No further doses needed: if previous dose given at or after age 15 months	8 weeks (as final dose): this dose only necessary for children age 12 months–5 years who received 3 doses before age 12 months	
Pneumococcal conjugate vaccine (PCV) (6 weeks)	4 weeks: if 1st dose given before age 12 months and current age is under age 24 months 8 weeks (as final dose): if 1st dose given at or after age 12 months or current age is 24–59 months No further doses needed: for healthy children if 1st dose given at or after age 24 months	4 weeks: if current age is less than 12 months 8 weeks (as final dose): if current age is 12 months or older No further doses needed: for healthy children if previous dose given at or after age 24 months	8 weeks (as final dose): this dose only necessary for children age 12 months–5 years who received 3 doses before age 12 months	

Sources: The Centers for Disease Control, the Advisory Committee on Immunization Practices, the American Academy of Pediatrics, and the American Academy of Family Physicians.

den is often on the medical provider or system of care to track children and ensure immunizations, and a lack of public health resources may affect this tracking. Those who have not received shots will require a special catch-up schedule, which is listed in the AAP's *Red Book: 2003 Report of the Committee on Infectious Diseases,* generally available in public health departments, health clinics, and medical providers' offices. A worker who is either monitoring the routine schedule or helping the family with the catch-up should ask for a copy of the most recently approved vaccine schedule to make sure the child returns at the right times to complete the series.

This schedule may change slightly each year if newer vaccines are developed or availability of a vaccine limits its use. Again, check with the local public health department regularly to inquire about vaccine availability or shortages.

☐   **Recommended Childhood Immunization Schedule for the United States, 2005**

Figure A.1 indicates the recommended ages for routine administration of currently licensed childhood vaccines, as of December 2004, for children through age 18. Any dose not given at the recommended age should be given at any subsequent visit when

Table A.2. Catch-Up Schedule for Children, Age 7 through 18

Minimum Interval between Doses

Done One to Dose Two	Dose Two to Dose Three	Dose Three to Booster Dose
Tetanus and diphtheria toxoids (Td): 4 weeks	Td: 6 months	Td: 6 months: if 1st dose given before age 12 months and current age is under 11 years
		5 years: if 1st dose given at or after age 12 months and 3rd dose given before age 7 years and current age is 11 years or older
		10 years: if 3rd dose given at or after age 7 years
Inactivated polio vaccine (IPV): 4 weeks	IPV: 4 weeks	IPV
Hepatitis B vaccine (HepB): 4 weeks	HepB: 8 weeks (and 16 weeks after first dose)	
Measles, mumps, and rubella vaccine (MMR): 4 weeks		
Varicella vaccine (VAR): 4 weeks		

Sources: The Centers for Disease Control, the Advisory Committee on Immunization Practices, the American Academy of Pediatrics, and the American Academy of Family Physicians.

indicated and feasible. The *shaded line bars with diagonal lines* indicate age groups that warrant special effort to administer those vaccines not previously given. Additional vaccines may be licensed and recommended during the year. Licensed combination vaccines may be used whenever any components of the combination are indicated and the vaccine's other components are not contraindicated. Providers should consult the manufacturers' package inserts for detailed recommendations.

Reference

American Academy of Pediatrics. (2003). Section 1: Active and passive immunization. In L. K. Pickering (Ed.), *Red book: 2003 report of the committee on infectious diseases* (pp. 1–98, 26th ed.). Elk Grove Village, IL: Author.

Appendix B

Developmental Stages of Infants and Children

Table B.1. Developmental Stages

Infancy: 0–6 Months Old

Physical Development	Cognitive/Language Development	Psychosocial Development
0–4 Weeks	**0–4 Weeks**	**0–8 Weeks**
Proceeds from head to foot and central part to extremities.	Smiles selectively at mother's voice.	Gazes at faces (birth).
Sucks reflexively.	Shows startle reflex to sudden noise.	Smiles responsively.
Visually tracks to midline.		Uses vocalization to interact socially.
Lifts head when held upright.	**3–6 Months**	**3–4 Months**
	Babbles and coos, squeals and gurgles (by 3 months).	Distinguishes primary caregivers from others and will react if removed from home.
3–4 Months	Anticipates food with vocalization.	
Prone: lifts head momentarily—rolls from stomach to back.	Laughs.	Smiles readily at most people.
Pulls to sit without head lag.		Plays alone with contentment.
Grasps rattle.		
5–6 Months		
Reaches for objects.		
Inspects objects with hands, eyes, and mouth.		

(*continued*)

Infancy: 6–12 Months Old

Physical Development	Cognitive/Language Development	Psychosocial Development
Gross Motor	**6–9 Months**	**6–9 Months**
6–9 Months	Smiles and vocalizes to own mirror image.	Discriminates strangers (e.g., frowns, stares, cries).
Creeps.	Says "ma-ma," "da-da" (nonspecific).	Stranger/separation anxiety begins.
Sits without support.	Shakes head "no-no."	Actively seeks adult attention; wants to be picked up and held.
Pulls to stand to cruise furniture.	Imitates playful sounds.	
9–12 Months	Responds to name with head turn, eye contact, and smile.	Plays peekaboo.
Crawls on all fours.		Rarely lies down except to sleep.
Attains sitting position unaided.	**9–12 Months**	Pats own mirror image.
Stands momentarily.	Recognizes voices of favorite people.	Chews and bites on toys.
Takes first steps.	Responds to verbal request such as "Wave bye-bye."	Begins to respond to own name.
Fine Motor		**9–12 Months**
6–9 Months	Calls parent "Mama" or "Dada."	Social with family, shy with strangers.
Transfers objects hand to hand.	Repeats performances that are laughed at.	Begins to show sense of humor.
Bangs with spoon.	Plays peekaboo.	Becomes aware of emotions of others.
Finger feeds part of meal.		
Shakes bell.		
9–12 Months		
Holds, bites, and chews a cracker.		
Grasps string with thumb and forefinger.		
Beats two spoons together.		
Begins to use index finger to point and poke.		

Toddler Years: 12–18 Months Old

Physical Development	Cognitive/Language Development	Psychosocial Development
Gross Motor	**12–15 Months**	
12–18 Months	Jabbers expressively.	
Walks alone.	Communicates by gesture.	
Stoops and stands up again.	Vocalizes more than cries for attention.	

Toddler Years: 12–18 Months Old (*continued*)

Physical Development	Cognitive/Language Development	Psychosocial Development
Climbs up on furniture. Walks up stairs with help. **Fine Motor** **12–18 Months** Builds tower of 2 cubes. Scribbles spontaneously or by imitation. Holds cup. Puts raisin or pellet in bottle. Turns book pages, 2–3 at a time. Holds spoon. **Self-Help** **12–15 Months** Feeds self with fingers. Removes hat, shoes, and socks. Inhibits drooling. **15–18 Months** Chews most foods well. Opens closed doors. Holds cup and drinks with some spilling. Imitates housework. Brings familiar object upon request.	Understands word "no." Shakes head to indicate *no.* Says 2–3 "words" other than "ma-ma" or "da-da." Looks in appropriate place when asked (e.g., "Where is the book?"). **15–18 Months** Vocalizes "no." Has vocabulary of 10–15 words. Fluently uses jargon. Points and vocalizes to indicate wants.	**12–15 Months** Shows strong dependence on primary caregiver with increasing difficulty separating. Shows difficulty quieting and relaxing into sleep. Wants to have caregiver nearby all the time. Gives toy to adult on request. Shows sense of "me" and "mine." **15–18 Months** Begins to distinguish "you" and "me." Imitates adult activities. Interested in strangers, but wary. Does not respond well to sharp discipline. Does not respond to verbal persuasion and scolding. Expressed autonomy through defiance. Plays alone or beside other children. Strongly claims "mine." Follows simple requests.

Toddler Years: 18–24 Months Old

Physical Development	Cognitive/Language Development	Psychosocial Development
Gross Motor **18–24 Months** Runs stiffly. Pushes and pulls large objects. Carries large teddy bear while walking.	**18–24 Months** Points to pictures in books. Points to one body part on request. Has vocabulary of 20 words—mostly nouns.	**18–24 Months** Moves about house without constant supervision. Plays primarily alongside children but not with them.

(*continued*)

Toddler Years: 18–24 Months Old *(continued)*

Physical Development	Cognitive/Language Development	Psychosocial Development
Comes downstairs on bottom or abdomen.	Understands "yours" versus "mine."	Has temper tantrums in situations of frustration.
Seats self in small chair.	Uses the words "me" and "mine."	Is conscious of family as a group.
Fine Motor	Enjoys simple stories.	Enjoys role playing.
18–24 Months	Speaks in 2-word sentences (e.g., "juice gone").	Mimics real-life situations during play.
Builds tower of 4–6 cubes.		Claims and defends ownership of own things.
Tries to fold paper imitatively.		Begins to call self by name.
Wiggles thumb.		Discriminates between edible and inedible substances.
Places rings on spindle toy.		
Turns pages singly.		
Turns knobs (television).		
Self-Help		
18–24 Months		
Helps dress and undress self.		
May indicate wet or soiled diapers.		
Pulls person to show.		
Asks for food and drink by vocalizing and gesturing.		
Uses spoon with little spilling.		
Replaces some objects where they belong.		

Toddler Years: 24–30 Months Old

Physical Development	Cognitive/Language Development	Psychosocial Development
Gross Motor	**24–30 Months**	**24–30 Months**
24–30 Months	Often calls self by first name.	Initiates own play activities.
Jumps in place.	Speaks 50 or more words.	Want routines "just so."
Walks on tiptoe (imitation).	Has vocabulary of 300 words.	Does not like change in routine.
Walks up and down steps, both feet on each step.	Uses phrases and 3- to 4-word sentences.	Cannot wait or delay gratification.

Toddler Years: 24–30 Months Old (*continued*)

Physical Development	Cognitive/Language Development	Psychosocial Development
Walks backward.	Understands and asks for "another."	Does not share.
Runs headlong.	Points to 4 body parts.	Knows identity in terms of sex and place in the family.
Fine Motor		Observes other children at play and joins in for a few minutes.
24–30 Months		
Holds pencil with thumb and forefingers.		
Zips and unzips.		
Builds tower of 6–8 cubes.		
Self-Help		
24–30 Months		
Learning to use buttons, zippers, and buckles.		
Pulls on socks.		
Pulls on pants or shorts.		
Drinks from cup without spilling.		
Helps put things away.		
Toilet training in progress.		

Toddler Years: 30–36 Months Old

Physical Development	Cognitive/Language Development	Psychosocial Development
Gross Motor	**30–36 Months**	**30–36 Months**
30–36 Months	Verbalizes toilet needs.	Begins playing "with," as opposed to "next to," others.
Builds tower of 6–8 cubes.	Uses plural.	Names or points to self in photos.
Completes 3-piece form board.	Increases use of verbs.	Joins in nursery rhymes and songs.
Fine Motor	Begins using adjectives and prepositions.	Likes praise.
30–36 Months	Has vocabulary of 900–1,000 words (36 months).	Dawdles.
Turns book pages singly.	Uses verbal commands.	Has auditory fears (noises).
Holds pencil with thumb and forefingers.	Gives full name when asked.	Shows sympathy, pity, modesty, and shame.
Can zip and unzip.	Asks "What's that?"	

(*continued*)

Toddler Years: 30–36 Months Old (*continued*)

Physical Development	Cognitive/Language Development	Psychosocial Development

Self-Help

30–36 Months

Toilet training in progress.

Dresses with supervision.

Eats with fork and spoon.

Pours from one container to another.

Gets drink unassisted.

Avoids simple hazards.

Preschool Years: 3 Years Old

Physical Development	Cognitive/Language Development	Psychosocial Development
Gross Motor	**Receptive Language**	Is ready to conform to spoken word.
Gallops.	Follows two unrelated commands.	Begins to take turns.
Balances on one foot (1–5 seconds).	Has concept of 2 or 3.	Plays simple group games.
Catches large ball, arms flexed.	Identifies same versus different with pictures.	Toilets self during the day.
Hops on one foot (3 times).	Responds to verbal limits and directions.	Shows fear (visual fears, heights, loss of parents, nightmares).
Turns somersaults.	Identifies 2–3 colors.	Uses language to resist.
Shows lack of coordination (3½ years)—stumbling, falling.	Listens attentively to short stories.	Is able to bargain with adults.
Fine Motor	Chooses objects that are hard/soft, heavy/light, big/little.	Tries to please.
Copies circle.		May masturbate openly.
Imitates cross.	**Expressive Language**	May have imaginary playmates.
Builds with Legos, bristle blocks, etc.	Converses in sentences.	Plays most often "with," as opposed to "next to," others.
Builds tower of 10 cubes.	Speaks intelligibly.	Shares upon request.
Spontaneously draws.	Answers simple yes/no questions.	
Handedness may shift.	Rote counts to 5.	
Imitates snipping with scissors.	Repeats nursery rhymes.	
	Counts 2–3 items.	
	Has 50–75% articulation of consonants.	
	Has vocabulary of 1,500 words (age 4 years).	
	Tells age using fingers.	

Preschool Years: 3 Years Old (*continued*)

Physical Development	Cognitive/Language Development	Psychosocial Development
	Cognitive	
	Uses words for ordering perceptions and experiences.	
	Understands past versus present.	
	Shows curiosity; asks endless questions.	
	Matches colors (2 or 3).	
	Completes 6-piece puzzles.	
	Answers sensibly to "Why do we have stoves?" etc.	
	Tells a simple story.	

Preschool Years: 4 Years Old

Physical Development	Cognitive/Language Development	Psychosocial Development
Gross Motor	Understands opposite analogies.	Is dogmatic and dramatic.
Runs smoothly, varying speeds.	Follows 3-stage commands.	Shows urge to conform/please is diminished.
Hops on one foot (4–9 times).	Listens eagerly to stories.	May have control issues.
Balances on one foot (8–10 seconds).	Follows directions with prepositions (e.g., "above," "under").	May be physically aggressive.
Bounces ball with beginning control.	**Expressive Language**	Is self-sufficient in own home.
Throws ball overhand.	Uses all parts of speech correctly.	Has nightmares.
Handles stairs with alternating feet using rail.	Has vocabulary of 2,000-plus words.	May argue, boast, and make alibis.
Fine Motor	Uses color names.	Calls attention to own performance.
Copies cross and square.	Defines words in terms of use (e.g., car, pencil).	Bosses and criticizes others.
Attempts to cut on straight line.	Asks many questions (e.g., why, what, how).	Rarely sleeps at nap time.
Has established hand dominance.	Has 100% production and use of consonants.	Separates from mother easily.
"Writes" on page at random.	Corrects own errors in pronunciation of new words.	Often has "special" friend.
May try to print own name.		Prefers peers to adults.
Draws person—arms and legs directly from head.		Washes face, brushes teeth, and dresses self.
		Uses bathroom unassisted.

(*continued*)

Preschool Years: 4 Years Old (*continued*)

Physical Development	Cognitive/Language Development	Psychosocial Development
	Has sense of humor and self-laughing.	
	Loves silly songs, names.	
	Increasing use of imagination.	
	Enjoys dress-up play.	
	Is interested in time concepts (e.g., yesterday, hour, minute).	
	Identifies several capabilities.	
	Rote counts to 10.	
	Counts 4 items.	
	Categorizes animals, food, toys.	
	Matches geometric forms.	
	Identifies missing part.	

Preschool Years: 5 Years Old

Physical Development	Cognitive/Language Development	Psychosocial Development
Gross Motor	**Receptive Language**	Enjoys small group cooperative play—often noisy.
Balances on one foot.	Listens briefly to what others say.	
Skips smoothly.		Listens and participates in 20-minute group activity.
Uses roller skates.	Understands 6,000 words.	
Rides bicycle with training wheels.	Categories words.	Knows when certain events occur.
Balances on tiptoes.	Guesses object by attribute or use of clues (e.g., "What bounces?").	Accepts adult help and supervision.
Fine Motor	Points to first and last in a line-up.	Is serious, businesslike, and self-assured.
Handedness firmly established.	**Expressive Language**	Wants to help and please adults.
Colors within lines.	Has vocabulary of 2,500-plus words.	
Cuts on line.		Enjoys competitive exercise games.
Copies circle, square, and triangle.	Repeats days of the week by rote.	Fears parental loss, thunder, and scary animals.
Is not adept at pasting or gluing.	Defines words and asks for word meanings.	More conscious of body, wants.
Draws within small areas.	Acts out stories.	
Ties knot in string after demonstration.	Gives rhyming word after example.	Respects peers and their property.

Preschool Years: 5 Years Old (*continued*)

Physical Development	Cognitive/Language Development	Psychosocial Development
	Cognitive	
	Is often ready to enter kindergarten.	
	Appreciates past, present, and future.	
	Can count 6 objects when asked, "How many?"	
	Begins to enjoy humorous stories and slapstick humor.	
	States address, age, name, and ages of siblings.	
	Acts out stories.	
	Learns left from right.	
	Matches 10–12 colors.	
	Predicts what will happen next.	
	School Milestones	
	Prints first name and simple words.	
	Writing is mostly capital letters.	
	Frequently copies left to right.	
	Reversals are common (e.g., writes *b* as *d*).	
	Reads letters in sequence.	
	Recognizes first name.	
	Recognizes several or all numerals on clock, phone, calendar.	
	Counts and points to 13 objects.	
	Writes 1–10 poorly— many reversals.	
	Adds and subtracts using 5 fingers.	
	Is capable of self-criticism.	

(*continued*)

Elementary School Years: 6 Years Old

Physical Development	Cognitive/Language Development	Psychosocial Development
Gross Motor	**Receptive Language**	Has poor ability to modulate feelings.
Is constantly active.	Uses picture dictionary.	Enjoys performing for others.
Shows smooth and coordinated movement.	Knows category labels.	
Stands on one foot, eyes closed.	Defines and explains words.	Has difficulty making decisions.
Has good balance and rhythm.	**Expressive Language**	Dawdles in daily routines but will work beside adult to complete tasks.
Bounces ball with good control.	Identifies likeness and differences between objects.	Shows jealousy of others; very competitive.
Hops through hopscotch course.	Identities consonant sounds heard at beginning of words.	Plays simple table games.
Fine Motor	Gives category labels.	Often insists on having own way.
Ties own shoes.	Likes to use big words.	Is easily excited and silly.
Makes simple, recognizable drawings.	Shows increasingly symbolic language.	Persists with chosen activities.
	Cognitive Development	Goes to bed unassisted but enjoys good-night chat.
	Names all colors.	
	Knows what number comes after 8.	Frequently frustrated—may have tantrums.
	Understands quantity up to 10.	May return to thumb sucking, baby talk, etc.
	Identifies similarities and differences among pictures.	Responds better to praise of positive behaviors versus focus on negative behaviors.
	School Milestones	
	Begins to recognize words.	Often takes small things from others and claims they found them.
	Matches words.	
	Identifies words by length or beginning sound/letter.	Begins to distinguish right and left on self.
	Rereads books many times.	
	Prints first and last name.	
	Invents spelling.	
	Reverses two-digit numbers (e.g., writes "13" as "31").	
	Rote counts to 30 or higher.	
	Adds amounts to 6.	
	Subtracts amounts within 5.	
	Uses simple measurement.	
	Names coins; states values of a penny, dime, and nickel.	
	Writes slowly and with effort with mixed capital and lowercase letters.	

Elementary School Years: 7 Years Old

Physical Development	Cognitive/Language Development	Psychosocial Development
Gross Motor	Speaks fluently.	Shows independence in completion of routines.
Shows variability in activity level.	Uses slang and clichés.	Is learning to screen out distractions and focus on one task at a time.
Rides bicycle.	Understands cause-effect relationships.	
Runs smoothly on balls of feet.	Recites days of week and months of year.	Becomes quiet and sullen when angry.
Fine Motor	Talks about own feelings in retrospect.	Has better control of voice and temper.
Has well-developed small muscles.	Often seems not to hear when absorbed in own activity.	Sets high expectations for self; frequently disappointed by own performance.
Has well-developed hand-eye coordination.	Shows concrete problem solving.	
Draws triangle in good proportion.	Organizes and classifies information.	Is anxious to please others; sensitive to praise and blame.
Copies vertical and horizontal diamonds.	Learns best in concrete terms.	Has not learned to lose games; will cheat or end game abruptly.
	Shows interest in issues of luck and fairness.	May have little sense of humor; thinks others are laughing at him/her.
	Internal sense of time emerging.	Is considerate of others.
	School Milestones	Is concerned about right and wrong.
	Shows increasing reading vocabulary.	
	Shows greater speed with writing.	
	Begins to self-monitor reversal errors (e.g., writing b rather than d).	
	Learns to solve addition and subtraction combinations.	
	Learns to tell time.	

Elementary School Years: 8 Years Old

Physical Development	Cognitive/Language Development	Psychosocial Development
Gross Motor	Easily expresses and communicates.	May be selfish and demanding of attention.
Shows rhythmical and somewhat graceful movement.	Is often out of bounds verbally (e.g., boasting, exaggerating, sharing private information).	May be cheerful.
Has frequent accidents due to misjudging abilities (e.g., broken arm).		Is curious about activity of others.
	Likes to use big words.	Learning to lose at games.

(*continued*)

Elementary School Years: 8 Years Old (*continued*)

Physical Development	Cognitive/Language Development	Psychosocial Development
Holds pencil, toothbrush, and tools less tensely. Enjoys exercise of both large and small muscles.	**Reading** Shows variable enjoyment of reading. Likes humor in stories. Reads new words through context and phonics. Stops and talks about what he or she reads. Omits words and reads out of order. Prefers silent reading. **Arithmetic** Knows addition and subtraction combinations—some by heart. Learning to carry in addition. Learning to borrow in subtraction. Knows a few multiplication facts. Knows ½ and ¼. Interested in money. **Written Language** Writes sentences. Begins cursive writing. Shows few reversal errors. Uses capital and lower-case letter forms. Tries to write neatly.	Is sensitive to criticism, especially in front of others. Shows strong interest in own past (e.g., stories, baby books, life books). Begins to have sense of humor for own jokes or riddles. May be snippy and impatient in talk with family members.

Elementary School Years: 9 Years Old

Physical Development	Cognitive/Language Development	Psychosocial Development
Gross Motor Becomes interested in competitive sports—social aspects of sports. Apt to overdo physical activities. Shows poor posture (e.g., slouches, head close to work).	Gains proficiency in reading, writing. Works and plays hard. Frequently discusses reproduction with friends. Associates scary daytime events with frightening dreams.	Appears emotionally more stable. Experiences quick, short-lived emotional extremes. Mostly cooperative, responsible, and dependable.

Elementary School Years: 9 Years Old (*continued*)

Physical Development	Cognitive/Language Development	Psychosocial Development
Works purposefully to improve physical skills.	Enjoys school; wants to operate at optimal level and may relate fears and failure more strongly to subject than to teacher.	Capable of concentrating for several hours.
May have somatic complaints (e.g., stomachache, dizziness, leg pains).	Can describe preferred methods of learning.	Likes to plan ahead.
		Is increasingly attentive to peer pressure.
	Likes to read for facts and information.	Begins to subordinate own interests to group purpose.
	Enjoys keeping a diary and making lists.	May take up collecting hobbies.
	Prefers to read silently.	Learns to lose at games.
	Usually prefers written to mental computation.	Begins to be neater about own room.
	Worries about doing well in school.	Chooses member of own sex for special friend.
		Overtly criticizes opposite sex.
		Makes decisions easily.
		Responds relatively easily to discipline.

Elementary School Years: 10 Years Old

Physical Development	Cognitive Development	Psychosocial Development
Girls and boys tend to be even in size and sexual maturity (early in 10th year).	Participates in discussion of social and world problems.	Seems relaxed and casual; describes self as "real happy."
Girls' bodies undergo slight softening and rounding at 10½.	Interest in reading varies greatly by child.	Boys show friendship with physical expression (e.g., punch, shove, wrestle).
Has decreasing somatic complaints.	Shows humor that is broad, labored, and often not funny to adults.	Girls show friendship with note writing, gossip, and hand-holding.
Is increasingly fidgety—more common for girls.	Repeats "dirty" jokes to parent, but often does not understand them.	Enjoys sharing secrets and discussing mysteries with friends.
Shows little awareness of fatigue.	Interested in his or her future as a parent and how he or she will treat own child.	Believes friends over parents.
Strongly refuses bathing.	Rarely interested in keeping a diary.	Does not respond well when praised or reprimanded in front of friends.
Loves outdoor exercise play (e.g., baseball, skating, jumping rope, running).	Mostly interested in material possessions, health and happiness for self and others, and personal improvement.	Shows infrequent and soon-resolved anger.

(continued)

Elementary School Years: 10 Years Old (*continued*)

Physical Development	Cognitive Development	Psychosocial Development
	Enjoys memorizing.	Yells and calls names.
	Prefers oral to written work in school.	Rarely cries except with hurt feelings.
	Shows short interest span—needs frequent shift of activity in school.	Tends to have sincere, trusting, and physically affectionate relationship with mother.
	Is decreasingly interested in movies and television.	Tends to have positive, adoring, admiring relationship with father.

Early Adolescence: Beginning Age, 11–13 Years Old

Physical Development	Cognitive Development	Psychosocial Development
Females	Begins to move from concrete toward abstract thinking (reasoning based on hypotheses or propositions rather than only on concrete objects or events).	Is anxious about peer acceptance.
Pubic hair pigmented, curled.		Is concerned with self-identity.
Auxiliary hair begins after pubic hair.		Depends on family but increasingly tests limits.
Height growth spurt.		Establishes independence through conflicts with peers and family.*
Breast development continues.	Increasingly interested in ideas, values, social issues; often narrow in understanding and dogmatic.	Is egocentric.
Labia enlarged.		Has abrupt mood and behavior swings.
Increase in subcutaneous fat.		Females highly concerned with body image, physical changes.
Menstruation begins.	Is very interested in music and personal appearance—especially common for females.	Increasingly interested in peers and peer culture.
Males		Changes in friends are common.
Prepubescent physical development.	Has increasing conflict with family—however, most place strong value on family and involved parents.	Has same-sex relationships most often, although has concerns, anxiety, and experimentation with opposite sex.
Beginning growth of testes, scrotum, and penis.		Has strong needs for achievement and recognition of accomplishment, although may be masked by feigned indifference.
Downy pubic hair.		
Consistent height growth.		

Midadolescence: Beginning Age, 13–15 Years Old

Physical Development	Cognitive Development	Psychosocial Development
Females Pubic hair fully developed. Auxiliary hair in moderate quantity. Continued breast growth. Menstruation well established. Decelerating height growth. Ovulation (fertility). Moderate muscle growth and increase in motor skills. **Males** Pubic hair pigmented, curled. Auxiliary hair begins after pubic hair. Penis, testes, and scrotum continue to grow. Height growth spurt. Seminal emissions but sterile. Voice lowers as larynx enlarges. Mustache hair.	Shows fully developed abstract thought (usually by age 15) and can apply in more situations. Anxiety, major distractions interfere with abstract thinking Has continued interest in ideas, ideals, values, social issues.	Increasingly independent from family; less overt testing.* Females somewhat more comfortable with body image and changes. Males highly concerned with body image and changes as puberty begins. Shows increase in relationships with opposite sex; same-sex relationship continues to dominate. Is reliant on and anxious about peer relationships. May experiment with drugs. Concerned with achievement, experiences, feelings of accomplishment, receiving recognition.* Continues to be interested in appearance, music, and other elements of peer culture.

Late Adolescence: Beginning Age, 15–16 Years Old

Physical Development	Cognitive Development	Psychosocial Development
Females Full development of breasts and auxiliary hair. Decelerated height growth (ceases at 16 years ± 13 months). **Males** Facial and body hair. Pubic and auxiliary hair denser. Voice deepens.	Shows well-established abstract thinking. Makes applications to own current and future situations and to broader issues (e.g., social concerns, academic studies).	May show increase in anxiety and avoidance behaviors as a major emancipation step becomes imminent (e.g., graduation, moving out of the house, going to college, partial or total self-support).* Increasingly concerned and interested in movement towards independence; generally not prepared emotionally or logistically for complete emancipation.*

(continued)

Late Adolescence: Beginning Age, 15–16 Years Old (*continued*)

Physical Development	Cognitive Development	Psychosocial Development
Testes, penis, and scrotum continue to grow.		Maintain more stable relationships with peers and adults.
Emissions of motile spermatozoa (fertility).		Has reasonably well-established body image, especially among girls.
Graduated deceleration of height growth (ceases by 17¾ years ± 10 months).		Has more realistic and stable view of self and others and nature of problems and is better at problem solving.
Muscle growth and increase in motor skills.		Has continued need for achievement and recognition for accomplishment.

Postadolescence: Beginning Age, 17–18 Years Old

Physical Development	Cognitive Development	Psychosocial Development
Females	Abilities for abstract thinking and for practical problem-solving skills are increasingly tested by the demands associated with emancipation and/or higher education.	Is partially or fully emancipated, although often with difficulty.
Uterus develops fully by age 18–21.		Shows decreased concerns about autonomy and increased concerns about resources.
Other physical maturation complete.		Often has less conflictual relationships with family; existing conflict tends to revolve around emancipation issues.
Males		
Full development of primary and secondary sex characteristics; muscle and hair development may continue.		Still directs attention toward peers and self-identity.*

*Given cultural differences in the development of "independence," it is important not to ascribe pathology to families and youth who may emphasize continuing connection to the family throughout adolescence and adulthood. In such families, rather, the focus may be on increasing responsibility and competence in performing a variety of roles for the benefit of the whole rather than individuation and separation.

Glossary

Compiled by Jesse Rainey

The terms appearing in this glossary were obtained and adapted from numerous sources, including previous publications of the American Humane Association, specifically *Helping in Child Protective Services: A Competency-Based Casework Handbook*. Other medical terms listed are adapted in part from *Dorland's Illustrated Medical Dictionary, 29th Edition* (Philadelphia: W. B. Saunders, 2000), and from *Merriam Webster's Medical Dictionary Online*, offered through Medline Plus (http://medlineplus.gov/, 2004).

abrasion Rubbing or scraping of the skin's surface.

acquired immune deficiency syndrome (AIDS) A virus that infects white blood cells and uses the cells to further replicate the virus. This affects the body's immune system.

acute Characterized by sharpness or severity; having a sudden onset, sharp rise, and short course.[1]

Adoption and Foster Care Analysis and Reporting System (AFCARS) A mandatory data collection system that collects automated case-level information on all children in foster care for whom the state child welfare agency has responsibility for placement, care, or supervision. Information is also collected on children whose adoptions from the foster care system have been finalized. The AFCARS data allow for analyses regarding the number and characteristics of children who are in foster care and who are adopted, the circumstances associated with children's removal from home, the length of time children spend in foster care, and many other factors.

Adoption and Safe Families Act (ASFA) (Public Law 105-89) Passed in 1997, ASFA provides both changes and clarification of policies of its antecedent legislation, the Adoption Assistance and Child Welfare Act. The legislation is intended to improve the safety of children, promote adoptions and permanent homes for children, and support families. Of significance, the legislation stipulates that child safety is of paramount importance during reunification efforts and provides exceptions to reasonable efforts requirements. The law also requires concurrent permanency planning; provides financial incentives and technical assistance to states to promote adoption activities; includes system accountability and reform provisions; and outlines state requirements for performance measures for state child welfare programs. It also promotes the study of kinship placement feasibility.

allergic shiners   The appearance of bruising around the eye area due to allergies.

alopecia   Loss of hair, due to any number of organic or nonorganic causes.

amylase   An enzyme that occurs in saliva and pancreatic juice and aids in digestion.

anal hematoma   Deep bruising of the anal tissue as a result of penile penetration. Can also occur from digital or object penetration.

anal fissure   A break or slit in the anal tissue.

anxiety disorders   Psychological conditions that cause children and youth to feel excessively frightened, distressed, and uneasy during situations in which most others would not experience such symptoms. Anxiety disorders can lead to poor school attendance, low self-esteem, deficient interpersonal skills, alcohol abuse, and adjustment difficulty.

apnea   Cessation of breathing.

asphyxiate   To make unconscious or kill by obstructing breathing.

assessment   A professional, systematic, and informed approach to gathering and evaluating specific information about the child and/or family for the purpose of making decisions regarding allegations of maltreatment, protection of the child, services to the family, and family progress.

attachment   An active, affectionate, reciprocal, enduring relationship between infant and caregiver that is thought to be essential to the development of the psychological foundation of the child. The establishment of attachment is based on how responsive the caregiver is to the infant's needs for physical care, nurturance, and social interactions. When the caregiver responds to the infant's needs, the infant comes to realize that he or she can count on the caregiver to meet any needs. This learned relationship is thought to be critical to the formation of trust and the development of future relationships.

attention deficit disorder (ADD) and attention deficit hyperactivity disorder (ADHD)   Neurochemical disorders that interfere with attention. ADD is a condition characterized by inattention and impulsivity. If children show these symptoms along with hyperactivity, they are considered to have ADHD. Most children identified as having ADD are also hyperactive and restless (ADHD), have poor impulse control, and are prone to outbursts of anger and aggression. Often, they are emotionally labile and immature and are resistant to discipline.

attenuate   To make thin; decrease in size.

avulsion   Tearing away or forceful separation of a part of a structure.

axonal injury   A condition in which the axon (single nerve-cell process) is stretched and cut by a sudden accelerational, decelerational, or rotational force to the head.

battered child syndrome   A medical condition, primarily of infants and young children, in which there is evidence of repeated inflicted injury to the nervous, skin, or skeletal system. Frequently the history, as given by the caregiver, does not adequately explain the nature of occurrence of the injuries.

bilateral   Refers to both sides of the body.

bipolar disorder   A mental illness in which mood and affect are maladaptive. Can be subcategorized as manic, depressed, and mixed (alternating between mania and depression).

bone scan   A process in which a small amount of radioactive phosphorus is injected into the bloodstream. The radiation, or "heat," from this injection is then photographed. Those areas of bone that are growing will demonstrate radioactivity. This method can detect fractures within 48 hours after they occur. It does not allow for dating of injuries. Also referred to as radionuclide skeletal scintography.

callus   New bone growth that forms around a fracture.

candida   Fungal/yeast infection.

capsule   A membrane that encloses a part or an organ.

caput succedaneum   A temporary swelling of the soft parts of an infant's scalp as a result of the use of forceps, vacuum suction, or passage through the birth canal.

caregiver   A person responsible for a child's health or welfare, including the child's parent, guardian, or other person within the child's own home, or a person responsible for a child's health or welfare in a relative's home, foster home, or residential institution. A caregiver is responsible for meeting a child's basic physical and psychological needs and for providing protection and supervision.

cauliflower ear   A deformation of the ear due to repeated injuries and regrowth of tissue.

caustic   A substance that burns or destroys organic tissue by chemical action.[2]

cephalhematoma   A usually benign swelling formed from a hemorrhage beneath the periosteum of the skull and occurring especially over one or both of the parietal bones in newborn infants as a result of trauma sustained during delivery.

cerebral edema   Excessive accumulation of fluid in the brain substance; causes include trauma, tumor, and increased permeability of capillaries as a result of anoxia (lack of oxygen) or exposure to toxic substances. This type of trauma can occur either laterally (on one side) or bilaterally (on both sides of the brain). Also referred to as brain edema and wet brain.

cerebrum   The largest and most highly developed part of the brain, composed of two cerebral hemispheres.

child development   Changes in physical characteristics, neurological makeup, behaviors, and personality traits that are observed in children and occur over time.

Chlamydia trachomatis   A sexually transmitted disease produced by bacteria. The most prevalent STD in teenagers and young adults.

chronic   Marked by long, indefinite duration, by frequent recurrence over a long time, and often by slowly progressing seriousness.[3]

closed fracture   A fracture of the bone with no skin wound.

coagulopathy   A disease or condition affecting the blood's ability to coagulate.[4]

coining/*cao gio***   Described in Asian cultures as a healing method. Warmed oil is applied to the child's skin, which is then rubbed with the edge of a coin or a spoon in a linear fashion, usually on the chest or back. Repetitive rubbing leads to linear bruises and welts.

collaterals   Individuals (often professionals) who have contact with the child and/or the child's family, such as medical personnel, teachers, neighbors, and clergy, and can provide information about the child's history and/or ongoing condition or situation.

complicated fracture   Occurs when a bone fracture injures an internal organ.

compound fracture   Open fracture; a fracture in which the bone is broken and protruding through the skin.

compression fracture   Occurs when bone is collapsed along the direction of force.

concussion   A limited period of unconsciousness, which may last for seconds or hours, caused by an injury to the brain; may cause a disturbance of cerebral function and sometimes marked by permanent damage.

Condyloma acuminata   Venereal warts, produced by a virus that enters into the skin.

congenital syndrome   A syndrome related to a physiological or structural abnormality that develops before birth but is not related to heredity.

congenital syphilis   A disease that causes bone irregularities.

contact burn   Occurs when the skin is burned from contact with an object, such as a cigarette or iron.

contact dermatitis   Irritation of the skin, caused by exposure to detergents, certain plants, etc.

contracture   A permanent shortening of a muscle or tendon, producing deformity or distortion.[5]

contusion   A bruise from accidental or nonaccidental causes.

corneal abrasion   A laceration or abrasion to the cornea (transparent layer in front of the eye).

corporal punishment   Physical punishment inflicted directly upon the body (e.g., spanking). Some abusive parents mistakenly believe that corporal punishment is the only way to discipline children, and some child development specialists believe that almost all parents must occasionally resort to corporal punishment to discipline or train children. Other professionals believe that corporal punishment is never advisable.

cradle cap   A condition in infants in which flaky, crusty skin appears on the scalp, face, and head.

CT scan (computed tomography scan)   A type of x-ray that takes sequential images and in head imaging. This is useful for seeing acute blood, brain swelling, masses such as tumors, and fractures.

cultural responsiveness   Efforts made by CPS workers to understand the unique experiences of the individual person, family, and community. Culturally responsive practitioners recognize and value multiple and diverse worldviews and histories. People's culture and history is the strongest influence in their relationships with their environments. A critical component of culturally responsive practice is relationship. Culturally responsive practitioners understand the history of the other, allow time for trust to develop, and are trustworthy in their capacity to keep commitments. Skills of the culturally responsive practitioner include humility, respect, being willing to learn, a capacity to listen deeply while tolerating silence, and awareness of personal biases and levels of power and privilege.

culture   The stable pattern of beliefs, attitudes, values and standards of behavior that is transmitted from generation to generation. Culture facilitates successful adaptation to the group and to the environment. It is dynamic, includes within itself group differences, and changes over time. In the "strengths perspective," culture transmits hope and resilience, and is the source of meaning, belonging, and identity. Culture also mediates response to trauma and healing.

cupping   A healing method described in Asian and Mexican cultures. In cupping, a cup is warmed and placed on the skin. A vacuum is created between the cup and the skin as the cup cools, which leads to a bruise.

cutaneous   Pertaining to the skin.

degeneration   Deterioration of a tissue or an organ.

depression   A serious medical illness that can affect a person's mood, concentration, sleep, activity, appetite, social behavior, and feelings that last for a sustained period of time (e.g., more than 2 weeks). It can include persistent feelings of helplessness, hopelessness, inadequacy, and sadness.

dermatitis herpetiformis   Chronic, recurrent papular skin condition that is usually symmetric. Lesions are usually small, clustered in groups, very itchy, and usually seen on the extremities, buttocks, back, and abdomen. It may be mistaken for cigarette burns.

dermis   The layer of skin beneath the outermost layer (epidermis).

developmental assessment   Assessment of a child's developmental progress that typically consists of a combination of observations of the child and questions to the caregiver on the child's behaviors. The observations and questions often target how the child's behaviors and skills compare to the developmental milestones typical for the age of the child being assessed.

diaphysis   The shaft (midportion) of a long bone.

differential diagnosis   A list of possible diagnoses.

displaced fracture   Occurs when a broken bone is no longer in alignment.

displacement   Transferring the feelings from one relationship or situation into another; for example, the battered wife who batters her children may be displacing her own hostility toward her husband onto someone less dangerous.

disseminated intravascular coagulation (DIC)   A bleeding disorder characterized by abnormal reduction in the elements involved in blood clotting due to their use in widespread intravascular clotting. It may be caused by any of numerous disorders; in the late stages, it is marked by profuse hemorrhaging.

distal   Far from the point of reference, for example, the distal femur, etc. The opposite of proximal.

dysuria   Painful urination.

duodenum   The first portion of the small intestine.

eczema   Allergic skin condition that causes reddened, dry areas on the child's skin, which may be mistaken for signs of abuse.

edema   Swelling due to excessive collection of serous fluid in body tissues.

Ehlers-Danlos (ED) syndrome   Rare inherited disorder of collagen, which is characterized by skin laxity, hyperextensible joints, and skin fragility. The skin of these children is extremely fragile. The diagnosis of this syndrome is made with the help of genetics.

emergency services   Services whose focus is protection of a child and prevention of further maltreatment through availability of a reporting mechanism on a 24-hour basis and immediate intervention. This intervention could include hospitalization of the child, assistance in the home, including homemakers, or removal of the child from the home to a shelter or foster home.

emotional abuse/emotional maltreatment   A pattern of behavior that impairs a child's emotional development or sense of self-worth. This may include constant criticism, threats, or rejection, as well as withholding love, support, or guidance. Also referred to as psychological abuse/psychological maltreatment.

encopresis   A condition in which older children (typically older than 4 years) regularly have stool or bowel movement accidents.

enuresis   The involuntary passage of urine; a common condition of children that may or may not be of psychological origin.

encephalomalacia   Softening of the brain, especially that caused by an infarct (necrosis due to blood clot or other blockage).

endocarditis   Inflammation of the lining of the heart and its valves.[6]

epidermis   The outer layer of the skin.

epidermolysis bullosa   A group of blistering skin disorders that may mimic burns. Blisters may develop in response to mechanical trauma.

epidural hematoma   Occurs when there is bleeding between the skull and the dura membrane (the membrane closest to the skull).

epiphysis   The ends of the bone: the part of the long bone that is developed from the center of ossification. In a growing child, the epiphysis is separated from the shaft by a layer of cartilage, called the epiphyseal plate, or "growth plate." Often not seen on the x-ray of infants and young children because it is not yet ossified.

erosive injury   Injury to a surface caused by erosion of the tissue.

erythema multiforme   A skin condition that produces red, targetlike lesions.

etiology   The cause of a disease or abnormal condition.

failure to thrive (FTT)   A nonspecific term applied to infants and young children who are failing to grow according to commonly described normal parameters. FTT may be organic, meaning that the growth failure is caused by an underlying disease, or nonorganic, meaning that the cause is psychosocial or environmental in origin. If the condition progresses, the undernourished child may become apathetic and irritable and may not reach milestones like sitting up, walking, and talking at the usual age. Inadequate nutrition may have permanent negative effects on a child's mental development in some cases. May be referred to as pediatric growth failure.

family violence   The intentional infliction of harm or injury by one intimate partner to another. May also be referred to as domestic violence, intimate partner violence, spouse abuse, battering, and partner violence.

fetal alcohol effect (FAE)   Behavioral and developmental symptoms of Fetal Alcohol Syndrome.

fetal alcohol syndrome (FAS)   A condition in infants resulting from heavy and continual prenatal exposure to alcohol. This syndrome consists of growth retardation before and/or after birth, central nervous system dysfunction, and at least two of the following: (1) small head, (2) short or small eyelids, (3) thin upper lip, and/or (4) underdeveloped jaw area. Following birth, the infant may suffer from alcohol withdrawal.

fomites   Objects, such as clothing, toilet seats, water, etc., that are able to harbor microorganisms and can potentially transmit infections.

fontanelles   Soft spots (areas not covered by bone) in a newborn's skull. Bone growth covers these areas within one year of age.

forensic evidence   Evidence that has legal implications.

frenulum   Skin connecting the lips to the gums, or the tongue to the floor of the mouth.

full thickness burns   Occurs when the entire thickness of the skin is burned, including the hair follicles. Formerly referred to as third- and fourth-degree burns.

Gardnerella vaginalis   A sexually transmitted disease that can be identified by a malodorous vaginal discharge.

gonorrhea   A sexually transmitted disease, produced by a bacteria, that is frequently characterized by inflammation of the genital mucous membrane.

greenstick fracture   Incomplete fracture; fracture in which the compressed side of the bone is partially bent/bowed and the other side is partially broken, as when a greenstick breaks but is not completely fractured. Caused by compression and angulation.

growth curve/growth chart   A curve on a graph depicting physical growth of a child over time and in comparison to the larger child population.

hairline fracture   A minor fracture in which the broken bone is in alignment.

Health Insurance Portability and Accountability Act (HIPAA)   Federal law, established in 1996, which mandates confidentiality regarding an individual's medical and health information, and allows an individual more control in accessing and releasing his or her own medical information.

hemangiomas   Red marks that are usually not present at birth but appear during the first 4 to 6 weeks of life. These marks represent blood vessel growth just below the surface of the skin. Also referred to as strawberry marks.

hematoma   Accumulation of blood in an organ or tissue due to a break in a wall of a blood vessel.

hemophilia   A hereditary disorder in which blood fails to clot adequately and abnormal bleeding can occur.

hemorrhage   Escape of blood from a ruptured blood vessel, either internally or externally.

hemothorax   Leakage of blood into any area of the chest; can be caused by broken ribs.

hemotympanum   Blood located in the middle ear behind the tympanic membrane or eardrum. May indicate a basilar (at the base) skull fracture.

Henoch-Schönlein purpura (HSP)   Vascular inflammation that causes areas of distinctive rash particularly on the lower extremities and buttocks, abdominal pain, and joint symptoms. The rash may resemble bruising. This illness is most commonly found in children between 3 and 10 years old.

hepatic injury   Injury to the liver.

hepatitis   A Virus contracted through oral-anal contact; can cause abdominal pain and illness with liver inflammation.

hepatitis B   A liver disease caused by a virus transmitted through birth, blood, or bodily fluids; causes chronic liver disease.

hepatitis C   A liver disease caused by a virus transmitted through birth, blood, or bodily fluids; causes chronic liver disease and accounts for most cases of non-A, non-B hepatitis.

herniation The abnormal protrusion of an organ or other body structure through a defect or natural opening in a covering, membrane, muscle, or bone.

herpes simplex virus (HSV) A sexually transmitted disease that causes blister lesions in the genital area or in the mouth.

human immunodeficiency virus (HIV) A virus that destroys cells of the immune system. Acute HIV infection progresses over time and may develop into AIDS.

human papilloma virus (HPV) A sexually transmitted disease that causes venereal warts in the genital area, as well as in the mouth and throat area, or on hands and feet, depending on the type of HPV contracted. This virus produces *Condyloma acuminata.*

hydrocephalus An abnormal increase in the amount of cerebrospinal fluid within the cranial cavity that is accompanied by expansion of the cerebral ventricles, enlargement of the skull and especially the forehead, and atrophy of the brain. In children it may occur prior to closure of the skull sutures and is typically characterized by enlargement of the head, prominence of the forehead, brain atrophy, mental deterioration, and convulsions.

hyperextension To extend beyond the normal distance between the bones of a joint.

hyperflexion To flex so that the distance between the bones of a joint is smaller than normal.[7]

hypertension Abnormally high arterial blood pressure.[8]

hyphema A collection of blood in the anterior chamber of the eye (the area in front of the lens).

hypopharynx The area in the back of the throat that is below the hyoid bone. Also referred to as the laryngopharynx.

hypoxia A condition in which an insufficient supply of oxygen reaches body tissues; may result in tissue damage or death.

idiopathic Arising spontaneously or from an obscure or unknown cause.[9]

idiopathic thrombocytopenic purpura (ITP) A bleeding disorder characterized by a marked decrease in the number of platelets in the system, resulting in multiple bruises.

ileum The end portion of the small intestine; extends into the large intestine.

immersion burn Occurs when the body is immersed into scalding water.

impacted fracture Occurs when one end of a broken bone is wedged into the interior of the other end.

impetigo Superficial bacterial infection of the skin typically caused by *Staphylococcus aureus*. This condition produces lesions that appear as pustules and then later form crusts. These lesions are of different sizes and may produce blisters similar in appearance to cigarette burns. These usually do not leave scars, whereas cigarette burns may.

infantile cortical hyperostosis (Caffey's disease)   Rare disorder present in infants up to 2 to 3 months of age as red, painful, swollen extremities.

infarction   An area of necrosis (death in a tissue) resulting from obstruction of the local circulation by a thrombus (clot of blood formed within a blood vessel and remaining attached to its place of origin) or embolus (an abnormal particle such as an air bubble) circulating in the blood.

intracranial   Within the cranium (skull).

intramural hematoma   Bleeding within the walls of an organ.

intraventricular hemorrhage   Bleeding that occurs within the ventricles (central spaces within the brain).

investigation   The activities that follow the process of intake in order to assess the safety of the child, initiate the appropriate intervention with the family, make a decision on the substantiation of the report if an investigation is conducted, and identify and initiate services for the child and family. Some locales use the term "initial assessment" to label this stage in the casework process.

ipsilateral   Pertaining to the same side of the body.

ischemia   Inadequate flow of blood to a part of the body.

jejunum   The middle portion of the small intestine.

laceration   A tear in the flesh producing a wound with irregular edges.

lap belt complex   Injuries to abdominal organs related to an automobile accident in which an individual wearing a lap belt is rapidly decelerated against the belt. A more common injury in children due to the size of the child and the location of the lap belt over major abdominal organs.

lateral   Refers to the side of the body.

learning disability   A condition in which there is a significant discrepancy between a child's achievement (in reading, spelling, written language, mathematics, and/or language skills) and ability. The discrepancy between actual and expected achievement is not the result of lack of educational opportunity, emotional disturbance, physical disability, or health impairment.

lethargy   Abnormal drowsiness.

leukemia   In this form of cancer there is a tremendous increase in the number of immature white blood cells that are unable to fight infection and an associated marked decrease in the production of platelets and red blood cells, often causing a child to "bruise easily."

lice   Small, wingless, parasitic insects that are found in body hair areas and are spread by direct body contact. Pubic lice are found specifically in the pubic hair region but can be found in other areas, such as eyelashes.

linear fracture   A hairline fracture that occurs in the skull.

luxate   To throw out of place or out of joint.

maculae ceruleae   Bluish spots on the skin that occur when lice are present.

maltreatment   An act (or failure to act) by a parent, caregiver, or other person as defined under state law that results in physical abuse, neglect, medical neglect, sexual abuse, or emotional abuse. Or an act (or failure to act) that presents an imminent risk of serious harm to a child.

mandated reporter   A person designated by state statutes who is legally responsible for reporting suspected cases of child neglect and abuse to the mandated agency. Such persons, held liable for failure to report, vary by state but often include professionals such as pediatricians, nurses, school personnel, childcare providers, police, and workers who have frequent contact with children and families.

medical neglect   Failure to provide necessary medical or mental health treatment.

Menkes kinky hair syndrome   Resulting from a copper deficiency; creates bone structure problems as well as neurological disorders.

meningitis   An illness characterized by inflammation of the meninges (membranes covering the brain and spinal cord), which can result in fever, headache, vomiting, and stiff neck and back.

metabolic   Relating to metabolism.

metaphyseal fracture   Occurs when a chip off a growing end of a bone is detached by a ligament.

metaphysis   The wider part of the long bone between the end and the shaft. It borders the growth plate. On the x-ray, it is identified as the flaring portion of the long bone.

microcephaly   Abnormal smallness of the head, usually associated with mental retardation.

Molluscum contagiosum   A virus that can be acquired either sexually or nonsexually (via fomites) that is characterized by round papules (inflamed sores) on the skin.

Mongolian spots   Grayish-blue, clearly defined areas of increased skin pigmentation that are most commonly found on the buttocks or the back. They are present at birth and usually fade after the first few years of life. These are most commonly found in darker pigmented children.

MRI (magnetic resonance imaging)   A type of x-ray that takes sequential images and a computer analyzes the magnetic spin of electrons. In head imaging, it is useful for seeing the posterior parts of the brain, brain stem, and spinal cord. MRI shows detailed three-dimensional views and can also use contrast dyes to image blood vessels.

multidisciplinary team   A group of professionals, and possibly paraprofessionals, representing a variety of disciplines (e.g., law enforcement personnel, social workers, psychologists, and the community). These members interact and coordinate their efforts to diagnose and treat specific cases of child abuse and neglect and may also address the general problem of child abuse and neglect in a community. Their goal is to pool their respective skills in order to comprehensively and effectively address the child maltreatment problem.

Munchausen's syndrome by proxy (MSBP) See *pediatric condition falsification.*

National Child Abuse and Neglect Data System (NCANDS) Authorized by the Child Abuse Prevention and Treatment Act (CAPTA); a voluntary system of reporting on the acceptance and investigation of child maltreatment allegations. CAPTA requires states that receive a State Child Abuse Grant to provide information on the extent and nature of child abuse and neglect to the extent practical. This information includes prevention services, the number of reports and investigations, child fatalities, types of maltreatment, characteristics of perpetrators, and services provided, as well as workforce information.

necrosis Death of a tissue.

neglect A type of maltreatment that refers to a caregiver's failure to provide needed, age-appropriate care, despite being financially able to do so or being offered financial or other means to do so.

Neisseria gonorrhea A sexually transmitted disease frequently characterized by vaginal, penile, anal, or pharyngeal pus-like discharge, genital or anal swelling and redness, and painful urination.

neonatal Occurring after birth, with reference to the newborn one month after birth.

neurological Relating to neurology, the study of the nervous system

neuromuscular Relating to both nerves and muscles.

nonorganic Arising from effects outside of the body; cause is psychosocial or environmental in origin.

organic Arising from an organ or organs, or caused by an underlying disease.

ossification Inflammation of bone caused by a bacterial organism.

osteogenesis imperfecta (OI) Group of rare, inherited connective tissue disorders that are characterized by bony fragility and skeletal deformity. The incidence of this disorder is 1 in 25,000 to 30,000 live births; it is diagnosed with the help of a geneticist.

osteomyelitis A bacterial bone infection that may produce bone weakness and subsequent fractures.

osteopenia of prematurity Weakened bones in a premature infant.

pair bonding A stage of psychosexual development in a child under 1 year of age, in which the child derives pleasure from body contact, sucking, cuddling, and touching.

pancreatitis Acute or chronic inflammation of the pancreas, which may be asymptomatic or symptomatic, and which is due to autodigestion of a pancreatic tissue by its own enzymes. It is caused most often by alcoholism or biliary tract disease; less commonly, it may be associated with abdominal trauma.

parenchyma   The functional part of an organ as opposed to the supporting tissue.

partial thickness burn   Occurs when a burn reaches the layer of skin beneath the epidermis. Formerly referred to as a second-degree burn.

pathologic fracture   Occurs when a diseased or weakened bone is broken.

pathology   Any deviation from a healthy, normal, or efficient condition.

pathophysiology   The physiology of abnormal states; specifically, the functional changes that accompany a particular syndrome or disease.

pediatric condition falsification   A disorder in which a parent or caregiver fabricates an illness in a child by faking or inducing the signs or symptoms. Also referred to as Munchausen's syndrome by proxy.

pediatric growth failure   See *failure to thrive.*

perinatal   Existing or occurring just before and after birth; generally between the twenty-eighth week of gestation and twenty-eight days after birth.

perineum   The space between the anus and the scrotum or vagina.

periorbital ecchymosis Bruising of the tissue surrounding the eye. Also referred to as "black eyes."

periosteal reaction   The creation of new bone by the periosteum, a membrane several cell layers thick that covers bone, when a bone is fractured.

periosteum   A specialized connective tissue covering all bones of the body and possessing bone-forming potentialities.

peritoneal cavity   Space formed when the parietal (walls) and visceral layers of the peritoneum spread apart.[10]

peritoneum Membrane lining the cavity of the abdomen.[11]

peritonitis Inflammation of the peritoneum.

petechiae Minute reddish or purplish spots containing blood that appear in skin or mucous membranes, especially in some infectious diseases.[12]

pharyngeal   Relating to the pharynx.

pharynx   A muscular tube lined with a mucous membrane that extends from the beginning of the esophagus to the base of the skull. Acts as a passageway for food from the mouth to the esophagus and as an air passage from the nasal cavity and mouth to the larynx.

physical abuse   Physical injury (ranging from minor bruises to severe fractures or death) as a result of punching, beating, kicking, biting, shaking, throwing, stabbing, choking, hitting, (with a hand, stick, strap, or other object), burning, or otherwise harming a child. Such injury is considered abuse regardless of whether the caregiver intended to hurt the child.

phytophotodermatitis   Skin reaction to psoralens (chemical compounds found in citrus fruits and other plants). Skin in contact with psoralens manifests red marks that may appear like bruises or burns if exposed to sunlight.

pinworms   A parasite that can be contracted due to lack of proper hygiene. Small, white worms that live in the large intestine; causes itching when the worm's eggs are laid on the skin surrounding the anus.

pneumothorax   Leakage of air into the space around the lungs; can be caused by broken ribs.

pneumopericardium   Presence of air within the membrane sac surrounding the heart.

posterior   Refers to the area of the body nearest the rear.

postnatal   Occurring immediately after birth, with reference to the newborn.

posttraumatic hypopituitarism   An injury to the area of the brain that produces growth hormones.

posttraumatic stress disorder   An anxiety disorder in which a traumatic event is repeatedly experienced in the person's mind to the point that it can interfere with daily functioning. These experiences can take the forms of flashbacks to the event, nightmares, daydreams, and so on.

prenatal   Existing or occurring before birth, with reference to the fetus.

prophylaxis   Prevention of a disease or an infection.

proximal   Nearest; closer to any point of reference; opposed to distal (e.g., the end of a bone closest to the body trunk).

psychological maltreatment   See *emotional abuse/emotional maltreatment.*

psychosocial dwarfism   See *psychosocial short stature.*

psychosocial short stature (PSS)   A disorder in which a child suffers from severe failure to thrive, in which a child is physically and emotionally neglected, and is characterized by depression, short stature, sleep disturbances, abnormal pain tolerance, and developmental delays, among others. Also referred to as psychosocial dwarfism.

psychosomatic symptoms   Physical symptoms that have psychological causes.

purpura fulminans   Purpura of an often severe progressive form, especially of children, that is characterized by widespread necrosis of the skin and that is associated with a severe illness, results from an inherited or acquired defect of a certain biochemical pathway, or is of unknown cause.

purulent   Consisting of pus.

recidivism   The recurrence of a situation; for example, repeated child abuse and neglect.

report   An allegation of child maltreatment that is typically provided by someone in the community who suspects a child of being abused and/or neglected. A report is also known as a referral.

rickets   Bone disease due to vitamin D deficiency, renal and hepatic disease, and certain medications that may cause bone irregularities similar to those caused by trauma. The radiographic findings in this disease are specific to the disease and usually not confused with abuse. The diagnosis is confirmed by laboratory studies.

risk assessment   A structured process used to assist in determining the future risk of harm to a child and is used to assist in key decision-making processes in child abuse and neglect situations. Effective risk assessment models focus on both the strengths and needs of the family environment.

safety assessment   A formal assessment that assists in determining whether a child is currently safe, and, if not, what needs to happen to ensure safety. It focuses on the potential harm to the child that could be immediate or in the near future; also focuses on the strengths and needs of the family environment.

safety plan   A plan that is developed by the worker and the family to ensure that the child will be conditionally safe. It is based on the strengths of the individual family members and their ability to monitor their own behavior. It is put in place during the investigation process and must be revisited at each contact. Such plans are often developed after the safety assessment has been completed.

salmon patches   Pink marks that are commonly seen on the nape of the neck, the eyelids, above the nose, or on the mid-forehead of newborns. Also referred to as "stork bites."

scabies   A contagious itch or mange caused by mites that burrow under the skin.

schizophrenia   A group of psychotic reactions characterized by fundamental disturbances in reality relations and concept formations, and behavioral, affective, and intellectual disturbances in varying degrees. There is often progressive deterioration and regressive behavior.

sclera   The opaque, white outer layer of the eyeball.

scurvy   Rare condition resulting from vitamin C deficiency, which may cause irregularities and fractures of the bones.

sepsis   A toxic condition resulting from the spread of bacteria or their products from a focus of infection.[13]

sequelae   Abnormal conditions resulting from a previous disease.

sexual abuse   Actions by a parent or caregiver such as fondling a child's genitals, penetration, incest, rape, sodomy, indecent exposure, and exploitation through prostitution or the production of pornographic materials.

shaken baby syndrome   A type of head injury in abused children. This type of abuse involves infants who are held by the arms or trunk and violently shaken. There may or may not be impact with an either hard or soft surface in addition to the shaking. Commonly, infants with this identified form of injury are less than 2 years of age and are usually less than 6 months of age. Presenting symptoms are often irritability, poor feeding, and lethargy. The child may present for medical care with a history of apnea (cessation of breathing), seizures, visual impairment, or as an unexplained infant death. The history given at the time of presentation is often vague or not present at all. The term is used interchangeably with the term shaken impact syndrome.

shaken impact syndrome See *shaken baby syndrome.*

shearing tears Tears in the parenchyma of the brain caused by the shearing forces of accelerational and decelerational injury.

skeletal survey A series of x-rays taken of the child's entire skeleton to look for indications of new or old injury. Includes the skull, chest, spine, and extremities. Should be done in cases of suspected physical abuse for all infants and children under 2 years of age; rarely used in children over 5 years of age.

skull sutures Immobile joints that separate the bones of the skull.

social isolation The limited interaction and contact of many abusing and/or neglecting parents with relatives, neighbors, friends, or community resources. Social isolation can perpetuate a basic lack of trust, which hinders both the identification and treatment of child abuse and neglect.

somatization A mechanism in which the person becomes preoccupied with physical symptoms disproportionate to any actual physical disturbance (common among sex abuse victims).

spiral fracture Occurs when a bone is diagonally broken.

splash burns Occurs when a hot liquid is thrown or poured onto the skin.

"stair step" growth A situation in which a child suffering from nonorganic failure to thrive grows drastically during periods of care by a nurse or other caretaker, then gains no weight during periods of care by the primary caregiver.

subarachnoid hematoma Occurs when there is bleeding between the arachnoid membrane (the membrane closest to the brain) and the brain.

subclinical Not detectable by the usual clinical tests.

subconjunctival hemorrhage Bleeding into the area of the eye below the conjunctiva.

subdural effusion A collection of fluid (pus, serum, blood, lymph, or any other fluid) in the subdural space. When referring to cerebrospinal fluid, this may be a normal finding during infancy.

subdural hematoma Bleeding outside the brain in the space between the dura and the arachnoid membranes.

subgaleal hematoma Separation between the scalp and the skull, which fills with blood.

sudden infant death syndrome (SIDS) The sudden death of an infant under 1 year of age that remains unexplained after a thorough case investigation, including performance of a complete autopsy, examination of the death scene, and review of the clinical history. SIDS has been linked etiologically in research studies to prone sleep position, sleeping on a soft surface, maternal smoking during or after pregnancy, overheating, late or no prenatal care, young maternal age, prematurity, low birth weight, and male gender.[14]

superficial burn   Occurs when the outer layer of the skin is burned. Formerly referred to as a first-degree burn.

syphilis   A sexually transmitted disease that is characterized by three stages: painless ulcers on the skin and mucous membranes of the genital and surrounding area; a rash on hands and feet, headache, joint pain and fever; and antibodies occurring in the blood that can affect bone, heart, and brain.

tattooing   Discoloration of skin from fabric dye, giving the appearance of a bruise.

thoracic   Relating to the chest area.

tin ear syndrome   Syndrome characterized by unilateral ear bruising, ipsilateral cerebral edema (occurring on the same side as the ear trauma), and retinal hemorrhage.

tinea capitis   A fungus that may cause circular patches of hair to fall out. Also referred to as ringworm.

torsion   Twisting or rotating about an axis.

traction   Pulling along an axis.

transection   A cut across a section of tissue.

transverse fracture   Occurs when the fracture line of a bone is perpendicular to the long axis of the bone.

Trichomonas vaginalis   Inflammation of the vagina caused by the trichomonas parasite.

trichotillomania   A psychological condition in which a person pulls out his or her own hair.

unilateral   Refers to one side of the body.

urinalysis   Chemical analysis of urine.[15]

urticaria pigmentosa   A darkened area on the skin that can erupt into "hives" when rubbed or irritated.

vaginitis   Inflammation of the vagina.

vasculitis   Inflammation of a blood or lymph vessel.

visceral   Relating to the area among the large organs located within the large cavity of the trunk (chest and abdomen area).

vulvovaginitis   Inflammation and irritation of the vaginal area. Also referred to as vaginitis.

Wood's lamp   A lamp that emits ultraviolet radiation used to detect various skin conditions and fungus infections.

Women, Infants, and Children (WIC)   A program operated by the Department of Health for low-income mothers and their children 0 to 3 years of age. It provides financial assistance for baby supplies and food, as well as medical care.

Notes

1–13. Definitions reprinted by permission. From *Merriam-Webster's Medical Dictionary* © 2002 by Merriam-Webster, Incorporated (www.Merriam-Webster.com).

14. Definition reprinted by permission of the American Academy of Pediatrics.

15. Definition reprinted by permission. From *Merriam-Webster's Medical Dictionary* © 2002 by Merriam-Webster, Incorporated (www.Merriam-Webster.com).

Index

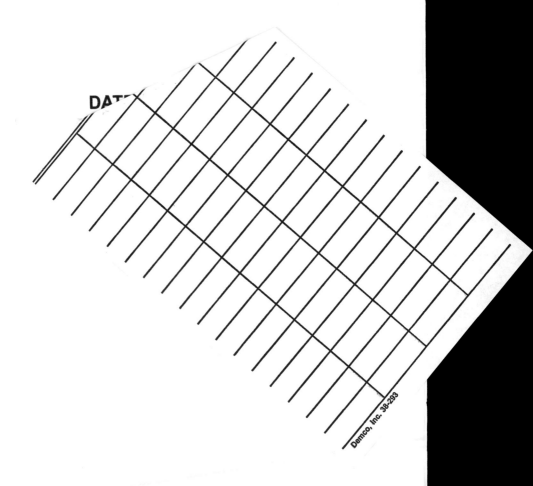

DAT

Demco, Inc. 38-293